"十三五"应用型本科院校系列教材/石油工程类

Professional English for Petroleum Engineering

石油工程专业英语

(第2版)

主 编 王洪秀

哈尔滨工业大学出版社
HARBIN INSTITUTE OF TECHNOLOGY PRESS

内 容 简 介

本书根据编者多年从事石油化工科技英语专业翻译工作及实际教学经验编写而成,系统、重点地阐述了石油工程英语的基础知识,同时也适当加入了部分高深内容,以及在实际工作中经常涉及的知识与内容。课程安排的目的是学以致用,培养学员实际操作能力。全书共分八章,主要内容包括油藏工程、钻井工程、固井工程、完井工程、采油工程、试井工程以及生产工程等。各章均配有"学习目的与要求"、"关键词"、"本章小结"及最新技术资料文摘,使学员能抓住学习重点及难点,进而不断拓展、更新知识;配有课后习题,题量少而精;为了培养学生实际操作能力,还在每章末尾编纂了诸如动机信、简历、摘要、说明书及标书广告等专业英文书写练习。

本教材适用于石油工程专业本科三年级学生使用,也可作为从事石油专业的在职人员专业英语进修的培训教材。

图书在版编目(CIP)数据

石油工程专业英语/王洪秀主编. —2版. —哈尔滨:哈尔滨工业大学出版社,2012.8(2021.1重印)
ISBN 978-7-5603-3152-2

Ⅰ.①石… Ⅱ.①王… Ⅲ.①石油工程-英语-高等学校-教材 Ⅳ.①H31

中国版本图书馆CIP数据核字(2012)第146868号

策划编辑　杜　燕
责任编辑　王桂芝
出版发行　哈尔滨工业大学出版社
社　　址　哈尔滨市南岗区复华四道街10号　邮编150006
传　　真　0451-86414749
网　　址　http://hitpress.hit.edu.cn
印　　刷　哈尔滨久利印刷有限公司
开　　本　787mm×960mm　1/16　印张15.75　字数330千字
版　　次　2010年11月第1版　2012年8月第2版
　　　　　2021年1月第4次印刷
书　　号　ISBN 978-7-5603-3152-2
定　　价　36.00元

(如因印装质量问题影响阅读,我社负责调换)

《"十三五"应用型本科院校系列教材》编委会

主　任	修朋月	竺培国		
副主任	王玉文	吕其诚	线恒录	李敬来
委　员	丁福庆	于长福	马志民	王庄严	王建华
	王德章	刘金祺	刘宝华	刘通学	刘福荣
	关晓冬	李云波	杨玉顺	吴知丰	张幸刚
	陈江波	林　艳	林文华	周方圆	姜思政
	庹　莉	韩毓洁	蔡柏岩	臧玉英	霍　琳
	杜　燕				

序

哈尔滨工业大学出版社策划的《"十三五"应用型本科院校系列教材》即将付梓,诚可贺也。

该系列教材卷帙浩繁,凡百余种,涉及众多学科门类,定位准确,内容新颖,体系完整,实用性强,突出实践能力培养。不仅便于教师教学和学生学习,而且满足就业市场对应用型人才的迫切需求。

应用型本科院校的人才培养目标是面对现代社会生产、建设、管理、服务等一线岗位,培养能直接从事实际工作、解决具体问题、维持工作有效运行的高等应用型人才。应用型本科与研究型本科和高职高专院校在人才培养上有着明显的区别,其培养的人才特征是:①就业导向与社会需求高度吻合;②扎实的理论基础和过硬的实践能力紧密结合;③具备良好的人文素质和科学技术素质;④富于面对职业应用的创新精神。因此,应用型本科院校只有着力培养"进入角色快、业务水平高、动手能力强、综合素质好"的人才,才能在激烈的就业市场竞争中站稳脚跟。

目前国内应用型本科院校所采用的教材往往只是对理论性较强的本科院校教材的简单删减,针对性、应用性不够突出,因材施教的目的难以达到。因此亟须既有一定的理论深度又注重实践能力培养的系列教材,以满足应用型本科院校教学目标、培养方向和办学特色的需要。

哈尔滨工业大学出版社出版的《"十三五"应用型本科院校系列教材》,在选题设计思路上认真贯彻教育部关于培养适应地方、区域经济和社会发展需要的"本科应用型高级专门人才"精神,根据前黑龙江省委书记吉炳轩同志提出的关于加强应用型本科院校建设的意见,在应用型本科试点院校成功经验总结的基础上,特邀请黑龙江省9所知名的应用型本科院校的专家、学者联合编写。

本系列教材突出与办学定位、教学目标的一致性和适应性,既严格遵照学科体系的知识构成和教材编写的一般规律，又针对应用型本科人才培养目标及与之相适应的教学特点，精心设计写作体例，科学安排知识内容，围绕应用讲授理论，做到"基础知识够用、实践技能实用、专业理论管用"。同时注意适当融入新理论、新技术、新工艺、新成果，并且制作了与本书配套的PPT多媒体教学课件，形成立体化教材，供教师参考使用。

《"十三五"应用型本科院校系列教材》的编辑出版，是适应"科教兴国"战略对复合型、应用型人才的需求，是推动相对滞后的应用型本科院校教材建设的一种有益尝试，在应用型创新人才培养方面是一件具有开创意义的工作，为应用型人才的培养提供了及时、可靠、坚实的保证。

希望本系列教材在使用过程中，通过编者、作者和读者的共同努力，厚积薄发、推陈出新、细上加细、精益求精，不断丰富、不断完善、不断创新，力争成为同类教材中的精品。

第 2 版前言

全球化计算机网络的飞速发展已使国与国之间的科技交流更加频繁、快捷与方便,进而也加快了全球经济由多元化向着一体化发展的进程,作为世界经济支柱产业之一的石油工业当然也不例外。我国石油工业正在与全世界一起同步快速向前发展,这就要求我们必须以科技为本,加速培养更多的高质量的高等应用型专业技术人才。目前,我国有很多石油工程技术人员专业能力强、综合素质好、技术过硬,就是因为对专业英语一知半解或根本不懂专业英语而无法与国外石油企业同行进行交流。本书根据国家教育部关于培养适应地方、区域经济和社会发展需要的"本科应用型高级专门人才"的精神,编写出既有一定理论深度,又注重实践能力培养的应用型本科院校石油工程专业英语教材,旨在培养既精通专业技术,又能熟练掌握专业英语,并且能直接与国外交流的专门型技术人才,使他们在今后国内外石油工业领域中发挥更大的骨干带头作用。

本教材注重应用性,具有极强的针对性,对编写体例做了科学调整,并且开创了许多具有前沿性的学习方法,主要特色如下:

1. 强调应用性

教学内容实用性强。本书为石油工程专业英语培训教程,培养对象是应用型大学本科石油工程专业技术人才,以及对生产工作第一线的石油工程技术人员进行在岗培训。许多专业书籍理论性很强,但很多内容在工作现场却用不上。而本书所强调的应用性,就是学用直接挂钩,高度重视现场操作能力的培养。我们既注重一定专业知识的积累,夯实基础,同时也注重应用能力的培养。如收录的国内外最新技术动态、实验报告、产品说明书,以及机械、仪表的使用指南等,另外还附有英文动机信、简历、摘要等书写方法,这不仅有利于提高学员阅读英文原文的能力,也能培养他们的翻译及书写能力,以便在今后的工作岗位上继续学习,不断提高。

2. 注重针对性

目前就业已经市场化,我们就要顺应这个发展,努力培养市场需要的人才。工作岗位上需要什么样的人才,就培养什么样的人才。例如,某石油公司急需出国钻井人员,我们就专门培养这样的人才;某些石油企业需要专业翻译人员,我们就输送这样的人员。

3. 坚持创新性

本教材编写目的明确、思路清晰,文字简洁明了,根据编者多年积累的翻译经验及技巧,按现场实际工作需求,剔除冗余、复杂的内容,直接切入学习要点及内容。每章、每节都首先列出关键词检索,文后附有中英文互译技巧——中心词法、对比排序法等,这些是本书教学的亮点。经过中心词法、对比排序法破解出来的中英文短句及长句易于理解,翻译方便、快捷、准确。

本书由王洪秀任主编,王昱、王浩任副主编。全书分为八章,其中第 1~5 章由王洪秀编写,第 6~7 章由王昱编写,第 8 章以及附录和各章的生词表由王浩编写。在编审过程中不仅收录了相关国外石油工程学英文原著,而且也编译了相当数量的国内外技术文献,在此衷心感谢博士生导师、东北石油大学华瑞学院院长王玉文教授,感谢同事们的通力协助与支持,也一并向提供文献资料及信息的各位专家及学者致以衷心的谢意。

由于编者水平有限,加之经验不足,在编纂过程中难免有错误、疏漏之处,在此敬请各位专家、同行批评指正,以便我们做进一步的修改和完善。

编　者

2012 年 6 月

目 录

Chapter 1 Reservoir Engineering 1
  1.1 Exploitation Designation of Oil Field 1
  1.2 Types of Petroleum Traps 2
  1.3 Porosity & Permeability of Reservoir Rock 3
  1.4 Reservoir Heterogeneity 9
  1.5 Evaluation of Reservoirs 11
  1.6 The Material Balance Equation (MBE) 15
  1.7 Reservoir Simulation 24
  Technical English Applications 25
  Exercises 28
  Reading Material 29

Chapter 2 Drilling Engineering 33
  2.1 Drilling Methods 33
  2.2 Rotary Rigs 34
  2.3 Drilling Fluids 41
  2.4 Trouble and Releasing 43
  2.5 A Brief Explanation of a Certain Drilling Program 46
  Technical English Applications 48
  Exercises 50
  Reading Material 51

Chapter 3 Cementing Engineering 53
  3.1 The Principal Objectives of the Primary Cementing Process 54
  3.2 The Principal Objectives of the Secondary Cementing Process 55
  3.3 The Dimensions and Strengths of Casing 55
  3.4 Primary Cementing 55
  3.5 Secondary Cementing 57
  3.6 A Case of Cementing Operation 58

Technical English Applications 59
Exercises 61
Reading Material 63

Chapter 4 Completion Engineering 64
    4.1 Conventional Completions 64
    4.2 Open-hole Completion 67
    4.3 Perforated Completion 67
    4.4 Cased hole Completions 69
    4.5 Wire-wrapped Screen Completions 70
    4.6 Tubing-less Completion 71
    Technical English Applications 72
    Exercises 75
    Reading Material 76

Chapter 5 Recovery Engineering 80
    5.1 Primary Recovery 80
    5.2 Secondary Recovery 86
    5.3 Tertiary Recovery 91
    5.4 Enhanced Oil Recovery (EOR) 95
    Technical English Applications 98
    Exercises 100
    Reading Material 101

Chapter 6 Well Testing 105
    6.1 Drawdown Test 106
    6.2 Pressure Buildup Test 111
    6.3 Horner Plot 112
    6.4 Miller-Dyes-Hutchinson Method 119
    6.5 Injectivity Well Testing 126
    6.6 Pressure Falloff Test 131
    Technical English Applications 138
    Exercises 142
    Reading Material 144

Chapter 7 Oil Production Engineering 146
    7.1 Downhole Components 146

7.2　Surface Flow Control Equipment ……………………………………………… 150
　　7.3　Pumping System ……………………………………………………………… 154
　　7.4　Surface Production Facilities ………………………………………………… 162
　Technical English Applications …………………………………………………………… 174
　Exercises …………………………………………………………………………………… 177
　Reading Material …………………………………………………………………………… 179
Chapter 8　Instrumentation & Computerization …………………………………… 183
　　8.1　Instruments on Drilling ……………………………………………………… 183
　　8.2　Mud Instruments ……………………………………………………………… 188
　　8.3　Computerizing Scheme for Drilling Data Management …………………… 191
　Exercises …………………………………………………………………………………… 195
附录 ……………………………………………………………………………………………… 196
　附录Ⅰ　中英文互译技巧 ………………………………………………………………… 196
　附录Ⅱ　专业英语常用时态及非谓语表达法 …………………………………………… 202
VOCABULARY ……………………………………………………………………………… 207
参考文献 ………………………………………………………………………………………… 237

Chapter 1

Reservoir Engineering

Purpose & Requirements

Reservoir Engineering is a branch of Petroleum Engineering. In this chapter, we mainly discuss reservoir traps, porosity and permeability of reservoir rock, classification of pores, permeability, wettability, reservoir heterogeneity, and evaluation of reservoirs. The purpose of this chapter is to get a general idea of a reservoir, know the principles and use MBE (the Material Balance Equation) to evaluate a reservoir. Reservoir engineers must learn to measure the reservoir, estimate the storage potential, and calculate the oil initially in place (OIIP).

Key Words   reservoir engineering

Reservoir engineering is a branch of petroleum engineering, which applies scientific principles to the drainage problems arising during the development and production of oil and gas reservoirs so as to obtain a high economic recovery. The working tools of the reservoir engineer are subsurface geology, applied mathematics, and the basic laws of physics and chemistry governing the behavior of liquid and vapor phases of crude oil, natural gas, and water in reservoir rock.

Reservoir engineers also play a central role in field development planning, recommending appropriate and cost effective reservoir depletion schemes.

1.1   Exploitation Designation of Oil Field

Key Words   oil field exploitation; oil field exploitation plan

After the initial exploration of finding industrial oil and gas, a reservoir is then exploited immediately and gradually. Oil Field Exploitation, aiming at enhanced oil and gas recovery according to the market requirement, based on the miscellaneous investigations to the commercialized oilfields, is the whole procedure in making reasonable exploitation plan, construction, and commission, together with estimating capacity and economic effect on planed productivities. Exploitation work must be carried out according to the bound technical policy, considering the factors of recovery velocity (the ratio of yearly rate of production to recoverable reserves in percentage), utilization and supplement of underground energy, the size of extraction ratio, years of stable production, economic effect and engineering etc.

Oil field exploitation plan is the must demonstration and carefully analysis of the factors of exploiting procedure, manner, subdivision of serious of strata, injection strategy, well spacing density, hole pattern and economic target and the final decision of exploitation designation.

1.2 Types of Petroleum Traps

Key Words origins of petroleum; a reservoir; a trap

1.2.1 Origins of petroleum

There are basically two opinions of origins of petroleum. One is that, generally speaking, petroleum was originated from the dead body of tiny plants and animals buried deeply underground with the condition of high temperature and pressure for millions of years. The other says that petroleum was formed from ethyne, which had been hydrolyzed from calcium carbide, with the condition of high temperature and pressure underground. Due to the force of gravity and the pressure created by the overlying rock layers, oil and gas move through the underground layers of sedimentary rocks until they either escape at the surface to form seeps or much of the oil and gas does not reach the surface. It migrates upward until its progress is blocked by an impermeable barrier or cap rock where it accumulates in place to form a reservoir.

The impermeable barrier and resulting reservoir is called a trap.

A trap requires three elements:

· a porous reservoir rock to accumulate the oil and gas (typically sandstone, limestone, and dolomite);

· an overlying impermeable rock to prevent the oil and gas from escaping;

· a source to origin oil and gas (typically black waxy shale).

1.2.2 Classification of traps

Key Words structural traps; anticlinic traps, salt dome traps; fault traps; normal fault trap; thrust fault trap; stratigraphic traps; truncation; pinch-out; lens trap; joints

There are two main types of impenetrable barriers that can impede the movement of petroleum and thus cause the formation of reservoirs: structural traps which are caused by a deformation in the rock layer that contains the hydrocarbons and stratigraphic traps which result from the reservoir bed being sealed by other beds, or by a change in porosity and permeability within the reservoir itself.

Anticlinic traps, salt dome traps, and fault traps belong to structural traps. Anticlinic traps are the kind of traps where, by the force of movement of the crust, rock layers are folded into anticlines and synclines. Oil and gas migrate upward to the crests of anticlines (not the synclines) within the reservoir rock and are trapped if overlain by an impermeable layer.

Salt dome traps are traps where a salt dome, under the weight of overlying rock layers, pushes its way upwards, forcing rock layers to folds and faults and thus trapping oil and gas around the dome. Porous ancient coral reefs also belong to this kind of traps, providing prolific oil and gas reservoirs, overlaying impermeable shale as seals to the reservoir.

Fault traps occur when petroleum rock is entrapped by a non-porous layer of rock moving into a position directly opposite the oil-bearing layer which consist of normal fault trap and thrust fault trap. Normal fault trap is a trap formed with faults dropping one side down and pushing the other side up to place the reservoir rock against impermeable sealing rock, whereas thrust fault trap is a trap with the original limestone layer being first folded and then thrust faulted over itself. Normal and reverse faults have vertical movement. Thrust and lateral faults mainly move horizontally.

Stratigraphic Traps result from the reservoir bed being sealed by other beds, or by a change in porosity and permeability within the reservoir itself. Truncation is a tilled layer of petroleum-bearing rock cut off by a horizontal, impermeable rock layer. Pinch-out is a petroleum-bearing formation gradually cut off by an overlying area. Lens trap, a porous layer surrounded by impermeable rock, joints, occur when rock is fractured as a result of Earth movement, also belong to this sort.

1.3 Porosity & Permeability of Reservoir Rock

Key Words   porosity; permeability

There are two attributes of reservoir rock — porosity and permeability. Porosity is the capacity for the pore spaces, or voids, within a rock to hold gas, oil or water. Permeability is the property of the porous medium that measures the capacity and ability of the formation to transmit fluids.

1.3.1 Porosity

Key Words   porosity; absolute porosity; effective porosity

The porosity of a rock is a measure of the storage capacity (pore volume) that is capable of holding fluids. Quantitatively, the porosity is the ratio of the pore volume to the total volume (bulk volume). This important rock property is determined mathematically by the following generalized relationship:

$$f = \frac{\text{pore volume}}{\text{bulk volume}} \qquad (1.1)$$

where f = porosity.

As the sediments were deposited and the rocks were being formed during past geological times, some void spaces that developed became isolated from the other void spaces by excessive cementation. Thus, many of the void spaces are interconnected while some of the pore spaces are completely isolated. This leads to two distinct types of porosity, namely:
- Absolute porosity
- Effective porosity

1. Absolute porosity

The absolute porosity is defined as the ratio of the total pore space in the rock to that of the bulk volume. A rock may have considerable absolute porosity and yet have no conductivity to fluid for lack of pore interconnection. The absolute porosity is generally expressed mathematically by the following relationships:

$$f_a = \frac{\text{total pore volume}}{\text{bulk volume}} \qquad (1.2)$$

or

$$f_a = \frac{\text{bulk volume} - \text{grain volume}}{\text{bulk volume}} \qquad (1.3)$$

where f_a = absolute porosity.

2. Effective porosity

The effective porosity is the percentage of interconnected pore space with respect to the bulk volume, or

$$f_e = \frac{\text{interconnected pore volume}}{\text{bulk volume}} \qquad (1.4)$$

where f_e = effective porosity.

The effective porosity is the value that is used in all reservoir engineering calculations because it represents the interconnected pore space that contains the recoverable hydrocarbon fluids.

1.3.2 Classification of pores

Key Words catenary pores; cul-de-sac pores; closed pores; primary pores; secondary pores

According to morphology, pores are divided into three types: catenary, which are those that communicate with others by more than one throat passage, cul-de-sac, or dead-end pores, which have only one throat connecting with another pore, and closed pores that have no throat connecting with other pores.

Fig. 1.1 shows the cross-section of such pores. (a) indicates that hydrocarbons can flow out pores freely in almost all directions, so hydrocarbons can be driven out naturally by the pressure underground or lately flushed out by artificial water drive or gas-cap drive. (b) demonstrates that hydrocarbons can hardly emerge from cul-de-sac pores because of the "sac" shape of pores, yet may still yield some hydrocarbons by dropping the pressure of reservoir to cause the expansion of pores. By dropping the pressure outside the pores, the pressure inside pores is then higher enough to expel the hydrocarbons. (c) shows that hydrocarbons firstly invaded an open pore, and then were shut in subsequently by the effect of compaction or cementation. Such pores are unable to yield hydrocarbons.

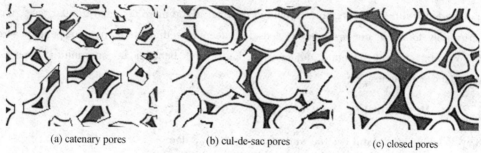

(a) catenary pores   (b) cul-de-sac pores   (c) closed pores

Fig. 1.1 Morphological pores

Of morphological types of pores, catenary and cul-de-sac pores constitute effective porosity, in that hydrocarbons can emerge from them. In catenary pores oil and gas can easily flow out naturally driven by the pressure underground, or afterwards by an artificial drive. Cul-de-sac pores are unable to yield hydrocarbons by flushing, but can still produce hydrocarbons by dropping reservoir pressure as much as possible to raise the pressure inside pores relatively, so that hydrocarbons can then flow out of pores just because of the pressure difference between inside and outside of pores. Closed pores are unable to expel hydrocarbons because such oil or gas, having invaded an open pore, was subsequently closed by compaction and/or cementation.

According to their time of formation, two main types of pores can be classified — primary pores and secondary pores. Primary pores, which are formed when a sediment is deposited, can then be divided into two subtypes — interparticle (intergranular) pores and intraparticle (intragrannular) pores. Secondary pores, which are developed laterly after deposition, are vuggy and moldic pores, fenestral pores, intercrystalline pores, as well as fracture pores.

Of primary pores, interparticle pores are initially present in all sediments and then often quickly lost in clays and carbonate sands because of the combined effects of compaction and cementation. Much of the porosity found in sandstone reservoirs is preserved primary intergranular porosity. Intraparticle pores, which are often cul-de-sac, are generally found within the skeletal grains of carbonate sands and, because of compaction and cementation, they are generally absent in carbonate reservoirs.

Secondary pores are caused by not only solution, but also cementation. Solution-induced porosity is commonly found in carbonate reservoirs. Vugs are pores whose bounderies cross-cut grains, matrices, while moldic porosity is fabric selective. Thus vugs tend to be larger than moldic pores. Fenestrial pores, which are characteristic of lagoonal pelmicrites, and in which dehydration has caused shringkage and buckling of the lamina, would appear to be primary than secondary. Intercristaline pores, which are those that occur between the crystal faces of crystalline rocks, tend to be polyhedral, with sheet-like pore throats in contrast to the more common tubular ones. Fracture pores are rarely found in unconsolidated, loosely cemented sediments, which respond to stress by plastic flow, but are often found adjacent to faults and beneath unconformities, especially in carbonates and sandstones.

1.3.3 Permeability

Key Words permeability; the unit of permeability; darcy

Permeability is the ability of fluids to pass through the porous rock. The unit of permeability is the Darcy, which is defined as the permeability that allows a fluid of 1 centipoise (cp) viscosity to flow at a velocity of 1 cm / s for a pressure drop of 1 atm /cm. Since most reservoirs have permeabilities much less than a Darcy, the milidarcy (md) is commonly used. Average permeabilities in reservoirs are commonly in the range of 5 to 500 md. The letter K generally refers to permeability.

Darcy's law is only valid when there is no chemical reaction between the fluid and the rock and when only one fluid phase completely fills the pores. According to the formula above, rate of flow depends upon the ratio of permeability to viscosity. Thus gas reservoirs may be able to flow at commercial rates with permeabilities of only a few milidarcies, whereas oil reservoirs need minimal permeabilities in the order of tens of milidarcies. For this reason permeability is measured in the laboratory using an inert gas rather than a liquid.

Permeability is seldom the same in all directions within a rock. Vertical permeability is generally far lower than permeability horizontal to the bedding. Permeability is thus commonly measured from plugs cut in both directions.

1.3.4 Wettability

Key Words wettability; the contact angle

Wettability is defined as the tendency of one fluid to spread on or adhere to a solid surface in the presence of other immiscible fluids. The concept of wettability is illustrated in Fig. 1.2. Small drops of three liquids—mercury, oil, and water—are placed on a clean glass plate. The three droplets are then observed from one side as illustrated in Fig. 1.2. It is noted that the mercury retains a spherical shape, the oil droplet develops an approximately hemispherical shape, but the water tends to spread over the glass surface.

The tendency of a liquid to spread over the surface of a solid is an indication of the wetting characteristics of the liquid for the solid. This spreading tendency can be expressed more conveniently by measuring the angle of contact at the liquidsolid surface. This angle, which is always measured through the liquid to the solid, is called the contact angle θ.

The contact angle θ has achieved significance as a measure of wettability. As shown in Fig. 1.2, as the contact angle decreases, the wetting characteristics of the liquid increase. Complete wettability would be evidenced by a zero contact angle, and complete nonwetting would be evidenced by a contact angle of 180°. There have been various definitions of intermediate wettability but, in much of the published literature, contact angles of 60° to 90° will tend to repel the liquid.

The wettability of reservoir rocks to the fluids is important in that the distribution of the fluids in the porous media is a function of wettability. Because of the attractive forces, the wetting phase tends to occupy the smaller pores of the rock and the nonwetting phase occupies the more open channels.

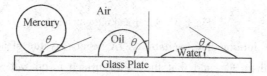

Fig. 1.2 Illustration of wettability

The contact angle is the angle at which a liquid/vapor or liquid/liquid interface meets a solid surface. The contact angle is specific for any given system and is determined by the interactions across the three interfaces. Most often the concept is illustrated with a small liquid droplet resting on a flat horizontal solid surface. The shape of the droplet is determined by the Young's relation. The contact angle plays the role of a boundary condition. Contact angle is measured using a contact angle goniometer. The contact angle is not limited to a liquid/vapor interface; it is equally applicable to the interface of two liquids or two vapors.

Consider a liquid drop on a solid surface. If the liquid is very strongly attracted to the solid surface (for example water on a strongly hydrophilic solid) the droplet will completely spread out on the solid surface and the contact angle will be close to 0°. Less strongly hydrophilic solids will have a contact angle up to 90°. On many highly hydrophilic surfaces, water droplets will exhibit contact angles of 0° to 30°. If the solid surface is hydrophobic, the contact angle will be larger than 90°. On highly hydrophobic surfaces the surfaces have water contact angles as high as 120° on low energy materials e. g. fluorinated surfaces. However some materials with highly rough surface may have water contact angle greater than 150°. These are called superhydrophobic surfaces.

1.3.5 Water wet & oil wet

Key Words　water wet; oil wet

Suppose water and oil drop intermingled on a highly hydrophilic flat solid surface, on which there then will be an interface between water and oil. If water has the angle of less than 90°, it is called water wet; if the angle is more than 90°, it is oil wet; and if just 90°, intermediate. See Fig. 1.3. A positive value of adhesion tension means the contact angle is less than 90° and the solid surface is preferentially water-wet. A zero value of adhesion tension indicates that the contact angle

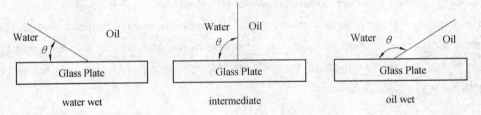

Fig. 1.3　Water and oil wettability

is equal to 90°, which is intermediate wettability. A negative value of adhesion tension means the contact angle is greater than 90° and that the solid surface is oil wet. Translated into geological terms, in water-wet pore systems the meniscus is convex with respect to water; in oil-wet system it is concave. Most reservoirs are water-wet, having a film of water on the surface of the grains of the reservoir rock, separating the pore boundaries from the oil. The film is called wetting water. Wetting water usually coats the grains of the reservoir rock. In other words, water is not only in the reservoir below the oil zoon but also within the pores along with the oil. The rare exceptions are oil-wet reservoirs, which have no film of water lining the pores but which may have an oil saturation of 100 percent of the available porosity.

1.3.6　Wettability influence on multiphase flow

The degree of rock preferential wettability influences greatly on the microscopic distribution of fluids in a porous medium. In a strongly water-wet reservoir, most of the water resides in dead-end pores in small capillaries, and on the grain surface. In strongly oil-wet reservoir, water is in the centre of the large pores as discontinuous droplets, while oil coats the surface of the grains and occupies the smaller capillaries.

Under strongly water-wet conditions the effective permeability to the non-wetting phase at irreducible water saturation is approximately equal to the absolute permeability of the rock. On the other hand, in strongly oil-wet systems, the effective permeability to oil at irreducible water saturation is greatly reduced by the water droplets in the larger pores.

Relative permeability become progressively less favourable to oil production as a rock comes less water-wet. The residual oil saturation increases as a rock becomes less water-wet. Weakly water-wet cores have more favourable relative permeability curves and lower residual oil saturation than strongly water-wet or oil-wet rocks.

Conceptually, this later behaviour seems reasonable since the capillary forces in strong water-wet cores are strong. The oil may be bypassed and trapped in larger pores by the tendency of a water-wet core to imbibe water into the smaller capillaries.

The bypassed oil in the larger pores is then surrounded by water and is immobile except at very high pressure gradients. The saturation interval for two-phase flow under this condition is probably short.

As the capillary forces are reduced by reduction in preferential water-wettability of a rock, the tendency toward rapid imbibitional trapping of oil in larger pores by movement of water through small pores should also diminish. The zone of two-phase flow should become broader and oil displacement to a lower residual saturation should be possible.

If other factors remain constant, higher flow rates and lower interfacial tensions are conductive to higher oil recovery.

1.4　Reservoir Heterogeneity

Key Words　reservoir heterogeneity ; vertical heterogeneity ; areal heterogeneity

It has been proposed that most reservoirs are laid down in a body of water by a long-term process, spanning a variety of depositional environments, in both time and space. As a result of subsequent physical and chemical reorganization, such as compaction, solution, dolomitization and cementation, the reservoir characteristics are further changed. Thus the heterogeneity of reservoirs is, for the most part, dependent upon the depositional environments and subsequent events.

The main geologic characteristic of all the physical rock properties that have a bearing on reservoir behavior when producing oil and gas is the extreme variability in such properties within the reservoir itself, both laterally and vertically, and within short distances. It is important to recognize that there are no homogeneous reservoirs, only varying degrees of heterogeneity.

The reservoir heterogeneity is then defined as a variation in reservoir properties as a function of space. Ideally, if the reservoir is homogeneous, measuring a reservoir property at any location will allow us to fully describe the reservoir. The task of reservoir description is very simple for homogeneous reservoirs. On the other hand, if the reservoir is heterogeneous, the reservoir properties vary as a function of a spatial location. These properties may include permeability, porosity, thickness, saturation, faults and fractures, rock facies and rock characteristics. For a proper reservoir description, we need to predict the variation in these reservoir properties as a function of spatial locations. There are essentially two types of heterogeneity:

· Vertical heterogeneity

· Areal heterogeneity

Geostatistical methods are used extensively in the petroleum industry to quantitatively describe the two types of the reservoir heterogeneity. It is obvious that the reservoir may be nonuniform in all intensive properties such as permeability, porosity, wettability, and connate water saturation. We will discuss heterogeneity of the reservoir in terms of permeability.

1.4.1 Vertical heterogeneity

One of the first problems encountered by the reservoir engineer in predicting or interpreting fluid displacement behavior during secondary recovery and enhanced oil recovery processes is that of organizing and using the large amount of data available from core analysis. Permeabilities pose particular problems in organization because they usually vary by more than an order of magnitude between different strata. The engineer must be able then to:

· Describe the degree of the vertical heterogeneity in mathematical terms, and

· Describe and define the proper permeability stratification of the pay zone. This task is commonly called the zoning or layering problem.

It is appropriate to be able to describe the degree of heterogeneity within a particular system in quantitative terms. The degree of homogeneity of a reservoir property is a number that characterizes the departure from uniformity or constancy of that particular measured property through the thickness of reservoir. A formation is said to have a uniformity coefficient of zero in a specified property when that property is constant throughout the formation thickness. A completely heterogeneous formation has a uniformity coefficient of unity. Between the two extremes, formations have uniformity coefficients comprised between zero and one.

1.4.2 Areal heterogeneity

Since the early stages of oil production, engineers have recognized that most reservoirs vary in permeability and other rock properties in the lateral direction. To understand and predict the behavior of an under ground reservoir, one must have as accurate and detailed knowledge as possible of the subsurface. Indeed, water and gas displacement is conditioned by the storage geometry (structural shape, thickness of strata) and the local values of the physical parameters (variable from one point to another) characteristic of the porous rock. Hence, prediction accuracy is closely related to the detail in which the reservoir is described Johnson and co-workers devised a well testing procedure, called pulse testing, to generate rock properties data between wells. In this procedure, a series of producing rate changes or pluses is made at one well with the response being measured at adjacent wells. The technique provides a measure of the formation flow capacity (kh) and storage capacity (h). The most difficult reservoir properties to define usually are the level and distribution of permeability. They are more variable than porosity and more difficult to measure. Yet an adequate knowledge of permeability distribution is critical to the prediction of reservoir depletion by any recovery process.

A variety of geostatistical estimation techniques has been developed in an attempt to describe accurately the spatial distribution of rock properties. The concept of spatial continuity suggests that data points close to one another are more likely to be similar than are data points farther apart from one another. One of the best geostatistical tools to represent this continuity is a visual map showing a data set value with regard to its location. Automatic or computer contouring and girding is used to prepare these maps. These methods involve interpolating between known data points, such as elevation or permeability, and extrapolating beyond these known data values. These rock properties are commonly called regionalized variables.

1.5 Evaluation of Reservoirs

Key Words oil reservoirs; gas reservoirs; undersaturated oil reservoir; saturated oil reservoir

1.5.1 Classification of reservoirs

In general, reservoirs are conveniently classified on the basis of the location of the point representing the initial reservoir pressure P_i and temperature T with respect to the pressure-temperature diagram of the reservoir fluid. Accordingly, reservoirs can be classified into basically two types. These are:

• Oil reservoirs—If the reservoir temperature T is less than the critical temperature T_c of the reservoir fluid, the reservoir is classified as an oil reservoir.

• Gas reservoirs—If the reservoir temperature is greater than the critical temperature of the hydrocarbon fluid, the reservoir is considered a gas reservoir.

1. Oil reservoirs

Depending upon initial reservoir pressure P_i, oil reservoirs can be sub-classified into the following categories:

(1) Undersaturated oil reservoir. If the initial reservoir pressure P_i is greater than the bubble-point pressure P_b of the reservoir fluid, the reservoir is labeled an undersaturated oil reservoir.

(2) Saturated oil reservoir. When the initial reservoir pressure is equal to the bubble-point pressure of the reservoir fluid, the reservoir is called a saturated oil reservoir.

(3) Gas-cap reservoir. If the initial reservoir pressure is below the bubble-point pressure of the reservoir fluid, the reservoir is termed a gas-cap or two-phase reservoir, in which the gas or vapor phase is underlain by an oil phase. The appropriate quality line gives the ratio of the gas-cap volume to reservoir oil volume.

Crude oils cover a wide range in physical properties and chemical compositions, and it is often important to be able to group them into broad categories of related oils. In general, crude oils are commonly classified into the following types:

• Ordinary black oil

• Low-shrinkage crude oil

• High-shrinkage (volatile) crude oil

• Near-critical crude oil

The above classifications are essentially based upon the properties exhibited by the crude oil, including physical properties, composition, gas-oil ratio, appearance, and pressure-temperature phase diagrams.

2. Gas reservoirs

In general, if the reservoir temperature is above the critical temperature of the hydrocarbon system, the reservoir is classified as a natural gas reservoir. On the basis of their phase diagrams and the prevailing reservoir conditions, natural gases can be classified into four categories:

• Retrograde gas-condensate

• Near-critical gas-condensate

- Wet gas
- Dry gas

1.5.2 Pressure system

As for every exploration and evaluation well, it is most important to determine the initial formation pressure accurately, plot relative diagram of pressure and buried depth, so that to judge the initial production and distribution type, as well as to establish the reserve parameters and evaluation.

In a reservoir with natural gas cap and edge water, according to its density, the fluids inside the reservoir bed form a vertically fluids distribution profile. In the profile, 5 exploration wells are drilled respectively on the oil and water section, 3 of which on the oil section, 1 on the interface of oil and water, and the last on the water section. The pressure gradient measured from the initial and media depth is shown on the right side of the profile. The oil and water interface locates just on the cross point of two lineal curves, which indicate the oil and water pressure gradient respectively.

The relationship between the formation pressure and the buried depth of different exploration wells is expressed as the equation bellow:

$$P_i = a + G_D D \tag{1.5}$$

where P_i = initial formation pressure, MPa;
a = static pressure after shut down, MPa;
G_D = static liquid pressure gradient inside the bore hole, MPa/m;
D = buried depth, m.

Static liquid pressure gradient inside the bore hole is expressed bellow:

$$G_D = dP_i/dD = 0.01\rho \tag{1.6}$$

where ρ = static liquid density inside the bore hole.

According to (1.2), pressure gradient and liquid density underground are in direct proportion, which means the gas top portion with less liquid density has smaller pressure gradient, comparing with the oil bearing or edge water portion with more liquid density. As pressure gradient times 100 equal to formation liquid density, it is possible to decide the liquid type and density of the formation by the size of pressure gradient. Meanwhile, the cross point of two lineal curves representing different formation liquids is exactly the interface point of formation liquids.

The initial static pressure can be measured using DST (Drill Stem Tester), RFT (Repeat Formation Tester) or MFDT (Modular Formation Dynamics Tester).

As for an oil field with multiple oil and water systems, due to the closed salinity of edge-bottom water in different bedding, the density of formation water is basically same, so that different oil layers can form a uniform hydrostatic gradient curve, using which the interface of oil and water in different layers can then be determined. The bigger the included angle between the pressure gradient of oil layer and that of water, the more oil bearing of the reservoir. The pressure system in different reservoir position (the ratio of initial formation pressure to static water pressure) is shown as bellow:

$$\eta_o = \frac{P_i}{P_{ws}} = 1 + \left(\frac{\rho_w - \rho_o}{\rho_w}\right)\left(\frac{D_{owc} - D}{D}\right) \quad (1.7)$$

where η_o ——pressure coefficient;
 P_i ——initial formation pressure, MPa;
 P_{ws} ——static water column pressure, MPa;
 ρ_w ——density of formation water, g/cm^3;
 ρ_o ——density of formation crude oil, g/cm^3;
 D_{owc} ——depth of interface of oil and water, m;
 D ——oil layer open depth, m.

According to (1.7), the pressure coefficient is different at various depth, usually high at top and low at flank bed. When $D = D_{owc}$, $\eta_o = 1$.

After pressure coefficient is determined, the following equation adapted from (1.7) can predict the position of oil and water interface:

$$D_{owc} = D\left[1 + \frac{(\eta_o - 1)\rho_w}{\rho_w - \rho_o}\right] \quad (1.8)$$

When only one well has reached the oil layer, but hasn't met the oil-water interface, the following equation can calculate the position of oil and water interface:

$$D_{owc} = D + \frac{100(P_i - P_{ws})}{\rho_w - \rho_o} \quad (1.9)$$

When one well has reached the oil layer, the other reached water layer, but neither has met the oil-water interface, the following equation can calculate the position of oil and water interface:

$$D_{owc} = \frac{(P_w D_w - \rho_o D_o) - 100(P_{iw} - P_{io})}{\rho_w - \rho_o} \quad (1.10)$$

where D_w ——depth into water layer, m;
 D_o ——depth into oil layer, m;
 P_{iw} ——initial formation pressure of water well, MPa;
 P_{io} ——initial formation pressure of oil well, MPa.

1.5.3 Temperature system

The temperature system of reservoir is the relationship between the static temperature measured in different exploration wells and the relative buried depth and, it can also be termed as static gradient diagram.

The static temperature is mainly subjected to the temperature of the crust rather than the influence of the lithology of the reservoir and the property of the fluids. Thus static gradient diagram in any regions is a straight line, and is shown as bellow:

$$T = A + BD \qquad (1.11)$$

where T——static temperature in different buried depth, ℃;
  A——even ground temperature, annually, ℃;
  B——static gradient, ℃/m;
  D——buried depth, m.

1.6 The Material Balance Equation (MBE)

Key Words the material balance equation; elastic drive reservoir

The reservoir can be thought of as a tank of pressurized fluids, in which reservoir pressure and producing characteristics change as fluids are produced. Observing these changes one can determine the type(s) of drive mechanism(s) in effect, the original volumes available, and the expected recovery. The MBE (Material Balance Equation) is the foundation of the reservoir engineer's analysis of a reservoir. Based on the law of conservation of mass converted to a volume relationship, it is simply expressed as:

volume in − volume out = net change in volume

This relationship can be restated in terms of reservoir quantities. For a given amount of production and the associated pressure change, the formula is as follows:

Reservoir withdrawal = Expansion of oil and originally dissolved gas + Expansion of gas cap + Reduction in hydrocarbon pore volume due to rock and water expansion + Water influx

As a relationship between pressure drop and volume changes, the material balance equation is very valuable because it enables one to make an estimate of the original volume of hydrocarbons based on the pressure-production performance. This estimate is relatively independent of the three-dimensional geological interpretation. Of course, in order to apply the equation to determine OOIP (Original Oil In Place), we must have some production and pressure data, along with some idea of the PVT (Pressure, Volume, Temperature) behavior of the reservoir fluids, the compressibility of the reservoir rock and the relative size of any gas cap.

The MBE, when properly applied, can be used to:
· estimate initial hydrocarbon volumes in place;

· predict reservoir pressure;
　　· calculate water influx;
　　· predict future reservoir performance;
　　· predict ultimate hydrocarbon recovery under various types of primary drive mechanisms.

Although in some cases it is possible to solve the MBE simultaneously for the initial hydrocarbon volumes, i.e., oil and gas volumes, and the water influx, generally one or the other must be known from other data or methods that do not depend on the material balance calculations. The accuracy of the calculated values depends on the reliability of the available data and if the reservoir characteristics meet the assumptions that are associated with the development of the MBE. The equation is structured to simply keep inventory of all materials entering, leaving, and accumulating in the reservoir.

Since oil, gas, and water are present in petroleum reservoirs, the MBE can be expressed for the total fluids or for any one of the fluids present. Three different forms of the MBE are presented below in details. These are:

(1) generalized MBE;
(2) MBE as an equation of a straight line;
(3) Tracy's form of the MBE.

1.6.1　Generalized MBE

The MBE is designed to treat the reservoir as a single tank or region that is characterized by homogeneous rock properties and described by an average pressure, i.e., no pressure variation throughout the reservoir, at any particular time or stage of production. Therefore, the MBE is commonly referred to as a tank model or zero-dimensional (0-D) model. These assumptions are of course unrealistic since reservoirs are generally considered heterogeneous with considerable variation in pressures throughout the reservoir. However, it is shown that the tank-type model accurately predict the behavior of the reservoir in most cases if accurate average pressures and production data are available.

Before deriving the material balance, it is convenient to denote certain terms by symbols for brevity. The symbols used conform where possible to the standard nomenclature adopted by the Society of Petroleum Engineers.

　　P_i　Initial reservoir pressure, psi

　　P　Volumetric average reservoir pressure

　　ΔP　Change in reservoir pressure $= P_i - P$, psi

　　P_b　Bubble point pressure, psi

N Initial (original) oil-in-place, STB

N_p Cumulative oil produced, STB

G_p Cumulative gas produced, scf

W_p Cumulative water produced

R_p Cumulative gas-oil ratio, scf/STB

GOR   Instantaneous gas-oil ratio, scf/STB

R_{si} Initial gas solubility, scf/STB

R_s Gas solubility, scf/STB

B_{oi} Initial oil formation volume factor, bbl/STB

B_o Oil formation volume factor, bbl/STB

B_{gi} Initial gas formation volume factor, bbl/scf

B_g Gas formation volume factor, bbl/scf

W_{ing} Cumulative water injected, STB

G_{inj} Cumulative gas injected, scf

W_e Cumulative water influx, bbl

m Ratio of initial gas cap gas reservoir volume to initial reservoir oil volume, bbl/bbl

G Initial gas cap gas, scf

PV   Pore volume, bbl

cw Water compressibility, psi^{-1}

cf Formation (rock) compressibility, psi^{-1}

Several of the material balance calculations require the total pore volume (PV) as expressed in terms of the initial oil volume N and the volume of the gas cap. The expression for the total PV can be derived by conveniently introducing the parameter m into the relationship as follows.

Define the ratio m as

$$m = \frac{\text{initial volume of gas cap in bbl}}{\text{volume of oil initially in place in bbl}} = \frac{GB_{gi}}{NB_{oi}} \qquad (1.12)$$

Solving for the volume of the gas cap gives:

$$\text{Initial volume of the gas cap}, GB_{gi} = mNB_{oi}, \text{bbl} \qquad (1.13)$$

The total initial volume of the hydrocarbon system is then given by

$$\text{Initial oil volume} + \text{initial gas cap volume} = (PV)(1-S_{wi}) \qquad (1.14)$$

$$NB_{oi} + mNB_{oi} = (PV)(1-S_{wi}) \qquad (1.15)$$

Solving for PV gives:

$$PV = \frac{NB_{oi}(1+m)}{1-S_{wi}} \qquad (1.16)$$

where S_{wi}——initial water saturation;
  N——initial oil-in-place, STB;
  PV——total pore volume, bbl;
  m——ratio of initial gas cap gas reservoir volume to initial reservoir oil volume, bbl/bbl.

1.6.2 MBE of Elastic Drive Reservoir

Elastic Drive Reservoir is the reservoir where there is neither edge or boundary water nor gas cap with initial pressure higher than saturated pressure.

This kind of reservoir originally drives crude oil from formation to well bore with the action of expansion of oil and water within rock fracture caused by pressure drop of formation.

When without considering the elastic expansion of rock and bound water, MBE of Elastic Drive Reservoir goes as below:

$$NB_{oi} = (N-N_p)B_o \tag{1.17}$$

where N——oil initially in place, m^2;
  B_{oi}——volume factor of oil in place with initial pressure psi;
  N_p——Cumulative oil produced, STB/m^2;
  B_o——Oil formation volume factor, bbl/STB.

Simplify (1.17):

$$N = \frac{N_p B_o}{B_o - B_{oi}} \tag{1.18}$$

Because $B_o - B_{oi} = C_o B_{oi} \Delta P$, then

$$N = \frac{N_p B_o}{C_o B_{oi} \Delta P} \tag{1.19}$$

Formula (1.19) is MBE of Elastic Drive Reservoir.

When considering the elastic expansion of rock and bound water, MBE of Elastic Drive Reservoir goes as below:

$$N_p B_o = C_o NB_{oi} \Delta P + C_p \frac{1}{S_{oi}} NB_{oi} \Delta P + C_w \frac{S_{wi}}{S_{oi}} NB_{oi} \Delta P = C_e NB_{oi} \Delta P \tag{1.20}$$

Imposing the above conditions on the MBE reduces the equation to the following simplified form:

$$N = \frac{N_p B_o}{C_e B_{oi} \Delta P} \tag{1.21}$$

where

$$C_e = C_o + \frac{S_{wi}}{S_{oi}} C_w + \frac{1}{S_{oi}} C_p \tag{1.22}$$

Examples:

(1) Calculate the elastic production rate

Rewrite (1.18) to:

$$K_1 = \frac{N_p}{\Delta P} = \frac{B_{oi}}{B_o} C_e N \tag{1.23}$$

where K_1——elastic production rate, m³/MPa.

Elastic production rate can be used to measure the elastic energy of an oil field. In general, The elastic production rate keeps stable in a closed elastic drive reservoir, thus the relation between total pressure drop and accumulated yield is usually a line equation.

(2) Define elastic oil production

Appraising from the compressibility of reservoir, only 0.2% ~ 0.5% of the IOIP (Initial Oil In Place) yields with a pressure drop of 1.0 MPa. This shows that elastic productivity is very low. Higher pressure difference can relatively boost elastic production rate.

Then the equation goes

$$N_{Pb} = \frac{B_{oi}}{B_o} C_e N (P_i - P_b) \tag{1.24}$$

where N_{Pb}——total elastic oil production, m³.

【Example 1.1】

An elastic drive reservoir exists at its initial oil in place (IOIP) of 526×10^4 t, initial pressure (P_i) of 38.5 MPa, and saturated pressure (P_b) 17.5 MPa, and the data of pressure and production rate annually are listed in Tab. 1.1. Calculate the elastic production rate (K_1) and the total production rate (η_{Pb}).

Tab. 1.1 A reservoir data of pressure & production

time	year	1971	1972					1973				
	month	12	2	4	6	8	10	2	4	6	8	10
total pressure drop/MPa		1.04	1.38	1.67	1.91	2.11	2.3	2.82	3.13	3.53	6.88	10.3
Accumulated production rate/10⁴t		1.5	2.1	2.5	3.2	3.4	3.6	4.7	5.1	5.6	12.0	18.3

Solution:

Step 1. Data from Tab. 1.1 are plotted up as a straight line across the origin of coordinates (as shown in Fig. 1.4). Then the slope of the line is measured as the elastic production rate of about 1.75×10^4 t/MPa.

Step 2. Calculate the max elastic production:

$$N_{Pb}/(10^4 t) = K_1(P_i - P_b) = 1.75 \times (38.5 - 17.5) = 36.75$$

Step 3. Calculate total production rate:

$$\eta_{Pb} = \frac{N_{Pb}}{N} = \frac{36.75}{526} \approx 7\%$$

[Example 1.2]

Using MBE calculate gas production

MBE of dry gas reservoir:

$$G_p B_g = G(B_g - B_{gi}) + C_t G B_{gi} \Delta P$$

where

$$C_t = \frac{C_p + C_w S_{wc}}{1 - S_{wc}}$$

$$G_p = G\left[\left(1 - \frac{B_{gi}}{B_g}\right) - \frac{C_t B_{gi} \Delta P}{B_g}\right]$$

according to equation

$$B_g = \text{constant} \times \frac{ZT}{P}$$

thus

$$\frac{B_{gi}}{B_g} = \frac{Z_{ip}}{Z_{pi}}$$

equation becomes

$$G_p = G - \left(\frac{GZ_i}{P_i}\right)\frac{P}{Z}(1 + C_t \Delta p)$$

because value C_t is usually very small, in earlier stage: $C_t \Delta P \ll 1$, then

$$G_p = G - A\frac{P}{Z}$$

where A is a constant value, and $A = \frac{GZ_i}{P_i}$.

So when there is no water invasion or no water, the curve for gas production vs. P/Z is a straight line, and when $P/Z = 0$, there is a intercept value at G. Fig. 1.5 can read directly a certain total gas production under a certain predicted abandonment pressure P_f.

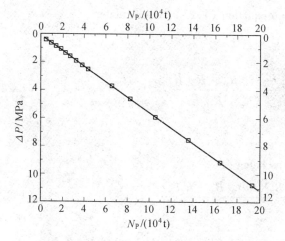
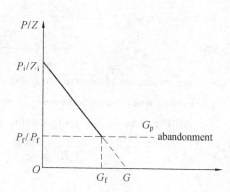

Fig. 1.4 accumulated production vs. total pressure drop for example 1.1

Fig 1.5 gas production vs. P/Z for example 1.2

1.6.3 MBE of Dissolved Gas Drive Reservoir

When not considering the elastic expansion of rock and bound water, MBE of Dissolved Gas Drive Reservoir goes as below:

$$NB_{oi} = (N-N_p)B_o + [NR_{si} - (N-N_p)R_s - N_p R_p]B_g \quad (1.25)$$

Simplifying (1.25) gives:

$$N = \frac{N_p[B_o + (R_p - R_s)B_g]}{B_o - B_{oi} + (R_{si} - R_s)B_g} \quad (1.26)$$

where N_p——well current cumulative oil production from pressure drop to saturated, m³;

N——well oil in place after saturated pressure, m³.

When considering the elastic expansion of rock and bound water, MBE of Dissolved Gas Drive Reservoir should be:

$$N = \frac{N_p[B_o + (R_p - R_s)B_g]}{B_o - B_{oi} + (R_{si} - R_s)B_g + \left(\dfrac{S_{wi}}{S_{oi}}C_w + \dfrac{1}{S_{oi}}C_p\right)B_{oi}\Delta P} \quad (1.27)$$

Where S_{wi}——initial water saturation, decimal;

S_{oi}——initial oil saturation, decimal;

C_w——water compressibility coefficient, 1/MP$_a$;

C_p——pore volume compressibility coefficient, 1/MP$_a$.

Application of the equation needs:

(1) Calculate or verify oil in place N.

Put all necessarily data and parameters into equation (1.23), to calculate.

(2) Calculate degree of reserve recovery

Rearrange equation (1.23):

$$\eta = \frac{N_p}{N} = \frac{B_o - B_{oi} + (R_{si} - R_s) B_g}{B_o + (R_p - R_s) B_g} \tag{1.28}$$

Where η ——degree of reserve recovery.

(3) Predict reservoir performance

This MBE can be rearranged accordingly as below:

$$N_p R_p = \frac{N(B_t - B_{ti}) - N_p(B_o - R_s B_g)}{B_g} \tag{1.29}$$

or

$$N_p R_p = \frac{N(B_t - B_{ti}) - N_p(B_t - R_{si} B_g)}{B_g} \tag{1.30}$$

And current oil saturation S_o is:

$$S_o = \frac{(N - N_p) B_o}{N B_{ob}/(1 - S_{wi})} = \left(1 - \frac{N_p}{N}\right) \frac{B_o}{B_{ob}} (1 - S_{wi}) \tag{1.31}$$

Where S_o——current oil saturation, decimal;

S_{wi}——connate water saturation, decimal;

B_{ti}——two phase volume factor at initial reservoir, m³/m³;

B_{ob}——oil formation volume factor at the bubble point pressure, m³/m³.

As well as instantaneous oil/gas ratio:

$$R = \frac{K_g}{K_o} \cdot \frac{\mu_o}{\mu_g} \cdot \frac{B_o}{B_g} + R_s \tag{1.32}$$

Where R——instantaneous oil/gas ratio;

K_g——effective permeability for gas;

K_o——effective permeability for oil;

μ_o——oil viscosity, cp;

μ_g——gas viscosity, cp;

B_o——oil formation volume factor, m³/m³;

B_g——gas formation volume factor, m³/m³;

R_s——gas solubility, m³/m³.

Then predict future dynamics:

(1) Choose a imagined reservoir pressure P_1, assume a cumulative oil production N_p, and solve

the problem value $N_p R_p$. Obviously N is a given value.

(2) Solve S_o using assumed N_p value in (1.27), isolate correspond K_g/K_o value from relative permeability curve, and calculate instantaneous oil/gas ratio R with equation (1.28).

(3) Calculate total cumulative oil production N_{p1} at pressure P_1:

$$\left(\frac{R_i + R_{i+1}}{2}\right) \times N_{P1} \tag{1.33}$$

Where R_i——initial oil/gas ratio, m³/m³;

R_{i+1}——instantaneous oil/gas ratio as cumulative oil production N_{p1} at pressure p_1;

N_{P1}——cumulative oil produced at the end of first period, m³.

(4) Compare the total gas production value using MBE (1.25) with that calculated using oil/gas ratio equation (1.28). If two values are equal, the assumed value N_p is right. If not, repeat calculating until reach the same value N_p.

(5) To simplify the calculation, three N_p values can be assumed. These values result three different gas production within two equations. If plot up these values on chart (N_p/N vs. G/N), two curves are sure to meet at the value N_p.

(6) Choose the second pressure value, and assumed N_{P2}.

(7) Solve $N_{P2}R_{P2}$, the value of which equals to the total gas production from the first period to the second. In order to calculate the second period gas production value, the following equation is then used:

$$G_2 = N_{P2}R_{P2} - N_{P1}R_{P1} = \frac{N(B_t - B_{ti}) - N_p(B_t - R_{si}B_g)}{B_g} - N_{P1}R_{P1} \tag{1.34}$$

(8) Using assumed value N_{P2} get S_o, verify K_g/K_o, and then calculate R_2 with equation (1.33).

(9) Calculate gas production in the second period with the following equation:

$$\left(\frac{R_{i+1} + R_{i+2}}{2}\right)(N_{P2} - N_{P1}) = G_2 \tag{1.35}$$

where G_2——total gas production in the second period, which is the total value while $(N_{P2} - N_{P1})$, m³.

(10) If the assumed value N_{P2} is right, the gas production value calculated with equation (1.30) and (1.31) is true. If not, assume three value N_{P2}, calculate three different gas production within two equations, plot up these values on chart N_p/N vs. G/N, and find out N_{P2} on the cross point of two curves.

(11) The process will continue until reaches the economic limit of recovery.

(12) Plot up above result on the relation curve of N_p/N—R and G/N—P.

(13) Replace value N_p with $\eta \times N$ to make calculation convenient.

The calculation can also be completed with a computer program:

step 1. input basic data;

step 2. choose a future reservoir pressure;

step 3. assume a value N_p;

step 4. calculate cumulative gas production G_{mb} with MBE;

step 5. calculate cumulative gas production G_{gor} with oil/gas ratio equation;

step 6. compare value G_{gor} and G_{mb} and adjust value N_p until $G_{gor} = G_{mb}$.

1.7 Reservoir Simulation

Key Words reservoir simulation

Reservoir simulation is an area of reservoir engineering in which computer models are used to predict the flow of fluids (typically, oil, water, and gas) through porous media.

Reservoir simulation models are used by oil and gas companies in the development of new fields. Also, models are used in developed fields where production forecasts are needed to help make investment decisions. As building and maintaining a robust, reliable model of a field is often time-consuming and expensive, models are typically only constructed where large investment decisions are at stake. Improvements in simulation software have lowered the time to develop a model. Also, models can be run on personal computers rather than more expensive workstations.

For new fields, models may help development by identifying the number of wells required, the optimal completion of wells, the present and future needs for artificial lift, and the expected production of oil, water and gas.

For ongoing reservoir management, models may help in improved oil recovery by hydraulic fracturing. Specialized software may be used in the design of hydraulic fracturing, then the improvements in productivity can be included in the field model. Also, future improvement in oil recovery with pressure maintenance by re-injection of produced gas or by water injection into an aquifer can be evaluated. Water flooding resulting in the improved displacement of oil is commonly evaluated using reservoir simulation.

The application of enhanced oil recovery (EOR) processes requires that the field possesses the necessary characteristics to make application successful. Model studies can assist in this evaluation. EOR processes include miscible displacement by natural gas, CO_2 or nitrogen and chemical flooding (polymer, alkaline, surfactant, or a combination of these). Special feature in simulation software is needed to represent these processes. In some miscible applications, the "smearing" of the flood front, also called numerical dispersion, may be a problem.

Reservoir simulation is used extensively to identify opportunities to increase oil production in heavy oil deposits. Oil recovery is improved by lowering the oil viscosity by injecting steam or hot water. Typical processes are steam soaks (steam is injected, then oil produced from the same well) and steam flooding (separate steam injectors and oil producers). These processes require simulators with special features to account for heat transfer to the fluids present and the formation, the subsequent property changes and heat losses outside of the formation.

A recent application of reservoir simulation is the modeling of coalbed methane (CBM) production. This application requires a specialized CBM simulator. In addition to the normal fractured (fissured) formation data, CBM simulation requires gas content data values at initial pressure, sorption isotherms, diffusion coefficient, and parameters to estimate the changes in absolute permeability as a function of pore-pressure depletion and gas desorption.

Summary

Reservoir is just like a giant underground storage facility, which is invisible but measurable and controllable. It is necessary knowing the storage capacity of a reservoir while making exploitation and during production period.

With the development of new technology and the help of modern computer, man can now easily measure oil and gas before and during production. Using of MBE (Material Balance Equation) to measure oil and gas reservoir and predict production is now feasible using computer programming technique. So, new technology always leads to new booming of oil and gas production.

Technical English Applications

Letter

When writing a letter, we must first consider what kind of letter we want to write. According to the usage, there are mainly three kinds of letters: official letter, social intercourse and commercial correspondence. Here we mainly discuss the social intercourse.

Here are the six elements for writing:

(1) Letter-heading

Generally, if there is already a printed title, there is no use to write this part. the letter heading includes the information of the name of the writer, address, phone number, e-mail etc.

In order to clarify the family name, now Chinese family name is printed in capital letters. eg. WANG Jian-nan.

In case that the date may misunderstood, we always first write the month with letter abbreviation, then the date and the year. Between the date and year, there must be a comma. eg. Oct. 10, 2010.

Letter heading is usually written on the top right of the letter, leftjustified.

(2) Name and mailing address of the writee (person you are writing to)

This part is written leftjustified, below the letter-heading, with a blank line.

(3) Salutation

If you don't know the name or sex, begin with "Dear Sir/Madam". But in a formal letter, always write "Gentlemen", no matter there is one person or persons.

(4) Body

And now you can write a letter. You may have personal statement, purpose, reason for writing the letter, and any inquire, etc. The body of a letter must be characterized of your own personality, attractive, moving.

(5) Closing

Commonly, at the end of the letter, you may write with:

"Looking forward to hearing from you"

"Awaiting your early reply"

"Best Regards"

"Best wishes"

etc.

(6) Ending & Signature

Ending words can be "Sincerely yours" or "Truly yours", and signature must be handwriting also, to show your regards.

If there are some documents, diploma, or certificates, you may write with: Encl. ⋯

【Example】

Letter of Motivation

WANG Hao

Petroleum Engineering Dep.

China University of Petroleum B. J.

Tel: +86-391-3987716

E-mail: wanghao98@sohu.com

Dean

Petroleum Engineering Dep.
East Texas University
Texas. USA. 8808

Dear Sir or Madam,

  When I was only eight years old, I was curious as to how petroleum can even drive a car. Such intense curiosity for new technology drove me to choose petroleum engineering as the focus of my undergraduate study. Today, I am certain I made the right choice. Information and communications technology has invaded every aspect of daily life from professional and educational uses to purely recreational ones. The integration of global technology is driving the modern world to a new unique one, which is where my interest and enthusiasm lies.

  With motivation and potential, I think my undergraduate studies are not nearly enough to fulfill my long-term goal: to be a superb researcher. So I am determined to study further. I am eager to apply for the master's degree in Information Technology at Texas University.

  I am always eager to embrace new challenges and surroundings. The master's program let me have the chance to receive an advanced education from the USA. Texas University has its area of specialization, which offers me a good opportunity to develop my interests and direction of study. One of the biggest challenges facing employers and educators today is the rapid advancement of globalization. Students who have experienced another culture firsthand are more likely to compete well globally when they graduate. Therefore, an international educational experience in different countries is a precious opportunity to enrich my life experience. Study in Texas University, I can develop intercultural competencies, such as critical and reflective thinking and intellectual flexibility.

  My uncle, who is an alumni of Texas University, strongly recommended that I pursue my studies there because Texas University is a pioneer of innovation and a leader in the field of petroleum engineering. Texas University so offers advanced resources and an inspiring academic atmosphere which are renowned throughout the world. My uncle told me Texas University would be the one place where my intelligence and diligence would be rewarded, even prized. I was deeply moved by his words and since that time studying at Texas University has become my dream. Now I feel this dream is nearly a reality.

  I would be much obliged if I can see you in your university. Looking forward eagerly to hearing from you.

Sincerely yours,
WANG Hao

Exercises

Part 1 Multiple choice

1. Crude oil and natural gas are trapped in _____ of the sedimentary rocks like water in a sponge.

   A. grinds and fractures   B. fractures and soil

   C. pores and soil   D. pores and fractures

2. A petroleum trap requires three requirements:

   A. a porous reservoir rock, silt and limestone

   B. an overlaying impermeable rock, limestone and silt

   C. a porous reservoir rock, an overlaying impermeable rock, and a source for the oil and gas

   D. an overlaying impermeable rock, imporus rock, and a source for the oil and gas

3. Most of the world's petroleum has been found trapped in _____.

   A. nonporous rocks above relatively permeable formations

   B. porous rocks under relatively impermeable formations

   C. porous rocks above relatively impermeable formations

   D. nonporous rocks under relatively impermeable formations

4. Crude oil is defined as "_____".

   A. a mixture of hydrocarbons that existed in the liquid phase in natural underground reservoirs

   B. a mixture of dead body of plants and animals underground

   C. the mixture of yellow, green and brown oil

   D. the mixture of gas and liquid underground

5. _____ are the most widely used sources of energy in the modern world.

   A. Petroleum, coal, and natural gas

   B. Gasoline, kerosene, and gas

   C. Petroleum, gasoline, and kerosene

   D. Gasoline, coal, and wood

Part 2 Translations

1. Translate the following phrases into Chinese:

   1) a branch of   2) so as to

   3) play a role in   4) due to

   5) the ratio of… to…   6) lead to

   7) with respect to   8) according to

   9) be defined as   10) be equal to

2. Translate the following sentences into Chinese:

1) After the initial exploration of finding industrial oil and gas, a reservoir is then exploited immediately and gradually.

2) The absolute porosity is defined as the ratio of the total pore space in the rock to that of the bulk volume.

3) It is noted that the mercury retains a spherical shape, the oil droplet develops an approximately hemispherical shape, but the water tends to spread over the glass surface.

4) After pressure coefficient is determined, the following equation adapted from equation (1.3) can predict the position of oil and water interface.

5) The reservoir can be thought of as a tank of pressurized fluids, in which reservoir pressure and producing characteristics change as fluids are produced.

Part 3 Reading comprehension

1. Classification of traps

2. Reservoir heterogeneity

3. The Material balance Equation (MBE)

4. Reservoir simulation

Part 4 Writing comprehension

Write a letter of motivation.

Reading Material: New Trend of Technology

Innovation, Automation Drive Oilfield Efficiencies, Increase Productivty

Traditionally, many companies have preferred to let others take perceived risks first, but that mentality is changing. New technology, including automation, is becoming widespread, implemented by more and more brand-name companies globally. New ideas and applications are significantly improving efficiencies while reducing costs, as old ideas about drilling operations are rapidly disintegrating.

A dual look at this changing mindset focusing on innovation and automation and mechanization illustrates this point.

Efficiency always matters

In today's worldwide economic downturn, operators want to drill wells even more efficiently. Everyone wants a competitive edge, and technology is usually the driving force.

One example illustrates how engineers are already turning remote drilling centers into reality. Picture a company drilling a dozen wells. Rather than having service company and operator personnel with varying degrees of skill and experience at each well, a remote drilling center is staffed with specialists who deal with typically encountered drilling problems.

All data feed into this centralized

support center, where information is reviewed by appropriate experts periodically to ensure that all operations are being handled properly at each drill site. At a desktop terminal they may receive certain types of data for which they can set alarm limits per job or per hole section.

For example, drilling parameters and performance can be evaluated in near real-time, and wellbore trajectories can be altered to mitigate instability problems or to connect to new production targets. By effectively becoming part of the drilling team, these technical specialists are already "up to speed" when any problem occurs because all are at a central site and not dispersed at different wells.

Centers such as these are ideal for companies with geographically far-flung drilling operations taking place under very harsh and dangerous conditions. By consolidating experienced technical personnel into one optimal protected environment, which could be in a major city, people in the remote areas can effectively manage risks and reduce exposure unnecessarily to hazards.

Additionally, companies have the flexibility to use centers through different business arrangements. Sometimes operators opt to benefit the oil company itself by locating the center within a company office. Others opt for a facility that houses multiple, smaller operators. In any event, the centers are affordable for most oil companies and allow them to monitor various drilling parameters at a single, consolidated location. Professionals based in the center may even be doing the actual directional control work by remotely steering downhole tools.

For offshore operations, a center's efficiencies are especially beneficial, saving helicopter and bed space along with catering charges in addition to technicians' service rates. When a technician is required, often a less experienced and less expensive person can be sent to the rig while the experienced office-based directional drilling hand oversees multiple wells.

Well manufacturing

The first steps involve mechanization — developing a machine that, for example, lifts more or reaches further than one person can handle. Next, control algorithms need to be developed that let the tool make some of its own decisions, leading to automation.

The advent of new drilling models, such as work recently produced by a Russian mathematician who uses fractal analysis and other highly complex mathematical criteria, will greatly aid the decision processes. Companies in the US, UK, and Norway also are working on drilling models. One Norwegian company has developed models providing envelope protection so a driller does not exceed a limit that could impact a wellbore's integrity. Some firms are starting to combine multiple models operating simultaneously, which present critical challenges to the control system manufacturers.

Historically, automation has been more easily accepted in downstream operations where pipelines, chambers, fluids, and contaminants are more homogenous than the complexities of a well bore. However, more accurate surface and downhole measurements added to the advanced drilling models have shown that parts of the drilling process are more predictable and more applicable for automated process controls. This can lead to "well manufacturing", essentially taking the drilling operation and seeing how to make it a standard, repeatable process rig-to-rig, formation-to-formation, and geography-to-geography.

When companies are drilling large numbers of wells, costs can be reduced dramatically through well manufacturing as rig designs and control systems are being designed to optimize the drilling processes.

As a result, NOV and NOV M/D Totco are building drilling operations appropriate for the "manufacturing" of wells.

Included within this environment are various new developments:

• Cruise control—auto drill or the mechanization whereby the driller sets up the machine and it drills automatically. The driller sets the parameter(s), and the machine ensures that those parameters are followed. Several elements are controlled simultaneously, including rate of penetration, weight on bit, torque, and differential pressure.

• Remote control—where technical experts in the support centers, which could be on a rig or in an office, review data and communicate instructions to the rig by phone, e-mail, or fax, and now by direct control. A current project in the arctic regions of northern Norway is investigating how to safely drill where conditions are dark, frigid, dangerous, and expensive. Siberia is another region where remote operations and maximum automation would be quite effective.

• Downlink control—existing rig control systems (originally introduced as DrillLink) can be augmented with a simple, low-cost option to automate downlinking to rotary steerables and other "smart tools" in the bottomhole assembly. DrillLink works with analog throttle signals. Newer rigs have programmable logic controllers (PLCs) that communicate digitally from joysticks or touch screens from the drillfloor. Today's CyberLink, with the same functionality as DrillLink, was developed for digital rigs. The first CyberLink job will be on offshore rigs with Cyberbase control systems. It will soon be on Amphion-controlled rigs manufactured by NOV in Houston.

The future

Inevitably, the industry is moving toward the highest degree of automation possible within the drilling process. Still, automation development and implementation are gradual, not swift, essentially getting closer to "full" automation on a part-by-part basis. Machines emerge that enhance human capabilities, and controls are continually improved to mechanize and streamline processes. Eventually, controls evolve into automation for smoother, more efficient, and more cost-effective solutions.

Yet, through a company anecdote, consider what sweeping change has already been accomplished by looking ahead rather than accepting the status quo. Ten years ago, a European drilling contractor wanted a control system — "to improve our processes and protect our people" — that instructed the user to type in the hole depth, then push the "trip button" and watch as the bit automatically tripped to bottom. Hardware to perform this operation existed at the time, and a model to automate the process was outlined, but many unknowns killed the project.

Controls continue to evolve, and today the industry is on the verge of tripping within cased hole and eventually tripping within certain formations subject to acceptable risks. As the evolution continues, it will require the same kind of visionary companies that see the value to push the industry beyond the status quo. As that happens, even more sophisticated mechanization and automation will be developed for field application in demanding drilling environments.

By http://www.epmag.com

Chapter 2

Drilling Engineering

Purpose & Requirements:

Drilling engineering is a subset of petroleum engineering. The purpose of this chapter is mainly about drilling mechanism, drilling procedures, as well as drilling equipments listed so as to let engineers have a complete concept of drilling engineering. Of the two drilling methods, rotary drilling is now the most used to meet with complicated circumstances. After learning, drilling engineers will plan and design procedures to drill wells as safely and economically as possible. The drilling engineer has the responsibility to confirm what he must do, get information and evaluate the formations while drilling, and from time to time, meet with new technology.

In this chapter, we mainly talk about a drilling rig. A rotary rig consists of four major systems. These include the power system, the hoisting system, the rotating system, as well as the mud system. Firstly, we discuss the mechanism separately, then put them together to form a whole rig.

2.1 Drilling Methods

Key Words cable-tool drilling; rotary drilling

There are mainly two methods in drilling a well: cable-tool drilling and rotary drilling.

Cable-tool drilling is a system that involves a cutting tool called a bit, a drilling stem that is raised and fall; the drill bit cuts or enlarge a hole by applying pressure to the workpiece, which forms chips at the cutting edge in solid materials and crushes the dirt or rock at the bottom of the well. When stem and bit are pulled up, the debris at the bottom of the well is removed. Then the bit is dropped again to crush more rock, and the process is repeated over and over again. Cable-tool drilling, because of less efficiency, is only used to drill shallow well on land and where there is hard rock to cut through.

Rotary drilling is a cutting system that uses a drill bit to cut or enlarge a hole in solid materials. The drill bit is a multipoint, end cutting tool. It cuts by applying pressure and rotation to the workpiece, which forms chips at the cutting edge. Rotary drilling methods, because of its excellent performance, is now commonly used to drill as deeply as it could into underground formation even in complicated working condition on land or off-shore.

2.2 Rotary Rigs

Key Words　power system; hoisting system; rotating system; mud system; a joint; making a joint; making a trip

Rotary rigs are variety sets of combined assemblies and drill the vast majority of wells today. There are mainly two kinds of rigs: onshore rigs and offshore rigs. Onshore rigs are all similar, and many modern rigs are of the cantilevered mast, or "jackknife" derrick type. This type of rig allows the derrick to be assembled on the ground, and then raised to the vertical position using power from the drawworks, or hoisting system. These structures are made up of prefabricated sections that are moved onto the location by truck, barge, helicopter, etc., and then placed in position and pinned together by large steel pins. Some cantilevered land rigs have their mast permanently attached to a large truck to enhance their portability. Fig. 2.1 shows a typical large land rig with a drilling mast. Rigs are rated as to how deep they can drill. Deeper wells require powerful engines and stronger derricks. A deep well could have a drill string weighing more than 500 000 lb suspended down the hole. The engines must be as powerful as they could to raise the drilling strings out of the hole and the derrick must be strong enough to support that weight. Offshore drilling rigs fall into one of several categories, each designed to suit a certain type of offshore environment:

- barge rigs
- submersible rigs
- jack-up or self-elevating rigs
- semisubmersible rigs
- drillships
- structure rigs

The derrick, or mast, supports the crown block and traveling block, which are operated via the drawworks and its drilling line. The derrick, and the substructure it sits upon, support the weight of the drillstem and allow vertical movement of the suspended drillpipe. The substructure also supports the rig floor equipment and provides workspace for its operation. The drillstring must be removed from time to time; the length of drillpipe section that can be disconnected and stacked to one side of

Chapter 2　Drilling Engineering

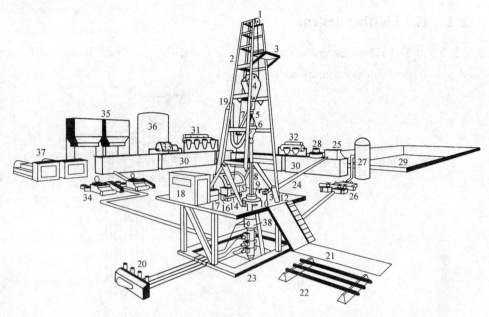

Fig. 2.1　A typical onshore rotary drilling rig

1—Crown block; 2—Mast; 3—Monkeyboard; 4—Traveling block; 5—Hook; 6—Swivel; 7—Elevators; 8—Kelly; 9—Kellybushing; 10—Master bushing; 11—Mousehole; 12—Rathole; 13—Backup tongs; 14—Makeup tongs; 15—Drawworks; 16—Weight indicator; 17—Driller console; 18—Doghouse; 19—Rotary hose; 20—Accumulator unit; 21—Pipe ramp; 22—Pipe rack; 23—Substructure; 24—Mud return line; 25—Shale shaker; 26—Choke manifold; 27—Mud-gas separator; 28—Degasser; 29—Reserve pit; 30—Mud pits; 31—Desilter; 32—Desander; 33—Centrifuge; 34—Mud pumps; 35—Dry mud components storage; 36—Water storage; 37—Engines and generators; 38—Blowout preventer stack

the derrick is determined by the height of the derrick. A joint of drillpipe is about 30 ft (9.1 m) long, and a derrick that will allow the pulling and stacking of pipe, in three-joint sections (90 ft or 27.4 m), is about 140 ft (42.7 m) high.

There are four major systems of the rotary rig. These include power system, hoisting system, rotating system, and mud system.

2.2.1　The power system

Originally, the rotary rig uses diesel engines to generate electrical power. And now more rigs use AC electric power. AC-powered motors have highly responsive and accurate speed and torque control. AC drives use induction motors, which are efficient, relatively quiet, and relatively low-maintenance.

2.2.2 The hoisting system

Fig. 2.2 and 2.3 shows the main components of the hoisting system. It is used to raise and lower and to suspend equipment in the well.

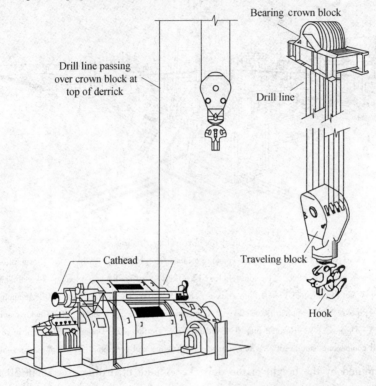

Fig. 2.2 Hoisting components of a rotary rig

The drawworks is a spool or drum upon which the heavy steel cable (drilling line) is wrapped. From the drawworks, the drilling line (wire rope) which is usually braided steel cable about 1 1/8 inches in diameter, is firstly wound around a reel in the drawworks and threaded up through the crown block at the top of the derrick and then through down the traveling block, which hangs suspended from the crown block. Below the traveling block is a hook to which equipment can be attached. The engines are connected to the drawworks and the drilling line in or out. By reeling in or letting out drill line from the drawworks drum, the traveling block and suspended drillstem can be raised or lowered.

In order to safely manage the movement of such a heavy load with precision, the driller relies on an electrical or hydraulic brake system to control the speed of the traveling block and a

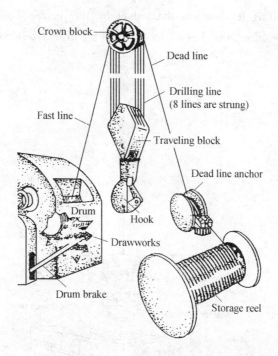

Fig. 2.3 Block diagram of the rotary rig

mechanical brake to bring it to a complete stop. The drawworks also features an auxiliary axle, or "catshaft", with rotating spools on each end called "catheads". One spinning cathead is used to provide power to tighten the drillpipe joints via a cable from the cathead to the rotary tongs. The other cathead is for "breaking out" or loosening the pipe joints when the pipe is being withdrawn in sections.

The wire rope drilling line that is spooled onto the drawworks drum undergoes a certain degree of wear as the block is raised and lowered in the derrick. For this reason the line is routinely "slipped" (moved onto the drawworks drum) and replaced with a new section from the continuous spool on which it is stored. The line is clamped at the storage spool end by a deadline anchor.

The hook is attached to the traveling block and is used to pick up the drillstem via the swivel and kelly when drilling, or with elevators when tripping into or out of the hole.

2.2.3 Rotating system

Fig. 2.4 shows the main components of the rotating system. Suspended on the hook directly below the traveling block is the swivel. The swivel allows the drillstem to rotate while supporting the weight of drillstring in the hole and providing a pressure-tight connection for the circulation of drilling fluid. The drilling fluid enters the swivel by way of the "gooseneck", a curved pipe connected to a high-pressure hose. Below the swivel is a four or six-sided pipe called the Kelly. The

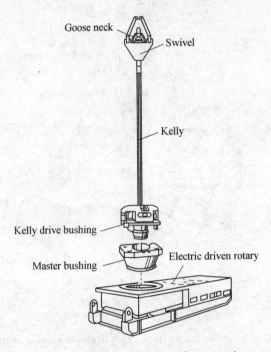

Fig. 2.4 Rotating components of a rotary rig

Kelly has sides so that it can be gripped and turned. The kelly cock is a special valve on the end of the kelly nearest the swivel, which can be closed to shut in the drillstem. A lower kelly cock is also available on the bottom end of the kelly to perform the same function when the upper kelly cock is not accessible. The flat-sided kelly fits through a corresponding opening in the kelly drive bushing, which in turn fits into the master bushing set into the rotary table. The kelly and swivel are connected to the drillstring and are suspended from the hook beneath the traveling block, allowing the kelly and drillstring to be turned by the rotary table. The term drillstem refers to the kelly and attached drillpipe, drill collars, and bit. The term drillstring refers to the drillpipe and drill collars. The rotary table is a circular table in the derrick floor. The rig engines turn the rotary table and the table turns the kelly. The kelly fits into the kelly bushing, the bushing turns the kelly and the kelly turns the drillpipe down to the bit.

　　The drill pipe is connected below the kelly. Steeldrill pipe come in 30 ft section that are threaded on both ends. The term a joint is "each section of drill pipe". The kelly must always be located on the top of the drill pipe. The term making a joint is " after drilling 30 ft, the kelly must be raised and another joint of pipe added below the kelly ", then another single is brought from the rack and placed in place (see Fig. 2. 5 and 2. 6).

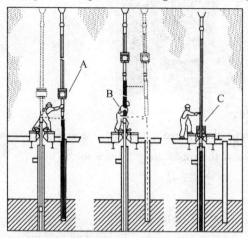 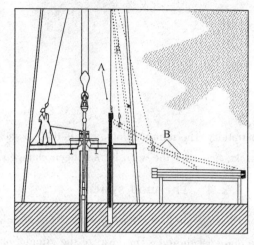

Fig. 2. 5　Making a connection　　　　　Fig. 2. 6　A new joint of pipe

Below the drill pipe are larger-diameter pipes called drill collars. Dill collars weigh more than drill pipe and are designed to put weight on the bottom of the drill pipe in case that drill pipe at that section may kink and break. Generally, two to twenty collars may often be placed. The bit screws into the bottom of the drill collars. Depending the different purposes, there are many kinds of bits (see Fig. 2. 7 and 2. 8). Different bits are used for different hardness formation. The most common bit is the tricone bit, which has tree rotating cones. The cones have teeth that are designed to chip and flake away the rock as the bit is rotated. Some tricone bits have hard tungsten carbide buttons

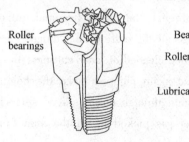 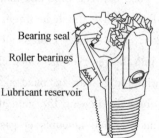 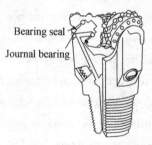

Fig. 2. 7　Tricone bit & diamond bit

instead of teeth. Another type of bit is the diamond or button bit, which has diamonds embedded in the bottom and sides. The button bit is the best for drilling limestones. Bits have an average wearing out time of 8 to 200 hours, so changing bit is necessary. A worn bit can be detected by: a. the noise on the derrick floor that the rotating drill pipe makes and, b. by a decrease in rate of drill

Fig. 2.8 Tricone bit & diamond bit

penetration. The term making a trip is that all the pipes are pulled out of the hole and stacked in the derrick, and after the worn bit has been changed, and the pipes are put back to the hole.

2.2.4 The mud system

The function of the mud system is the circulation of the drilling fluids to carry cuttings up the hole and cool the bit. The heart of the circulation system is the mud pumps, which are powered by the rig's prime power source, as are the rotary table and drawworks. Drilling fluids (also called drilling mud) are first stored in steel mud pits beside the rig. Mud pumps, called mud hogs, force a volume of drilling fluids from the mud pits or tanks up the standpipe to a point on the derrick where the rotary hose connects the standpipe to the swivel. This flexible, high-pressure hose allows the traveling block to move up and down in the derrick while maintaining a pressure-tight system. The circulating drilling fluids move through the swivel, kelly, drillpipe, and drill collars, exiting through the bit at the bottom of the hole, picking rock chips (cuttings) from the bottom of the well. The fluids then move up the annular space between pipe and hole (or casing), carrying the wastes in suspension. At the surface, the fluids leave the hole through the return line and fall over a vibrating screen called the shale shaker. This device screens out the cuttings and dumps. Some of them into a sample trap and the rest into the reserve pit. Once cleaned of large cuttings, the fluids are returned to a mud tank, from which they can be once again pumped down the hole. Fine particles are removed by centrifugal force by flowing the mud through desanders, desilters, or a centrifuge. A degasser is used to remove small amounts of gas picked up in the mud from the subsurface formations. See Fig. 2.9.

At the bottom of the well, there are two fluid pressures. Pressure on fluids in the rock tries to cause the fluids to flow into the well. Pressure exerted by the weight of the drilling fluids try to force the drilling fluids into the surrounding rocks. If the pressure on the fluids in the subsurface rock is greater than the pressure of the drilling fluids, the water, gas, or oil will flow out of the rock into the well. This often causes the sides of the well to cave in and trapping the equipment and may cause a

Chapter 2 Drilling Engineering

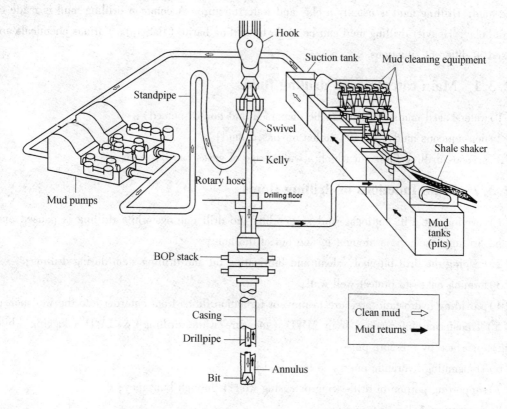

Fig. 2.9 Components of the circulating system for a rotary drilling rig

blowout. So the weight of the drilling fluids must be adjusted to exert a greater pressure on the bottom of the well. This is called overbalance, and the drilling fluids are then forced into the surrounding rocks. The rocks act as a filter and the solid mud particles cake to the sides of the well as the fluids enter the rock. This filter of mud cake is very hard. Once the filter cake has formed, the sides of the well are stabilized and subsurface fluids cannot enter the well.

2.3 Drilling Fluids

Key Words drilling fluid; main categories of drilling fluids; main functions of drilling fluids; types of drilling fluid; trouble and trouble shooting

In geotechnical engineering, drilling fluids are fluids used to drill boreholes into the earth. It is often used while drilling oil and natural gas wells and on exploration drilling rigs. Drilling fluids are also used for much simpler boreholes, such as water wells. Liquid drilling fluids are often called drilling mud. Drilling mud is usually a clay and water mixture. A common drilling mud is made of bentonite clay. Heavier drilling mud can be made by adding barite ($BaSO_4$). Various chemicals are also used in different situations.

2.3.1 Main categories of drilling fluids

(1) water-based muds (which can be dispersed and non-dispersed);
(2) non-aqueous muds, usually called oil-based mud;
(3) gaseous drilling fluid, in which a wide range of gases can be used.

2.3.2 Main functions of drilling fluids

(1) carrying out drill cuttings, and suspending the drill cuttings while drilling is paused and when the drilling assembly is brought in and out of the hole;
(2) keeping the drill bit cool, clean and lubricating bit and drilling stem during drilling;
(3) forming cakes to protect well wall;
(4) providing hydrostatic pressure to prevent formation fluids from entering into the well bore;
(5) Transfering information from MWD (measure while drilling) & LWD (logging while drilling) to surface by pressure pulse;
(6) Transmiting hydraulic energy to tools and bit;
(7) supporting portion of drill-string or casing weight through buoyancy;
(8) preventing or limiting corrosion.

2.3.3 Types of drilling fluids

Many types of drilling fluids are used on a day-to-day basis. Some wells require that different types be used at different parts in the hole, or that some types be used in combination with others. The various types of fluid generally fall into a few broad categories:

Air: Compressed air is pumped either down the bore hole's annular space or down the drill string itself.

Air/water: The same as above, with water added to increase viscosity, flush the hole, provide more cooling, and/or to control dust.

Air/polymer: A specially formulated chemical, most often referred to as a type of polymer, is added to the water & air mixture to create specific conditions. A foaming agent is a good example of a polymer.

Water: Water by itself is sometimes used.

Water-based mud (WBM): A most basic water-based mud system begins with water, then clays and other chemicals are incorporated into the water to create a homogenous blend resembling something between chocolate milk and a malt (depending on viscosity). The clay (called "shale" in its rock form) is usually a combination of native clays that are suspended in the fluid while drilling, or specific types of clay that are processed and sold as additives for the WBM (Water Based Mud) system. The most common of these is bentonite, frequently referred to in the oilfield as "gel". Gel likely makes reference to the fact that while the fluid is being pumped, it can be very thin and free-flowing (like chocolate milk), though when pumping is stopped, the static fluid builds a "gel" structure that resists flow. When an adequate pumping force is applied to "break the gel", flow resumes and the fluid returns to its previously free-flowing state. Many other chemicals (e. g. potassium formate) are added to a WBM system to achieve various effects, including: viscosity control, shale stability, enhance drilling rate of penetration, cooling and lubricating of equipment.

Oil-based mud (OBM): Oil-based mud can be a mud where the base fluid is a petroleum product such as diesel fuel. Oil-based muds are used for many reasons, some being increased lubricity, enhanced shale inhibition, and greater cleaning abilities with less viscosity. Oil-based muds also withstand greater heat without breaking down. The use of oil-based muds has special considerations. These include cost and environmental considerations.

Synthetic-based fluid (SBM): Synthetic-based fluid is a mud where the base fluid is a synthetic oil. This is most often used on offshore rigs because it has the properties of an oil-based mud, but the toxicity of the fluid fumes are much less than an oil-based fluid. This is important when men work with the fluid in an enclosed space such as an offshore drilling rig.

2.4 Trouble and Releasing

1. Control of mud properties

Trouble: Drilling mud weight is in excess of that needed to balance the pressure of surrounding rock (formation pressure), so mud weight is not usually increased for hole cleaning purposes.

Higher rotary drill-string speeds introduce a circular component to annular flow path. This helical flow around the drill-string causes drill cuttings near the wall, where poor hole cleaning conditions occur, to move into higher transport regions of the annulus.

Releasing: Increased rotation are the best methods in high angle and horizontal beds.

Trouble: Drill cuttings that settle causes bridges and fill, which can cause stuck-pipe and lost circulation. Weight material that settles is referred to as sag, this causes a wide variation in the density of well fluid, this more frequently occurs in high angle and hot wells.

High concentrations of drill solids are detrimental to:

Drilling efficiency (it causes increased mud weight and viscosity, which in turn increases maintenance costs and increased dilution)

Releasing: Mud properties that suspended must be balanced with properties in cutting removal by solids control equipment.

For effective solids controls, drill solids must be removed from mud on the 1st circulation from the well. If re-circulated, cuttings break into smaller pieces and are more difficult to remove.

Conduct a test to compare the sand content of mud at flow line and suction pit (to determine whether cuttings are being removed).

2. Control of formation pressures

Trouble: Unbalanced formation pressures will cause an unexpected influx of pressure in the wellbore possibly leading to a blowout from pressured formation fluids.

Releasing: If formation pressure increases, mud density should also be increased, often with barite (or other weighting materials) to balance pressure and keep the wellbore stable.

Hydrostatic pressure = density of drilling fluid × true vertical depth × acceleration of gravity.

Trouble: If hydrostatic pressure is greater than or equal to formation pressure, formation fluid will not flow into the wellbore.

Well control means no uncontrollable flow of formation fluids into the wellbore.

Hydrostatic pressure also controls the stresses caused by tectonic forces, which may make wellbores unstable even when formation fluid pressure is balanced.

Releasing: If formation pressure is subnormal, air, gas, mist, stiff foam, or low density mud (oil base) can be used.

In practice, mud density should be limited to the minimum necessary for well control and wellbore stability. If too great it may fracture the formation.

3. Seal of permeable formations

Trouble: When mud column pressure exceeds formation pressure, mud filtrate invades the formation, and a filter cake of mud is deposited on the wellbore wall.

Releasing: Mud is designed to deposit thin, low permeability filter cake to limit the invasion.

Trouble: Problems occur if a thick filter cake is formed; tight hole conditions, poor log quality, stuck pipe, lost circulation and formation damage.

In highly permeable formations with large pore throats, whole mud may invade the formation, depending on mud solids size.

Releasing: Use bridging agents to block large opening, then mud solids can form seal.

For effectiveness, bridging agents (e.g. calcium carbonate, ground cellulose) must be over the half size of pore spaces / fractures.

Depending on the mud system in use, a number of additives can improve the filter cake (e. g. bentonite, natural & synthetic polymer, asphalt and gilsonite).

4. Maintain wellbore stability

Chemical composition and mud properties must combine to provide a stable wellbore. Weight of the mud must be within the necessary range to balance the mechanical forces.

Trouble: Wellbore instability can cause tight hole conditions, bridges and fill on trips (same symptoms indicate hole cleaning problems).

If the hole is enlarged, it becomes weak and difficult to stabilize, resulting in problems such as low annular velocities, poor hole cleaning, solids loading and poor formation evaluation

Releasing: In sand and sandstones formations, hole enlargement can be accomplished by mechanical actions (hydraulic forces & nozzles velocities). Formation damage is reduced by conservative hydraulics system. A good quality filter cake containing bentonite is known to limit bore hole enlargement.

Trouble: In shales, mud weight is usually sufficient to balance formation stress, as these wells are usually stable. With water base mud, chemical differences can cause interactions between mud & shale that lead to softening of the native rock. Highly fractured, dry, brittle shales can be extremely unstable (leading to mechanical problems).

Releasing: Various chemical inhibitors can control mud/shale interactions (calcium, potassium, salt, polymers, asphalt, glycols and oil-best for water sensitive formations).

Oil (and synthetic oil) based drilling fluids are used to drill most water sensitive shales in areas with difficult drilling conditions.

To add inhibition, emulsified brine phase (calcium chloride) drilling fluids are used to reduce water activity and creates osmotic forces to prevent adsorption of water by Shales.

5. Minimizing of formation damage

Skin damage or any reduction in natural formation porosity and permeability (washout) constitutes formation damage

Trouble: Mud or drill solids invade the formation matrix, reducing porosity and causing skin effect. Swelling of formation clays within the reservoir, reduced permeability.

Precipitation of solids due to mixing of mud filtrate and formations fluids resulting in the precipitation of insoluble salts.

Mud filtrate and formation fluids form an emulsion, reducing reservoir porosity.

Releasing: Specially designed drill-in fluids or workover and completion fluids minimize formation damage. Cool, lubricate, and support the bit and drilling assembly.

Trouble: Heat is generated from mechanical and hydraulic forces at the bit and when the drill string rotates and rubs against casing and wellbore.

Releasing: Cool and transfer heat away from source and lower to temperature than bottom hole. If not, bit, drill string and mud motors would fail more rapidly.

6. Lubricity based on Coefficient of friction

Trouble: Poor lubrication causes high torque and drag, heat checking of drill string but aware these problem also caused by key seating, poor hole cleaning and incorrect bottom hole assemblies design.

Releasing: Lubricity based on Coefficient of friction. Oil- and synthetic-based mud generally lubricate better than water-based mud (but can be improved by the addition of lubricants).

Amount of lubrication provided by drilling fluid depends on type & quantity of drill solids and weight materials + chemical composition of system.

7. Control of drill string pressures

Trouble: Drill string pressure loses higher in fluids higher densities, plastic viscosities and solids.

Releasing: Low solids, shear thinning drilling fluids such as polymer fluids, more efficient in transmit hydraulic energy.

8. Control corrosion (in acceptable level)

Trouble: Drill-string and casing in continuous contact with drilling fluid may cause a form of corrosion.

Dissolved gases (oxygen, carbon dioxide, hydrogen sulfide) cause serious corrosion problems;

Cause rapid, catastrophic failure;

May be deadly to humans after a short period of time.

Releasing: Low pH (acidic) aggravates corrosion, so use corrosion coupons to monitor corrosion type, rates and to tell correct chemical inhibitor is used in correct amount.

Trouble: Mud aeration, foaming and other O_2 trapped conditions cause corrosion damage in short period time.

Releasing: When drilling in high H_2S, elevated the pH fluids + sulfide scavenging chemical (zinc).

2.5 A Brief Explanation of a Certain Drilling Program

Before drilling a well, a drilling program must be ready. Generally, the planned total depth of a well is 2 450 m with the conductor pipe being set at 36 m and the surface casing at 150 m. Some times it doesn't need the intermediate casing.

The diameter of the conductor pipes and that of the surface casing and the production casing are 20", 14 3/4" and 7", respectively. For running casing, drill a 24" hole for the conductor pipe, and then the surface hole and production hole with 17 1/2" and 9 5/8" bits. The mud program goes with Lime polymer mud system. The maximum density is 1.89 g/cm^3 and the viscosity is about 60 seconds. During drilling, a BOP drill and fire drill are very important.

Furthermore, Enough LCM (Lost circulation Material) and kill material must be prepared. The main pay zone is approximately from 1 650 to 2 300 m. So when reaching to the depth of 1 500 m, the related drills and slow pump stroke test must be performed. The pressure gradient is 1.2 MPa/100 m, and the parameters for drilling the conductor hole are 80 RPM, 110 SPM with double pumps, 2~6 ton WOB (Weight on Bit), and the ROP (Rate of Penetration) is less 40 m/h. The parameters for drilling the surface hole are 120 RPM, 105 SPM with single pumps, 4~8 ton WOB.

During drilling, instruments are used. They are: weight indicator, pump pressure gauge, flow rate gauge, rotary gauge, torque gauge, and mud recorder, etc. Pump pressure, weight on bit, rotary speed, flow rate torque etc are drilling parameters, and viscosity, water loss, mud weight, solid content, sand content etc are mud parameters. The weight indicator is used to show the parameter of the weight on bit and the hook load, the rotational viscosimeter to indicate the plastic viscosity of the mud, and the drilling fluid level sensor to identify and warn of the kick and lost circulation and so on. Some of the instruments are powered by air source and the others by electricity.

Summary

Well Drilling is the most important part of Petroleum Engineering. Exploitation well and evaluation wells are commonly drilled during the exploration period and infilled wells are needed later on. Drilling machines are composed of power, hoisting, rotating and mud system. Power system consists of giant diesel motors and diesel generating sets, and so far the powerful electric motors have been used in most fields, rotating system has swivel, kelly, rotating table, drill string, bit, hoisting system includes draw works, pulley block, and receiving storage reel, and mud system is equipped with mud pumps, shale shakers, suction tanks, mud tanks (mud pits), as well as mud cleaning equipment.

After everything is ready, it is time to begin. First drill the surface hole, set conductor and do the cementing job; then begins to spud in, the kelly, as well as strings and bit, is run by rotating table; bit cuts strata, while the circulating mud carries debris up to the surface; when to certain depth, set surface casing, intermediate casing and tubing successively in case of caving in and protecting superficial water from pollution; the cementing job is then done; the next step is to do the completion job by perforating or other ways to finish the well; fitting the christmas tree, testing the well and delivering the well to production unit is the last step.

Technical English Applications

Instruction

Generally, instruction writing is mainly divided into two parts: title and body. When writing an instruction, pay attention to the following points:

(1) Title must be a noun, noun phrases or verbid. Never use a sentence to form a tile.

(2) Use simple sentences with brief words and expressions. The language used must be short, exact, and easily understood.

(3) Use imperative sentences in the instruction manual.

(4) Instruction parts are listed with letters and figures to indicate the order or schedule, in case of misunderstanding.

(5) noun phrases, compound nouns, abbreviations, and verbid are frequently used in instructions.

【Example】

Drilling Instruction

From: TOTAL Rep- Well KH 13 Date: 18 June, 2002	To: -Rig Supt Cc: Toolpushers-Drillers-Services Comp

Subject: PRE SPUD TEST

TDS:

Install and test top drive (full test)

Change out saver sub

Re-calibrate torque

Emergency shut down

DRILLER PANEL:

All sensors must be calibrated

Test all SCR's

Test all alarms (flow panel…)

Test emergency shut down

Test no Pb with hydraulic bundle in the mast

Function test tuggers

Test crown "O" matic

Check GEOSERVICES sensors calibration

Check monkey board camera is ready

Check gas and smoke detectors are calibrated and at the right place

Test fire pump, foam unit and water transfer pump

Connect fire pump to emergency power supply& test

Check verticality of the mast

Test casing stabbing board

MUD TANK AND SURFACE LINES:

Line up line in order to have the return on shale shakers

Fill up, flush all surface lines and check if we have any leaks step by step

Check all underflow mud guns lines

Test all agitators, shale shakers, mixing unit

Function test desilter, desander, centrifuge, degasser (flow rate and vacuum)

Secure all surface lines

MUD PUMPS:

Make sure water-cooling on pump lines is working fine

Stop if any problems

Install safety device on each pump to shut down power

Make sure that all HP lines are secured with safety chains

Start circulation with 50 spm/100 spm and check spm and pressure sensors

Rig and Geoservices

PRESSURE TESTS:

Fill up and flush lines:

All test to be performed at 500 psi to 4 500 psi for 10 min

Set pop off valve on mud pump at 300 psi

Thanks

SMITH

Excercises

Part 1 Multiple choice

1. Drilling mud is usually a mixture of _____.

   A. water, clay, gas and a few chemicals

   B. oil, chemicals, weighting material and clay

   C. chemicals, weighting material and clay

   D. water, clay, weighting material, and a few chemicals

2. Everything but _____ is considered part of _____, a term that refers to all of the special equipment.

   A. the host; the rig B. the casing; the rig

   C. the tubular; the casing D. the host; the tubular

3. The cementing job is _____.

   A. to pull the drill string and the bit out, and force liquified cement down through the casing to the space between the formation and casing

   B. force liquified cement down through the drill string to the space between the formation and casing

   C. pulling the casing and the bit out, and force liquified cement down through the space between the formation and drill string

   D. to push the drill string and the bit out, and force liquified cement down the space between the formation and drill string

4. The mud goes through _____ and return through _____ up to the ground.

   A. the drill string, bit; the annular

   B. the casing; the drill string

   C. the drill string; the annular

   D. the casing, bit; the drill string

5. In _____, a hole is punched or pounded into the ground with special cutting tools, while in _____ a circular motion like the one a carpenter uses to make a hole in a piece of wood is used to penetrate the ground.

   A. remote drilling; cable-drilling

   B. cable-tool drilling; rotary drilling

   C. rotary drilling; directional drilling

   D. cable-tool drilling; directional drilling

Part 2　Translation Practice

1. Translate the following phrases into Chinese:

1) be made up of
2) spud in
3) from time to time
4) be connected to
5) by way of
6) in turn
7) be attached to
8) in case that
9) be applied to
10) be in excess of

2. Translate the following sentences into Chinese:

1) Rotary drilling is a cutting system that uses a drill bit to cut or enlarge a hole in solid materials.

2) The derrick, or mast, supports the crown block and traveling block, which are operated via the drawworks and its drilling line.

3) Fig. 2.3 shows the main components of the rotating system.

4) Below the drill pipe are larger-diameter pipes called drill collars.

5) The function of rotary drilling rig is the circulation of the drilling fluids to carry cuttings up the hole and cool the bit.

Part 3　Reading comprehension:

1. Classify the Drilling system.
2. Give a brief explanation of a drilling procedure.
3. Give a brief explanation of mud system.

Part 4　Writing comprehension

Try to write a drilling instruction.

Reading Material: New Trend of Technology

Enhanced Technology Promises Improved Well Planning, Drilling Engineering Workflows

Enterprise software provider Paradigm recently launched its upgraded well planning and drilling engineering application aimed at reducing nonproductive time. Known as Sysdrill 2009, the technology reduces drilling risk and cost by enabling the drilling engineer to model all phases of wellbore construction within a single application.

The company states that by combining advanced well planning and drilling engineering in a single application, Sysdrill 2009 allows drilling engineers to plan wells quickly, safely, and accurately to reduce drilling uncertainty. The application suite incorporates several components, including:

(1) The well planning module allows geometrically constrained wellpaths and sidetracks to be validated against the prospect.

A casing design module that allows the driller to safely design the minimum number of casing strings required to safely complete a well, which can reduce well capital costs

(2) A well planning module that provides easy and efficient well design by offering automated well planning from a surface location to multiple targets

(3) A hydraulics optimization and analysis system that models downhole circulating pressures during drilling, tripping, and running casing

(4) A torque and drag component, used to model the forces acting on drilling assemblies, casing strings, sand screens, and completion strings to eliminate drilling string failure.

The 2009 version reportedly delivers tighter integration, improved ease-of-use, and enhanced functionality. Additional benefits of this release include a significant reduction in data entry time for engineering analyses, advanced input-output interface for loading third-party data, results-driven analysis for faster identification of drilling problems, and the ability to incorporate geological data for improved planning and visualization.

Sysdrill integrates well planning, drilling engineering analysis, and visualization to allow drilling engineers to perform quick and accurate well design by incorporating the geological model.

Sysdrill 2009 is also integrated with Paradigm's Geolog petrophysical log interpretation application to provide a commercially available, real-time geosteering solution. The contractor-independent Geolog platform offers unique workflows to support the fast creation of log-scale geosteering models ahead of drilling, facilitate interactive updates to geosteering models while drilling, and enable the replanning of wells using updated models.

The interactivity between Sysdrill and Geolog is an example of the multidisciplinary workflows enabled by Paradigm's solutions continuum known as Paradigm Higher Order Workflows (H.O.W.). Paradigm H.O.W. advance the science of hydrocarbon detection and extraction with fit-for-purpose and customizable geophysical, geological, petrophysical, and engineering solutions.

"In today's challenging market conditions, there is even greater need for accurate well design that minimizes nonproductive rig time," said Robert Innes, Paradigm Director of Well Planning and Drilling. "Paradigm Sysdrill 2009 enables high levels of integration and engineering analysis to achieve these goals."

Ted Moon is the Technology Editor of JPT Online. He brings information on emerging technologies, R&D successes, new field applications, updates from SPE papers about recent innovations, and more. If you have a question or suggestion for future article topics, email Ted at teched@spe.org.

http://www.spe.org/jpt/2009/04/enhanced-technology-promises-improved-well-planni

Chapter 3

Cementing Engineering

Purpose & Requirements

Cementing Engineering is the last and the most key procedure of drilling engineering. The purpose of cementing engineering is to seal off the loose, cavy, and leaking formations, to isolate oil, gas and water layers against crossflow, and to assemble well head, as well as control the stream. The basic requirements are: after the cementing job, an integral sheath between casing and cement and cement and well wall must be well formed, and layers between oil, gas and water be isolated completely.

Key Words cementing engineering; cementing; principal objectives of the primary cementing process; the dimensions and strengths of casing; the principal objectives of the secondary cementing process

Cementing engineering: During drilling of a well, in order to protect the borehole face, seal off oil, gas and water layers, when reaching a certain depth, it is needed to set a kind of annular steel tube called casing into the well, then the cement slurry (a mixture of cement and water, as well as hardwares) fills the annulus around the centralized string of casing, wait it solidified, and go on with another smaller sized casing (see Fig. 3.1). The working of running a casing into the well and pumping cement slurry into the annulus is called cementing. It is one of the most critical operations performed during the drilling and completion of a well.

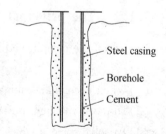

Fig. 3.1 Cementing casing strings

3.1 The Principal Objectives of the Primary Cementing Process

(1) To isolate and control formations restricting fluid movement and sealing-off lost circulation or thief zones.

(2) To support and bond the casing to the formation.

(3) Act as a conduit or pipeline for oil and gas to flow from the reservoir to the surface during production.

(4) To protect the casing from corrosion and reinforce it against the shock loads in drilling deeper.

(5) To control the pressure and flow rate.

3.1.1 The principal objectives of the surface casing

(1) To prevent the rig foundation from collapsing.

(2) To isolate the upper loose, cavy and leaky formation.

(3) To assemble well head, support intermediate casing and tubing; some deeper surface casing can also be used to install blowout preventer (BOP).

(4) To provide protection for fresh water formation.

(5) To prevent the hole from caving in.

(6) To control fluids crossflow.

3.1.2 The principal objectives of the intermediate casing

To seal off the complicated formations that are difficult to control with drilling fluids, usually in case that:

(1) When encounter leaking, high pressure, caving in, and shrinking layers.

(2) To meet with high pressure, thief zone, rock salt, and shrinking layers.

(3) To solve some troubles encountered with unpredicted formation pressure, so that the BOP must be installed to prevent blowing out.

3.1.3 The principal objectives of the production casing

(1) To prevent the oil-bearing from caving in.

(2) To isolate the hydrocarbon zone from other fluids and the hydrocarbon zone with different pressure.

3.2 The Principal Objectives of the Secondary Cementing Process

(1) To mechanically anchor the casing in place.
(2) To seal the borehole in order to prevent vertical movement of fluids from zone to zone.
(3) To abandon a well or isolate zones.
(4) When directional drilling, lost circulation control, or formation testing is required.

3.3 The Dimensions and Strengths of Casing

The dimensions and strengths of casing is identified by its outside diameter (OD), measured in inches. Casing sizes range from 4 1/2 to over 30 in. OD. Casing lengths are generally supplied in three ranges: Range 1 casing lengths range from 19~26 ft; Range 2 casing 26~32 ft; Range 3 casing 32~42 ft. The most common lengths are 31 ft and 42 ft. Longer casing joints are generally preferred because, since there are fewer connections per foot of casing, there are fewer points of possible failure. Running longer casing is also more economical because making the connection adds to the cost of the casing.

Casing is further classified by weight and grade. Casing weights are given as pounds per foot (lb/ft) with the extra weight of the coupling averaged over the joint of casing. For example, $5^1/_2$-in. casing is a common size that can be obtained in casing weights ranging from 13~26 lb/ft. Since the OD of the casing is always held constant for one size, the inside diameter (ID) varies according to the casing weight. For example, $5^1/_2$-in. 13-lb/ft casing has an ID of 5.044 in., compared to 4.548 in. for a $5^1/_2$-in. 26-lb/ft casing. These small differences in inside diameter are very important in selecting bit sizes and other tools to be run inside the casing. For the same size casing, heavier-weight casing is stronger with greater collapse and tensile strengths. Casing collapse occurs when the external forces and pressures cause the sides of the casing to flatten and push together. Tensile strength is a measure of the actual steel strength of the pipe, which shows how much weight or loading the casing can support. Heavier casing weighs more and also costs more, since there is a larger amount of steel in the casing on a per-foot basis.

3.4 Primary Cementing

Key Words primary cementing; running casing; cementing; cement displacement; wait on cement

Primary cementing is the cementing that takes place immediately after casing has been run into the hole during the drilling operation. A good primary cementing job is one in which the cementing completely fills the annulus. Cementing job includes running casing and cementing.

Running casing is a job of connecting a joint of casing (or a joint) with its attachments needed together into the well. The joint has a tube or body with screw-type connectors on each end, commonly a pin, or male connector on the bottom and a box, or female, connector on the top of the tube (Top and bottom here refer to the position of the casing after it has been run into the hole). A joint on site usually consists of two parts: 1. box coupling and 2. casing (Fig. 3.2).

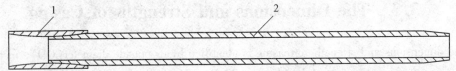

Fig. 3.2 a single casing

Box coupling and casing are fabricated separately and have already been screwed together before leaving the factory.

Cementing is the job of firstly pumping slurry into the inner side of the casing, then pushing it out into the annulus with drilling fluids after setting the casing. Fig. 3.3 is a typical conventional primary cementing procedure.

The device fixed at the top end of the casing string is the cement head, inside which fit an upper and a lower rubber plug. The function of the lower plug, together with spacer fluid, is to separate the slurry and the drilling fluids, in case that the drilling fluids may affect the property of slurry after they meet each other. The lower plug is a hollow one, on top of which is a rubber membrane which can be broken with the pressure exerted on it.

The upper plug is a solid one, the function of which is to separate drilling fluids for replacement from slurry and, after it has seated on the lower plug against the float collar, the surface pressure goes up rapidly to a certain value (it is called "squeezing pressure"), the signal indicates that the slurry has been in position. There is a guide shoe fixed on the bottom of the casing string for good casing. Float collar is exactly a check valve, the function of which is preventing the slurry inside the annulus flowing back into the string (as the density of the slurry is higher than that of drilling fluids), as well as being used for seating the rubber plug.

When reaching the designed depth, it is time to clean the shale shaker, mix the chemicals, unscrew the circulating head, fix the cementing head, inject about 5 barrels of spacer fluid, unpack the backing pin of the lower rubber plug, put the rubber plug into the cementing head, and then pump the slurry. The programmed slurry weight is about 16 ppg (pound per gallen), the amount of

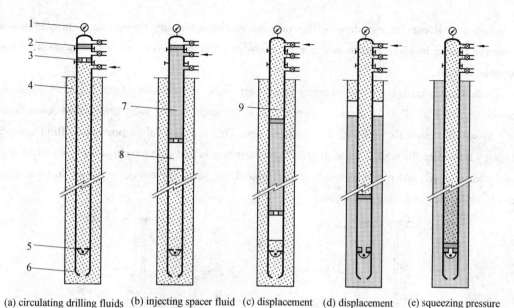

(a) circulating drilling fluids (b) injecting spacer fluid and slurry (c) displacement (d) displacement (e) squeezing pressure

Fig. 3.3 Cementing engineering flow diagram

1—pressure gage; 2—upper rubber plug; 3—lower rubber plug; 4—drilling fluids; 5—float collar; 6—guide shoe; 7—cement slurry; 8—spacer fluid; 9—drilling fluids

about 600 bags of cement will be pumped. After the injection, unpack the backing pin of upper rubber plug, put the rubber plug into the cementing head, and displace the slurry with drilling fluids. The process of displacement of the slurry with drilling fluids is called cement displacement. After the lower rubber plug has been seated on the float collar, the rubber membrane breaks with the pressure on it; The cement displacement will not stop until the upper and lower plug meets.

Mud pump is used to do the displacement job, first the double pump, then the single pump at a rate of 75 strokes per minute. The squeezing pressure is 2 500 psi (pound per square inch), and hold on for 5 minutes after squeezing the cement, then release the pressure. It will take 6 to 8 hours to wait on cement. The time of waiting for the cement to solidify is called wait on cement.

3.5 Secondary Cementing

Key Words   secondary cementing; purpose of the secondary cementing; two main types of secondary cementing; squeeze cementing; plug-cementing

Secondary cementing is a remedy job in which the cementing completely fills up the zone to be isolated, the specific intervals to be sealed, or controls a lost circulation and performs a formation test before a well can be completed. The purpose of the secondary cementing is to mechanically anchor the casing in place and to seal the borehole in order to prevent vertical movement of fluids from zone to zone.

There are two main types of secondary cementing: squeeze cementing (see Fig. 3.4) and plug-cementing (see Fig. 3.5). Squeeze cementing is the process that uses pressure to force cement slurry to specific intervals in a well to provide a seal. This seal is vital in preventing fluid migration between zones after the well is perforated. Plug-cementing is that cement plugs are used when a well is to be abandoned, when a zone needs to be isolated, or when directional drilling, lost circulation control, or formation testing is required.

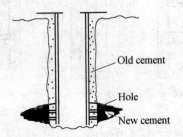
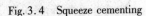

Fig. 3.4 Squeeze cementing

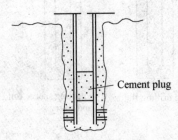

Fig. 3.5 Setting cement plugs

3.6 A Case of Cementing Operation

Preparation for cementing:

Mix the cementing chemicals and prepare 3 bottles of water slurry samples.

Test the pressure of cementing line: 3 000 psi, keep away from the high-pressure line while the pressure testing.

Check the inside capacity of the casing: 0.149 62 lb/ft

Put the plugs into the cementing head and check if they work well (the release sign is working or not), and connect the cementing line.

The programmed slurry weight is 16 ppg (pound per gallen).

Prepare 5 barrels of spacer and 600 bags of cement. The additional amount of cement is 15%.

Cementing:

Pump slurry into the inner side of the casing.

About 25 minutes later, first use the double pump, then the single pump to do the displacement at 75 strokes per minute.

The squeezing pressure is 2 500 psi.

Wait on cement time: 6~8 hours, depending on the cement samples.

Hold on the pressure for 5 minutes then release after the squeezing of the cement.

An hour later, cut the $13^3/_8"$ casing.

The cement plug will be pumped to 1 200 m deep near the casing shoe.

Run in 5" pipes to about 1 200 m.

Connect one $4^1/_2"$ IF×2" union with the cement line.

The depth of the cement top is 1 850 m deep at the choke ring.

The top cementing is set in the annular clearance between the 20" casing and $13^3/8"$ casing.

Check the interpolation cementing head for 20" casing top-cementing.

Connect 10 pieces of 2" tubes and prepare the adaptor to connect the rotary hose.

Check the top of cement in the cellar with a long pipe (it is about 1 m below the surface of the cellar)

Pump 60 barrels of high viscosity gel before pumping the cementing plug.

After pumping the cement plug, pull 3 stands out of the hole, and then make up the kelly for circulation.

After cementing:

Pump out the mud from all the tanks, clean them and pump fresh water into them.

Summary

Development of Cementing technology approaches simultaneously with that of petroleum profession, from single step to multi-step cementing, from shallow to deep even super-deep (tens of thousands of meters), from simple calculation to the using of computer software control, from the purpose of simply production to the protection of hydrocarbon zone, and from merely slurry cementing to modern MTC tech. Development of Cementing technology goes on with broad aspects, mainly of cementing equipment, slurry system, additives, tool accessories, software, etc. Not only can modern cementing tech. solve problems like absorption well, high pressure well, extended reach well, horizontal well etc, but also expand to the protection of hydrocarbon zone and stimulation. Modern computer programming has driven cementing unit to higher level and more complicated tech.

Technical English Applications

Resume

In finding a job, applying for a higher position, we need writing a resume.

Here introduces the procedure of writing a resume.

Resume writing mainly consists of:

1. Title

On the top middle of the paper, write the capital letter "RESUME".

2. Heading

Below the title, interlined, on the top right, write your heading. This includes your name, address, telephone number and e-mail.

3. Body

Interlined, left-justified, put your body of resume. This consists of:

1) OBJECTIVE
2) EDUCATION
3) EXPERIENCE
4) ACHIEVMENTS & ACTIVITIES
5) SCHOLARSHIPS & AWARDS
6) SELF EVALUATION
7) REFERENCES

Suggestions on writing a resume:

1. Write with noun phrases for indication, verb phrases for explanation;

2. Use present, present perfect and past tense, never use future tense; never use "I" in sentences; had better not use too many abbreviations;

3. Use block, italic and underlined letters to emphasize the key points;

4. Had better write your resume on just one piece of paper and, make it look more special.

【Example】

RESUME

WANG Hao

Hegang, Heilongjiang Province, China

Cell Phone: 13613677504

E-mail: wanghao1988@sohu.com

OBJECTIVE Engineer in Petroleum Engineering

EDUCATION Hua Rui, Daqing Petroleum University

Major: Petroleum Engineering & Professional English for Petroleum Engineering

	Minor: Computer Programming
EXPERIENCE	Practice on oil field, 2006
	Fieldwork in Tech. Center, Summer, 2008
ACHIEVMENTS & ACTIVITIES	
	President and Founder of the Costumer Committee
	Established the organization as a member of BIT
	President of Communications for the Marketing Association
	Representative in the Student Association
COMPUTER ABITITIES	
	Skilled in using of MS Frontpage, Win 95/NT, Sun, Visual Interdev, Distributed Objects, CORBA, C, C++, Project 98, Office 97, Rational RequisitePro, Pascal, PL/I and SQL. Software
ENGLISH SKILLS	A good command of both oral and written English
	Passed CET-4 & CET-6
SCHOLARSHIPS & AWARDS	
	Guanghua Third-class Scholarship for graduate, Sep. 2006
SELF EVALUATION	Honest, progressive, independent, and able to work under a dynamic environment, coordination, teamwork, study and dedication
REFERENCES	Diploma, Achievements, Certificates, and Awards

Exercises

Part 1   Reading comprehension

1. What is cementing engineering?
2. What is cementing?
3. How is casing classified?
4. What is the purpose of the secondary cementing?
5. How many basic types of secondary cementing are there? What are they?
6. What are the functions of surface casing?

Part 2   Reading comprehension

1. Elaborate the primary cementing work.
2. Give a simple explanation of secondary cementing.
3. Tell the reason why the cementing plugs are used.
4. Explain squeezing pressure.

Part 3 Translation practice

1. Translate the following phrases into Chinese:

1) seal off
2) in order to
3) protect … from …
4) pounds per foot
5) adds to
6) at the top end of
7) as well as
8) in place

2. Translate the following sentences into Chinese:

1) Cementing Engineering is the last and the most key procedure of drilling engineering.

2) The purpose of cementing engineering is to seal off the loose, cavy, and leaking formations, to isolate oil, gas and water layers against crossflow, and to assemble well head, as well as control the stream.

3) The dimensions and strengths of casing is identified by its outside diameter(OD), measured in inches.

4) The device fixed at the top end of the casing string is the cement head, inside which fit an upper and a lower rubber plug.

5) The lower plug is a hollow one, on top of which is a rubber membrane which can be broken with the pressure exerted on it.

Part 4 Pair off the following phrases

annular steel tube	井口
cement slurry	下套管
well head	碰压
outside diameter(OD)	隔离液
spacer fluid	橡皮膜
Running casing	地层试验
cement head	引鞋
lower plug	水泥浆
rubber membrance	钢制套管
squeezing pressure	外径
formation test	水泥头
guide shoe	下胶塞

Part 5 Writing comprehension

Write a resume.

Reading Material: New Trend of Technology

BP to Use New BJ Cementing Unit in GoM

HOUSTON—BJ Services Co. has developed a new-generation, high-performance cementing unit for Pride International's drillship PS 1 which is scheduled for BP operations in the Gulf of Mexico. The drillship is expected to begin operations in ultra deepwater during 3Q 2010.

The unit provides a range of performance capabilities for offshore cementing, including faster mixing rates for high-volume tophole cementing, faster displacement rates for a variety of operations, and greater redundancy and backup capacity.

The Seahawk dual-skid cementing unit features automated twin-mixing capabilities and 2 300 bhp, ensuring density control and zonal isolation across long, complex intervals. Slurry consistency is maintained with two independent automatic cement control systems, Coriolis mass metering technology, and hydraulically driven recirculating blending systems. The power unit and pump combination also enables the unit to be configured as a temporary replacement for mud pumps for selected displacement operations, the company says.

The custom design also incorporates automated liquid additive components, variable-speed electric drives, and a high-speed fiber-optics package, enabling personnel to transmit information anywhere in the world. The self-contained model isolates the crew from high-powered components and manifolds to minimize noise, vibration, dust, and fume exposure, the company says.

BJ Services Soups up Units for Deepwater Cementing

HOUSTON—In order to meet operators' demands for reduced mixing and pumping times during deepwater cementing, BJ Services continues to develop higher horsepower cementing units with a wider array of configuration options.

In recent months a 1 600-brake horsepower (BHP) version and a powerful 2 300-BHP model were developed to handle displacement tasks at higher rates and pressures. High-speed fiber optics let the equipment communicate via remote.

Twin-mixing capabilities are being developed for the 2 300-BHP Seahawk unit for blending rates to 20 bpm to be deployed on an ultra-deepwater drillship in theGulf of Mexico in 2009.

By www.offshore-mag.com

Chapter 4

Completion Engineering

Purpose & Requirements

Key Words completion; requirements

Completion is the process of making a well ready for production, which, according to geological characters of hydrocarbon reservoir and the technical requirement of exploration and recovery, builds up the reasonable connections between reservoir and wellbore, involving preparing the bottom of the hole to the required specifications, running in the production tubing and its associated down hole tools as well as perforating and stimulating as required. The reasonable completion methods must fulfill the following requirements: connections between hydrocarbon zones and borehole must be in the optimum condition; the effluent seepage area of hydrocarbon zones to borehole should be larger; isolate zones effectively in case of gas breakthrough (GBT) or water break through (WBT); control sand production, and prevent borehole face from caving in. The completion engineers must understand and master the completion methods, and can design optimum methods in various complicated reservoir conditions.

Completion is as important as drilling a well, so we need to know the specific steps involved in the completion. Completion equipment and the methods are quite varied. This requires completion engineers have a broad view of this technology and make the correct decision for every individual well scientifically. Here are the mostly used completion methods:

Single-zone completion; Multiple-zone completion; Open-hole completion; Perforated completion; Cased hole completion; Wire-wrapped Screen completion; Tubing-less completion; Single-zone tubing-less completion; Multiple-zone tubing-less completion.

4.1 Conventional Completions

Key Words conventional completions; single-zone completions; multiple-zone completions

Conventional completion is that one or more production strings (tubings) are used for safety and other reasons. Inside the well casing there is commonly a tubing, the fundamental characteristic of which is that it is located completely inside the casing and that it is not cemented, therefore easy to replace.

4.1.1 Single-zone completion

Single-zone completion is the way the well is equipped with a single tubing. There are two main types of single-zone completions, depending on whether the tubing has a production packer on its lower end. See Fig. 4.1.

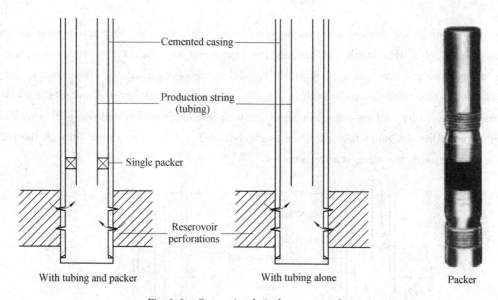

Fig. 4.1 Conventional single-zone completion

Single-zone completion, which is with just a tubing and no production packer, is used when the only aim is to have the right pipe diameter with respect to the flow rate. Obtaining enough velocity can thus lift the heavy part of the effluent but not too much in order to limit pressure drops, thereby minimize energy consumption. Single-zone completions may sometimes be considered as a variation on single-zone tubingless completion, since the hanging tubing has more of a repair and maintenance function, for example kill string to neutralize the well for workover jobs. They may be suitable for wells that produce a fluid that causes no problems at a very high flow rate.

Single-zone completions with a tubing and a production packer are the most widely used because of the safety due to the packer and their relative simplicity in comparison with multiple or other types of completion, in terms of installation, maintenance and workover.

4.1.2 Multiple-zone completion

Originally, Producing several zones together through the same tubing was used, but the subsequent reservoir and production problems that were experience have now caused this technique to be developed.

Multiple-zone completion is the technique that two more zones are produced in the same well at the same time but through different strings of pipe. Usually, one or two more separate tubing strings with packers are run inside the production casing for each producing zone. For another example, in a triple completion, three tubing strings and three packers can be utilized in a single production string.

Commonly used are double-zone completions, and there are three, four and even more zones produced separately. This surely complicates the equipment and makes any workover operations much more complex. Here, see Fig. 4.2(a): parallel string completions with two tubings, one for each of the two zones and two packers to isolate the zone from one another and protect the annulus. Also see Fig. 4.2(b): tubing-annulus completion with one single tubing and one packer, which is located between the two zones that are to be produced, with one zone produced through the tubing and the other through the tubing-casing annulus.

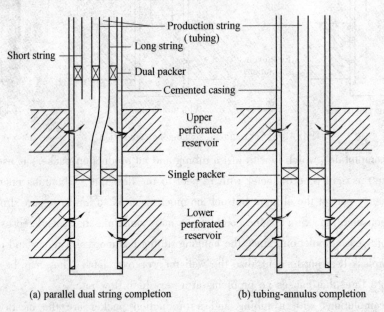

Fig. 4.2 (a) Parallel dual string completion (b) Tubing-annulus completion

4.2 Open-hole Completion

Key Words open-hole completion

Open-hole completion, or barefoot completion, has the procedure that casing is set just above the pay zone, and drilling proceeds into the productive zone as far as necessary to complete the well (see Fig. 4.3).

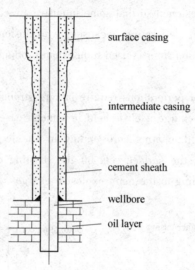

Fig. 4.3 Open-hole completion

Open-hole completion has no production casing or liner set opposite the producing formation. Reservoir fluids flow unrestricted into the open wellbore.

Open hole completions are used where there is only one zone which is either very well consolidated or provided with open-hole gravel packing for sand control. This is valid as long as there are, theoretically at least, no interface problems.

Because of this, open hole completions are seldom chosen for oil wells. On the other hand, this type of connection may be suited to a gas well. This type of completion, which is rarely used and is generally restricted to limestone reservoirs, is useful where only one productive zone and low-pressure formations exist.

4.3 Perforated Completion

Key Words perforated completion

Perforated completion is the process of piercing the casing wall and the cement to provide openings through which formation fluids may enter the wellbore (see Fig. 4.4). This method requires a good cementing job and a proper perforating. Perforating is accomplished by lowering a perforating gun down the production casing or the tubing until is opposite the zone to be produced. Since perforation can be placed very accurately in relation to the different zones and interfaces between fluids, this method gives better selectivity for zones and produced fluids. After reached the designed depth, a gun is fired to shoot bullets or, to say accurately, to set off special explosive charges known as shaped charges which are designed so that some intense, directional explosions are formed. This kind of perforating is called jet perforating because the explosion is actually a jet of high-energy gases and particles. If a production liner is used rather than production casing, the liner is perforated to complete the well.

Perforating: Wider, longer perforations require larger, stronger jet charges, and, accordingly, larger guns to hold them. The charge itself is held in a metal case (see Fig. 4.5) that is linked to similarly shaped charges by a detonating cord ending in an electric detonator. When the gun is fired, an electric current from the surface sets off the blasting cap detonator, which secondarily ignites the detonating cord leading to the main explosive charges.

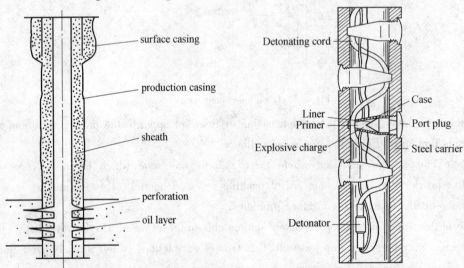

Fig. 4.4 Perforated casing

Fig. 4.5 Schematic of a steel, hollow-carrier, shaped-charge gun assembly, showing a cross section of a shaped charge

Retrievable hollow carrier guns have cylindrical steel bodies with closed ports opposite each jet charge (Fig. 4.6(a)). Fully expendable guns enclose the charges in a frangible aluminum or ceramic case that disintegrates on firing (Fig. 4.6(b)), whereas semiexpendable guns consist of wire. or metal strip carriers that are retrieved after firing (Fig. 4.6(c)). Through-casing and through-tubing guns of these types differ primarily in the diameter of the gun and in the size of the jet charges.

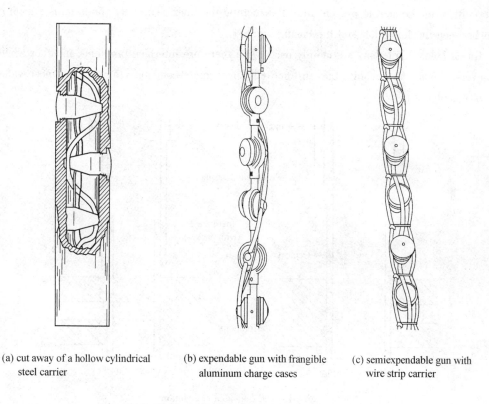

(a) cut away of a hollow cylindrical steel carrier

(b) expendable gun with frangible aluminum charge cases

(c) semiexpendable gun with wire strip carrier

Fig. 4.6　Perforating charge carriers

4.4　Cased Hole Completions

Key Words　cased hole completion

Cased hole completion (see Fig. 4.7) involves running casing or a liner down through the production zone, cementing it opposite the layer and perforating it opposite the zone that is to be produced in order to restore a connection between the reservoir and the well. Connection between the well bore and the formation is made by perforating. The perforations will have to go through the casing and the sheath of cement before they penetrate the formation. The preceding drilling phase was stopped just above the reservoir or at some distance above it and an intermediate casing was then run in and cemented.

Since perforations can be placed very accurately in relation to the different zones and interfaces between fluids, and perforation intervals can be precisely positioned, this method gives better selectivity for zones and produced fluids and affords good control of fluid flow, although it relies on the quality of the cement to prevent fluid flow behind the liner. The only condition is a good cement bond between the formation and the casing string.

Cased hole completions are mainly used when there are interface problems and/or when there are several zones. As a result, they are not only much more common, they are the most widespread type of completion.

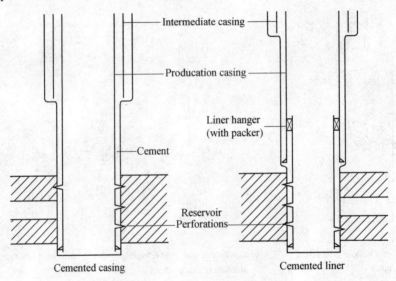

Fig. 4.7 Cased hole completion

4.5 Wire-wrapped Screen Completions

Key Words wire-wrapped screen completion

Wire-wrapped screen completion is a kind of completion method which has a short length of pipe that has openings in its sides and is wrapped with a specially shaped wire screen. The wire-wrapped screen involves attaching the screen to the bottom of the tubing string and lowering it into a well that has been perforated.

Wire-wrapped screens are usually run in conjunction with a gravel pack, which is a kind of packing device in which gravel is placed in the hole outside the screen to stop sands from flowing into the wellbore. In this way, well fluids flow through the gravel pack, through the wire-wrapped screen, and then into the tubing. Wire-wrapped screen completion method is used where the producing zone or zones are likely to produce sand as well as oil and gas.

4.6 Tubing-less Completion

Key Words tubing-less completion

Tubing-less completion is another completing method that production flows through a cemented and perforated pipe without tubing. This method is used because the diameter of casing is too small to hold tubing. Tubing-less completion is used mostly in small gas reservoirs that produce few liquids and are low in pressure. It can be further classified as single-zone tubing-less completion and multiple-zone tubing-less completion.

4.6.1 Single-zone tubingless completion

Key Words single-zone tubingless completion

Single-zone tubingless completion is that production flows directly through relatively a larger diameter casing, usually of large diameter (see Fig. 4.8(a)). Wells that are big producers of trouble-free fluids can be exploited in this way with minimum pressure losses and the lowest possible initial investment. This system is found particularly in the Middle East.

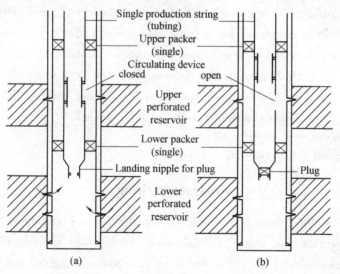

Fig. 4.8 Single-zone tubing-less completion

4.6.2 Multiple-zone tubing-less completion

Key Words multiple-zone tubing-less completion

Multiple-zone tubing-less completion is that production flows directly through several casings whose diameters may be very different from one another depending on the production expected from each zone, see Fig.4.8(b).

Several zones with mediocre production can be produced in this way with a minimum number of wells and downhole equipment, i.e. with a minimum initial investment. This is true provided there are no safety or production problems (such as artificial lift, workover, etc.)

Summary

Generally speaking, a well has a multi-casing system, from conductor casing, surface casing, intermediate casing, production casing, and liner to tubing. The annular space between the casing and the formation, casing and casing needs cementing. The main function of casing is to tighten borehole face and prevent it from caving in. After drilling through the reservoir, a completion job is then necessary. Completion job includes running of casing, perforating and well testing.

Completion methods mainly consist of single-zone completion, multiple-zone completion, open-hole completion, perforated completion, cased hole completion, and wire-wrapped screen completion etc. Open-hole completion has no production casing or liner, and the casing is only set on the top of the reservoir, with a barefoot. Open-hole completion method fits for lime and dolomite reservoirs, perforating method suits sandstone reservoir, and wire-wrapped screen completion combined with grave-packing method meets the needs of unconsolidated sandstone reservoir. For small sized wellbore, tubing-less completion method can be applied.

Technical English Applications

Abstract Writing

There are three kinds of papers: dissertation, journal paper and conference paper. Dissertation takes the basic conception of an article, the purpose is simple, clear and valuable and, let readers understand what your research is as well as the way of your analyses. Journal paper tries to make the readers feel that the article has a firm systematical theory base, and reads academically. Conference paper carries out a strong brand new idea independently of the theory, systematically and academically.

Chapter 4　Completion Engineering

Before writing a paper, it is most important to write a good abstract. Here we mainly discuss the abstract of dissertation.

Main content of an abstract:

(1) Background Information / Literature Review;

(2) Principal Purpose;

(3) Methodology;

(4) Results and discussion;

(5) Conclusions and Recommendation;

(6) Key words

Rules of writing an abstract:

· tense: use present and past tense

· format: write one whole paragraph only

· words range: 200 ~ 500

· key words range: 3 ~ 6 words or phrases

· word size: "Times New Roman 3" for "title"

"Times New Roman 4" for writer's name

"Times New Roman 4" small for "body"

"Times New Roman 4" for "key words"

Useful Patterns:

(1) Background information/Literature review:

This paper reviews the method on… 本文概述了关于……的方法

This article summarizes the theory on… 本文综述了关于……的理论

This paper is based on… 本文基于……

The frequently used verbs: present; summarize; review; outline.

(2) Principal purpose:

The purpose of this study is to (explore new methods of)… 此项研究的目的是(探索……的新方法)

The paper attempts to define… in terms of … 本文尝试从……的角度来定义……

The study is aimed at finding out the basic similarities between … and … 本研究旨在找出……与……之间的基本相似点

The main objective of… is to justify … 此项研究的主要目的是论证……

The primary goal of this research is… 这项研究的基本目标是……

The main objective of this investigation is to (obtain some knowledge of)… 我们调查的主要目的是(获得有关……的知识)

Frequently used verbs: aim; attempt to; initiate; intend to; seek

Frequently used nouns and phrases: aim; purpose; objective; goal; in terms of

(3) Methodology:

The article describes the principles and methodology of… 本文描述了……的原则和方法

This article discusses the method of… 本文讨论了……的方法

The principle of… is proposed. 本文提出了建立……的原则

This paper states the reasons for… 本文阐明了……的原因

The article adopts themethodology of… 本文采用了……的方法

This paper uses the principle of… 本文应用了……的原则

useful verbs: analyze; consider; discuss; examine; study; investigate; state; contain; cover; include; outline

useful nouns: scope; field; domain

(4) Results and discussion:

The result of… shows that… ……的结果表明……

The result provides a sound basis of… 结果为……提供了可靠的依据

It is noted that… 注意到……

It is worth confirming that… 值得确认的是……

Useful verbs: confirm; demonstrate; find; summary; lead to

Useful phrases: to sum up

(5) Conclusions and recommendation:

We concluded by experiment that… 我们根据试验得出的结论是……

To sum up, the article has revealed… 总结起来，文章已经揭示了……

The argument proceeds on… 论证得出的结论是……

The research has led to the discovery of…… 这项研究工作发现了……

Useful verbs: conclude; summary; result

Useful phrases: in conclusion; lead to

Here is a model of an abstract:

【Example】

Abstract: China is one of the largest petroleum consuming countries with limited oil and gas resources. It is estimated that by the year of 2020, China will need 480 million tons of petroleum, among which 290 million tons have to be rely on imports. It is obvious that China has to use petroleum from both domestic and foreign sources to meet its increasing energy demand. Yet China is rich in coal, having large deposit of it. Burning coal wastes resources, emits more carbon dioxide and causes the biggest environment pollution problem. Coal-to-oil strategy will certainly make China turn around the narrow corner. This paper demonstrates the strategy, discusses the feasibility of this new technology, and describes the bright future of petroleum industry in China.

Key words: petroleum; coal-to-oil strategy; feasibility

Excercises

Part 1　Reading comprehension

1. What is completion?
2. What are required in the completion job?

Part 2　Pair off the following phrases

production strings	采油封隔器
Open-hole completion	技术套管
production packer	产油带
intermediate casing	回收式射孔枪
gravel packing	修井作业
pay zone	生产套管
workover operation	聚能射孔
retrievable hollow carrier guns	井下设备
downhole equipment	绕丝筛网
jet perforating	砾石充填
wire-wrapped screen	注水泥套管
cemented casing	裸眼完井

Part 3　Fill in the blanks with the following phrases and expressions

with respect to　　　according to　　　be equipped with

depending on　　　as long as　　　be accomplished by

1. Single-zone completion is the way the well _____ a single tubing.

2. There are two main types of single-zone completions, _____ whether the tubing has a production packer on its lower end.

3. This is valid _____ there are, theoretically at least, no interface problems.

4. Single-zone completion is used when the only aim is to have the right pipe diameter _____ the flow rate.

5. Completion is the process of making a well ready for production, which, _____ geological characters of hydrocarbon reservoir and the technical requirement of exploration and recovery, builds up the reasonable connections between reservoir and wellbore.

6. Perforating _____ lowering a perforating gun down the production casing or the tubing until is opposite the zone to be produced.

Part 4 Translation practice

Translate the following sentences into English：

1. 这就要求完井工程师们开阔眼界,科学地对每口单井做出正确的处理决定。

2. 这口井的设计井深为 2 450 m,导管下深 36 m,表层套管下深 150 m,技术套管下深 500 m。

3. 射孔将不得不先穿透套管和水泥环,然后穿透油层。

4. 以这种方式,井内流体穿过砾石充填,流出绕丝筛管,然后进入油管。

5. 这种方法之所以被使用,是因为套管直径太小,不能托住油管。

Part 5 Writing comprehension

Write an abstract.

Reading Material: New Trend of Technology

Completion System Offers Multizone Stimulation in a Single Trip

A completion technology that promises economic and efficiency gains over conventional multiple-trip completion and stimulation is receiving a great deal of attention, onshore and off. In numerous field trials, BJ Services' ComPlete MST (multizone, single-trip) completion system has eliminated several operational steps compared with traditional multizone frac-pack/gravel-pack completions, providing at least a 20 to 40% reduction in completion costs and nonproductive time (NPT).

"The MST is part of BJ's ComPlete line of tools, all designed to help a client save rig time and money by minimizing the number of trips in and out of a hole," explained David Walker, Director of Completion Tools for BJ Services. "One tool replaces several different pieces of equipment, and the same ultimate goal is accomplished."

"The MST is used for single-trip perforating and gravel packing in many kinds of wells, including horizontal wells," Walker continued. "We designed the system to accomplish two purposes: to gravel pack multiple zones and to isolate the zones such that they could be selectively produced. The tool was aimed for those reservoirs with large gross-pay zones and numerous stress layers, which often present completion and stimulation challenges that single intervals do not."

Conventional gravel packs are often difficult and costly to perform in multi layer formations. Frac packs must be carefully planned and executed to avoid overstimulation situations, where the fracture breaches water zones, or understimulation, in which potential productive areas have poor reservoir-to-wellbore connectivity.

These stimulation challenges increase in reservoirs with large variations in formation properties. While mathematical modeling might provide some assistance in designing perforation or treatment scenarios that can circumvent these problems, the most effective method is to isolate and complete or stimulate each zone separately, according to Walker.

"Zonal isolation has been a major focus for us, historically. Ensuring that you only open a reservoir to treat it and then close it up again until you are ready to produce is good for several reasons: it prevents you from inadvertently putting damaging fluids in the formation, it prevents loss of fluids into the formation, and it keeps the well under control so that it doesn't surge in on you when you are busy doing something else."

Traditional methods for multizone treatment with zonal isolation call for the bottom zone to be treated first, followed by running bridge plugs into the hole and then repeating for successive zones uphole. At the end of the process, the bridge plugs are drilled out.

However, this can be a time-consuming process, requiring many trips into the well and increasing both NPT and expense. If the cost of the many downhole trips is not greatly exceeded by the expected production gains, the operator may have to make an economic decision on which zones to stimulate. "The result may be some combination of over- and understimulated zones, with other zones receiving no stimulation at all," Walker said.

The large costs associated with multiple trips downhole is significantly greater offshore, such as in the ultradeep Lower Tertiary play in the Gulf of Mexico (GOM), where daily rig costs are higher and tripping times are longer because of the extreme water and well depths. To meet economic targets, operators need either exceptionally prolific reservoirs or new technologies that can safely and reliably enable completions, sand control, and stimulation in fewer trips.

According to Walker, these challenges were the basis for the development of the ComPlete MST system, which reportedly eliminates much of the NPT. "We had the original idea for this concept during a discussion with Total, who came to us with some problem formations in Indonesia. These formations had multiple stacked pays, all at the same pressure, but they wanted to do different things with the zones," Walker said. "They wanted to gravel pack two or three zones in the same well with two nongravel-packed zones, and they wanted to do all of this as economically as possible."

Novel installation, completion method attracts operator interest

BJ designed the MST to operate as follows. During installation, all sleeves are run in hole in the closed position to provide positive pretreatment zonal isolation. After the ComPlete MST assembly's upper gravel-pack / production packer is hydraulically set and tested, the work string and service tool are released from the completion assembly.

The service tool is then positioned so the sleeve-opening tool is above the lower production sleeve. Downward movement opens the sleeve, allowing communication through the screen. Next, the service tool sets the isolation packer, and then it opens the gravel-pack/frac-pack sleeve, allowing stimulation treatment fluid to be pumped down the work string and into the annulus. Pumping continues until sandout. Picking up the service tool allows excess slurry to be reversed out by pumping down the annulus and taking returns through the work string.

Pushing the sleeve-closing tool below the lowermost sleeve and then raising the tool through the zone closes all sleeves, positively isolating the treated zone. This is verified by applying pressure at surface to ensure integrity.

The process is then applied to subsequent zones uphole. After the last zone is completed, the work string and service tool are removed from the wellbore, leaving a large-bore, full-open ID completion with selective-flow capability. Production may be initiated by means of a run into the hole with coiled tubing, wireline, or tubing with a sleeve-opening tool.

"After the initial discussion with Total, we proposed this same technology to BP," said Walker. "They gave us the money to develop the tool, and they gave us two test wells."

"The first system we developed was a 7-in. tool for BP's smaller casing sizes. We tested two onshore wells in 2004 and 2005, where we fractured three zones on the first well, came back in and made some modifications, then went back out and fractured three zones on the second well. These were south Louisiana water zones; they were wells that depleted out and they just plugged them out, and we fractured three zones in one trip. The test went very well, we then made some minor modifications to the tool and commercialized it."

The tool's first commercial applications were in two two-zone wells offshore Indonesia, where all components of the MST system performed as designed, including multiple manipulations of the autolocator, sleeves, and valves as planned during the stimulation program.

To date, the functionality of the ComPlete MST system has been field-proven in three two-zone wells and one four-zone well offshore Indonesia and in the GOM. Planning is underway for 23 four-zone wells in Indonesia and several GOM deepwater wells over the next 10 to 20 months.

The system is currently available for use in 7- through 10-in. casing sizes with no restrictions on zone length. Individual zones are produced through production sleeves incorporated in the well screen design below blank pipe and a gravel-pack or frac-pack sleeve with an isolation production packer. Up to five internal profiles are available with the current production sleeves to provide zonal selectivity for production.

No theoretical limit to number of zones

Walker indicated that there should be no theoretical limit to the number of zones the MST can isolate in a given trip, but there are practical limitations in terms of material durability. "Depending on overall length of the system, the only limit we have right now is the erosion resistance of the service tools and equipment. In some of these wells, particularly Lower Tertiary wells, you might pump fracturing treatments on the order of 500 000 lbm per zone for five zones. You'll be pumping 3-4 million lbm through your service tool, and the wear on the equipment internals will take a toll.

"However, we're pretty limitless in terms of the length of service we can do," Walker confirmed. "We've run a system as long as 3 000 ft into the wellbore already, and while there are some challenges at these lengths, such as temperature, pressure, even tubing movement, it is not impossible."

Cost savings significant, and growing

In terms of cost and NPT savings, BJ reported that results from the numerous field trials showed that the MST system afforded a 20 to 40% effective reduction in completion-cycle time and cost compared to standard multizone, multitrip completion technologies. "Depending on the number of zones, the savings might even be greater than that," Walker said. "For some of the jobs I've been involved in, I've seen a 25% savings for two zones, and it could be 50-60% for four to five zones easily. For the multizone wells in Indonesia, they were talking about saving 60% on completions, and cutting the total time from 9 days to 4."

The company further estimated that by eliminating one-third of a typical 12-day completion schedule on a multizone deepwater well, an operator can save as much as USD1 million on the total operation cost even with a conservative USD250 000 day rate for the rig.

"The speed with which the industry has been accepting this technology is incredible," Walker concluded. "After being technically selected by Total and BP, we've tested it for China National Offshore Oil Corporation, and Chevron wants to use this for a deepwater GOM project. All this activity has taken place in the last 2 to 3 years."

To learn more about the ComPlete MST contact Walker by email.
http://www.spe.org/jpt

Chapter 5

Recovery Engineering

Purpose & Requirements

When extracting crude oil, it normally starts by drilling wells into the underground reservoir. Historically, some oil fields existed where the oil rose naturally to the surface, but most of these fields have long since been used up. Often many wells (called multilateral wells) are drilled into the same reservoir, to ensure that the extraction rate will be economically viable. Also, some wells (secondary wells) may be used to pump water, steam, acids or various gas mixtures into the reservoir to raise or maintain the reservoir pressure, and so maintain an economic extraction rate.

The main objectives of this chapter are to introduce and give a detailed discussion of the various recovery methods and their effects on the overall performance of oil reservoirs and give a detailed explanation of enhanced recovery.

Key Words   duty of recovery engineering

The duty of recovery engineering is to design, control and manage scientifically the production wells and injection wells according to the requirement of oil exploitation to improve oil well production, stimulate oil recovery as well as exploit reservoir by taking a serious of technological measures.

5.1 Primary Recovery

Key Words   primary recovery; six driving mechanisms

The recovery of oil by any of the natural drive mechanisms is called primary recovery. The term refers to the production of hydrocarbons from a reservoir without the use of any process (such as fluid injection) to supplement the natural energy of the reservoir. Primary oil recovery describes the production of hydrocarbons under the natural driving mechanisms present in the reservoir without supplementary help from injected fluids such as gas or water. In most cases, the natural driving mechanism is a relatively inefficient process and results in a low overall oil recovery. The lack of sufficient natural drive in most reservoirs has led to the practice of supplementing the natural reservoir energy by introducing some form of artificial drive, the most basic method being the injection of gas or water.

There are basically six driving mechanisms that provide the natural energy necessary for oil recovery:
- Rock and liquid expansion drive
- Depletion drive
- Gas cap drive
- Water drive
- Gravity drainage drive
- Combination drive

These driving mechanisms are discussed as follows.

5.1.1 Rock and liquid expansion drive

Key Words undersaturated oil reservoir. reservoir rock compressibility; rock and liquid expansion drive

When an oil reservoir initially exists at a pressure higher than its bubble-point pressure, the reservoir is called an undersaturated oil reservoir. At pressures above the bubble point pressure, crude oil, connate water, and rock are the only materials present. As the reservoir pressure declines, the rock and fluids expand due to their individual compressibilities. The reservoir rock compressibility is the result of two factors:
- Expansion of the individual rock grains
- Formation compaction

Both of the above two factors are the results of a decrease of fluid pressure within the pore spaces, and both tend to reduce the pore volume through the reduction of the porosity.

Rock and liquid expansion drive: as the expansion of the fluids and reduction in the pore volume occur with decreasing reservoir pressure, the crude oil and water will be forced out of the pore space to the wellbore. Because liquids and rocks are only slightly compressible, the reservoir will experience a rapid pressure decline. The oil reservoir under this driving mechanism is characterized by a constant gas-oil ratio that is equal to the gas solubility at the bubble point pressure.

This driving mechanism is considered the least efficient driving force and usually results in the recovery of only a small percentage of the total oil in place.

5.1.2 The depletion drive

Key Words   the depletion drive

This driving form may also be referred to by the following various terms:
- Solution gas drive
- Dissolved gas drive
- Internal gas drive

In this type of reservoir, the depletion drive is a result of gas liberation from the crude oil and the subsequent expansion of the solution gas as the reservoir pressure is reduced. As pressure falls below the bubble-point pressure, gas bubbles are liberated within the microscopic pore spaces. These bubbles expand and force the crude oil out of the pore space. These bubbles expand and force the crude oil out of the pore space as shown conceptually in Fig. 5.1.

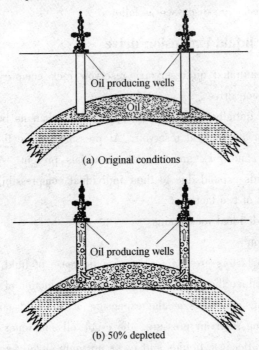

Fig. 5.1   Solution gas drive reservoir

Gas-cap-drive reservoirs can be identified by the presence of a gas cap with little or no water drive as shown in Fig. 5.2.

Due to the ability of the gas cap to expand, these reservoirs are characterized by a slow decline in the reservoir pressure. The natural energy available to produce the crude oil comes from the following two sources:

- Expansion of the gas-cap gas
- Expansion of the solution gas as it is liberated

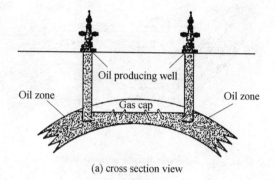

(a) cross section view

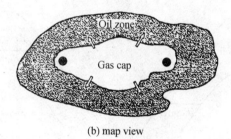

(b) map view

Fig. 5.2 Gas-cap-drive reservoir

5.1.3 Water-drive

Key Words   water drive

Many reservoirs are bounded on a portion or all of their peripheries by water bearing rocks called aquifers. The aquifers may be so large compared to the reservoir they adjoin as to appear infinite for all practical purposes, and they may range down to those so small as to be negligible in their effects on the reservoir performance.

The aquifer itself may be entirely bounded by impermeable rock so that the reservoir and aquifer together form a closed (volumetric) unit. On the other hand, the reservoir may be outcropped at one or more places where it may be replenished by surface water as shown schematically in Fig. 5.3.

As illustrated in Fig. 5.4. Regardless of the source of water, the water drive is the result of water moving into the pore spaces originally occupied by oil, replacing the oil and displacing it to the

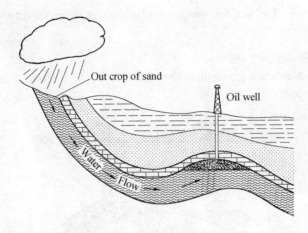

Fig. 5.3 Reservoir having artesian water drive

producing wells.

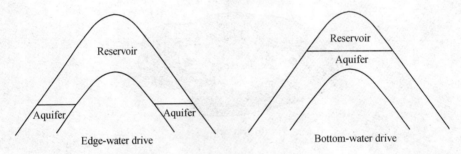

Fig. 5.4 Aquifer geometries

It is common to speak of edge water or bottom water in discussing water influx into a reservoir. Bottom water occurs directly beneath the oil and edge water occurs off the flanks of the structure at the edge of the oil.

5.1.4 The gravity-drainage-drive

Key Words mechanism of gravity drainage drive; effects of gravitational forces

The mechanism of gravity drainage drive occurs in petroleum reservoirs as a result of differences in densities of the reservoir fluids. The effects of gravitational forces can be simply illustrated by placing a quantity of crude oil and a quantity of water in a jar and agitating the contents. After agitation, the jar is placed at rest, and the more denser fluid (normally water) will settle to the bottom of the jar, while the less dense fluid (normally oil) will rest on top of the denser fluid. The fluids have separated as a result of the gravitational forces acting on them.

The fluids in petroleum reservoirs have all been subjected to the forces of gravity, as evidenced by the relative positions of the fluids, i. e., gas on top, oil underlying the gas, and water underlying oil. The relative positions of the reservoir fluids are shown in Fig. 5.5. Due to the long periods of time involved in the petroleum accumulation-and-migration process, it is generally assumed that the reservoir fluids are in equilibrium. If the reservoir fluids are in equilibrium, then the gas-oil and oil-water contacts should be essentially horizontal. Although it is difficult to determine precisely the reservoir fluid contacts, best available data indicate that, in most reservoirs, the fluid contacts actually are essentially horizontal.

Gravity segregation of fluids is probably present to some degree in all petroleum reservoirs, but it may contribute substantially to oil production in some reservoirs.

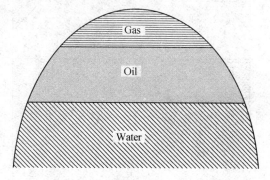

Fig. 5.5 Initial fluids distribution in an oil reservoir

During the primary recovery stage, reservoir drive comes from a number of natural mechanisms. These include: natural water displacing oil downward into the well, expansion of the natural gas at the top of the reservoir, expansion of gas initially dissolved in the crude oil, and gravity drainage resulting from the movement of oil within the reservoir from the upper to the lower parts where the wells are located. Recovery factor during the primary recovery stage is typically 5-15%.

While the underground pressure in the oil reservoir is sufficient to force the oil to the surface, all that is necessary is to place a complex arrangement of valves (the Christmas tree) on the well head to connect the well to a pipeline network for storage and processing.

5.1.5 The combination-drive

Key Words driving mechanism of the combination-drive

The driving mechanism of the combination-drive most commonly encountered is one in which both water and free gas are available in some degree to displace the oil toward the producing wells.

The most common type of drive encountered, therefore, is a combination-drive mechanism as illustrated in Fig. 5.6.

Two combinations of driving forces can be present in combination-drive reservoirs. These are (1) depletion drive and a weak water drive and; (2) depletion drive with a small gas cap and a weak water drive. Then, of course, gravity segregation can play an important role in any of the aforementioned drives.

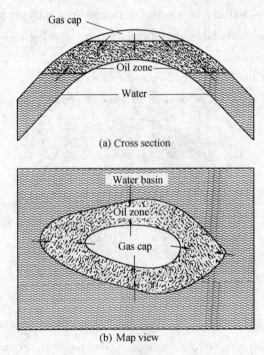

Fig. 5.6 Combination-drive reservoir

5.2 Secondary Recovery

Key Words secondary recovery

Secondary recovery is the artificial recovery method by injecting natural gas or water through injection wells to maintain reservoir pressure and push oil out of the rock. Over the lifetime of the well, the pressure will fall, and at some point there will be insufficient underground pressure to force the oil to the surface. After natural reservoir drive diminishes, secondary recovery methods are applied. Normally, gas is injected into the gas cap and water is injected into the production zone to sweep oil from the reservoir. They rely on the supply of external energy into the reservoir in the form of injecting fluids to increase reservoir pressure, hence replacing or increasing the natural reservoir drive with an artificial drive. Secondary oil recovery refers to the additional recovery that results from the conventional methods of water injection and immiscible gas injection. Usually, the selected secondary recovery process follows the primary recovery but it can also be conducted concurrently with the primary recovery. There are many artificial drive methods, most of which are variations or combinations of three basic processes:

(1) decreasing the weight of the hydrostatic column by injecting gas into the liquids some distance down the well (gas lift; water flooding);

(2) using of mechanical device inside the well, such as subsurface pumping (beam pumps, hydraulic pumps, electric submersible centrifugal pumps);

(3) piston-like displacement of liquid slugs (plunger lift).

5.2.1 Gas lift

Key Words gas lift; continuous flow gas lift; intermittent gas lift

Gas lift is a widely used artificial method with which gas is injected with injection well to reduce the weight of the hydrostatic column, thus reduce the back pressure and allow the reservoir pressure to push the mixture of produce fluids and gas up to the surface. The gas decreases the fluid density of the column and lowers the bottomhole pressure, allowing the formation pressure to move more fluid into the wellbore. Injected gas bubbles also expand as they rise in the tubing above their injection point, pushing oil ahead of them up the tubing. The degree to which each of these mechanisms affects the well's production rate depends on the type of gas lift method applied: continuous flow or intermittent flow.

Continuous flow gas lift relies on the constant injection of gas into the production stream through a downhole valve. The installation can be designed to allow for injection from the casing/tubing annulus into the tubing (most common), for injection into a smaller concentric tubing string within the production tubing ("macaroni" string), or for injection from the tubing into the casing/tubing annulus (annular flow installation). The fluid column above the injection point is lightened by the aeration caused by the relatively low density gas. The resulting drop in bottomhole pressure causes an increase in production rate.

Intermittent gas lift allows for the buildup of a liquid column of produced fluids at the bottom of the wellbore. At the appropriate time, a finite volume of gas is injected below the liquid and propels it as a slug to the surface.

5.2.2 Waterflooding

Key Words　waterflooding; water flooding patterns; irregular injection patterns; peripheral injection patterns; regular injection patterns

waterflooding is a method of secondary recovery in which water is injected into the reservoir formation to displace residual oil. The water from injection wells physically sweeps the displaced oil to adjacent production wells. Potential problems associated with waterflood techniques include inefficient recovery due to variable permeability, or similar conditions affecting fluid transport within the reservoir, and early water breakthrough that may cause production and surface processing problems.

1. Water flooding patterns

One of the first steps in designing a water flooding project is flood pattern selection. The objective is to select the proper pattern that will provide the injection fluid with the maximum possible contact with the crude oil system. This selection can be achieved by (1) converting existing production wells into injectors or (2) drilling infill injection wells. When making the selection, the following factors must be considered:

- Reservoir heterogeneity and directional permeability
- Direction of formation fractures
- Availability of the injection fluid (gas or water)
- Desired and anticipated flood life
- Maximum oil recovery
- Well spacing, productivity, and injectivity

In general, the selection of a suitable flooding pattern for the reservoir depends on the number and location of existing wells. In some cases, producing wells can be converted to injection wells while in other cases it may be necessary or desirable to drill new injection wells. Essentially four types of well arrangements are used in fluid injection projects:

- Irregular injection patterns
- Peripheral injection patterns
- Regular injection patterns
- Crestal and basal injection patterns

2. Irregular injection patterns

Surface or subsurface topology and/or the use of slant-hole drilling techniques may result in production or injection wells that are not uniformly located. In these situations, the region affected by the injection well could be different for every injection well. Some small reservoirs are developed for primary production with a limited number of wells and when the economics are marginal, perhaps only few production wells are converted into injectors in a non-uniform pattern. Faulting and localized variations in porosity or permeability may also lead to irregular patterns.

3. Peripheral injection patterns

In peripheral flooding, the injection wells are located at the external boundary of the reservoir and the oil is displaced toward the interior of the reservoir, as shown in Fig. 5.7. In an excellent review of the peripheral flood, points out the following main characteristics of the flood:

· The peripheral flood generally yields a maximum oil recovery with a minimum of produced water.

· The production of significant quantities of water can be delayed until only the last row of producers remains.

· Because of the unusually small number of injectors compared with the number of producers, it takes a long time for the injected water to fill up the reservoir gas space. The result is a delay in the field response to the flood.

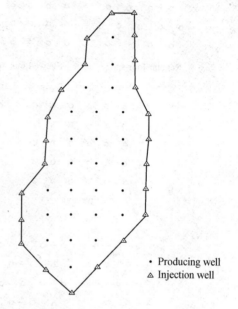

Fig. 5.7 Typical peripheral waterflood

For a successful peripheral flood, the formation permeability must be large enough to permit the movement of the injected water at the desired rate over the distance of several well spacings from injection wells to the last line of producers.

To keep injection wells as close as possible to the waterflood front without bypassing any movable oil, watered-out producers may be converted into injectors.

However, moving the location of injection wells frequently requires laying longer surface water lines and adding costs.

· Results from peripheral flooding are more difficult to predict. The displacing fluid tends to displace the oil bank past the inside producers, which are thus difficult to produce.

· Injection rates are generally a problem because the injection wells continue to push the water greater distances.

4. Regular injection patterns

Due to the fact that oil leases are divided into square miles and quarter square miles, fields are developed in a very regular pattern. A wide variety of injection-production well arrangements have been used in injection projects. The most common patterns, as shown in Fig. 5.8, are the following:

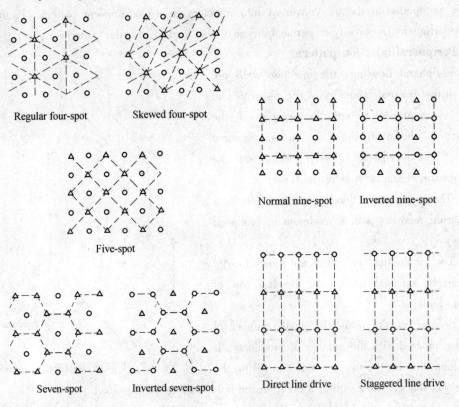

Fig. 5.8 Flood patterns

• Direct line drive. The lines of injection and production are directly opposed to each other. The pattern is characterized by two parameters: a = distance between wells of the same type, and d = distance between lines of injectors and producers.

• Staggered line drive. The wells are in lines as in the direct line, but the injectors and producers are no longer directly opposed but laterally displaced by a distance of a/2.

• Five spot. This is a special case of the staggered line drive in which the distance between all like wells is constant, i.e., a = 2d. Any four injection wells thus form a square with a production well at the center.

• Seven spot. The injection wells are located at the corner of a hexagon with a production well at its center.

• Nine spot. This pattern is similar to that of the five spot but with an extra injection well drilled at the middle of each side of the square. The pattern essentially contains eight injectors surrounding one producer.

The patterns termed inverted have only one injection well per pattern. This is the difference between normal and inverted well arrangements. Note that the four-spot and inverted seven-spot patterns are identical.

5. Crestal and basal injection patterns

In crestal injection, as the name implies, the injection is through wells located at the top of the structure. Gas injection projects typically use a crestal injection pattern. In basal injection, the fluid is injected at the bottom of the structure. Many water-injection projects use basal injection patterns with additional benefits being gained from gravity segregation. A schematic illustration of the two patterns is shown in Fig. 5.9.

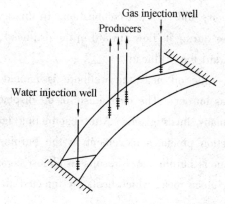

Fig. 5.9 Well arrangements for dipping reservoirs

5.3 Tertiary Recovery

Key Words tertiary (enhanced) oil recovery; thermally enhanced oil recovery methods

Tertiary (enhanced) oil recovery is that additional recovery over and above what could be recovered by primary and secondary recovery methods. Tertiary recovery begins when secondary oil recovery isn't enough to continue adequate production, but only when the oil can still be extracted profitably. This depends on the cost of the extraction method and the current price of crude oil. When prices are high, previously unprofitable wells are brought back into production and when they are low, production is curtailed. Various methods of enhanced oil recovery (EOR) are essentially designed to recover oil, commonly described as residual oil, left in the reservoir after both primary and secondary recovery methods have been exploited to their respective economic limits. In tertiary recovery, steam is injected into many oil fields where the oil is thicker and heavier than normal crude oil.

5.3.1 Thermal recovery

Key Words thermal processes; in-situ combustion; steam injection; steam assisted gravity drainage; wet combustion

When petroleum reservoirs contain a low-gravity (less than 20°API), high-viscosity oil and have a high porosity, secondary recovery methods are not effective for displacement of oil. For such reservoirs, thermal processes have received the most attention. The injection of steam reduces the oil viscosity which causes an increase in the oil mobility. Depending on the way in which the heat is generated in the reservoirs, the thermal processes can be divided into three categories: (1) in-situ combustion; (2) steam injection; and (3) wet combustion. In this approach, various methods are used to heat the crude oil either during its flow upward in the drillhead, or in the pool, which would allow it to flow more easily toward the drillhead.

In-situ combustion: the crude oil near the wellbore is ignited using chemicals, downhole electric heaters or downhole gas burners. The mechanism of oil displacement by in-situ combustion was extensively reported by many investigators. After completing ignition in the vicinity of the wellbore, continuous air injection promotes movement in the burning zone toward the producing wells. Propagation of a continuous burning zone results in almost complete removal of all reservoir liquids and leaves behind hot, clean rock, which heats the injected air before it reaches the burning zone.

Steam injection: steam is injected into the reservoir either continuously or in cycles. Continuous steam injection, or steam drive or steam flooding, involves both injection and production wells. In this process, steam is injected through injection well and the fluids are displaced toward production wells that are drilled in a specific pattern.

Whereas cyclic injection, also called steam stimulation, or steam soak, or the huff and puff process, involves one well only which serves as both injection and production well. Steam is injected into a producer for a specific period; the well is then closed for a while (soak process), and finally open for production.

Steam flooding is easier to control than in-situ combustion. For the same pattern size, the response time is 25% to 50% lower than the response time for additional production by in-situ combustion.

Steam Assisted Gravity Drainage (SAGD) is also an enhanced oil recovery technology for producing heavy crude oil and bitumen. It is an advanced form of steam stimulation in which a pair of horizontal wells are drilled into the oil reservoir, one a few metres above the other. Low pressure steam is continuously injected into the upper wellbore to heat the oil and reduce its viscosity, causing the heated oil to drain into the lower wellbore, where it is pumped out.

In the SAGD process, two parallel horizontaloil wells are drilled in the formation, one about 4 to 6 metres above the other. The upper well injects steam, possibly mixed with solvents, and the lower one collects the heated crude oil or bitumen that flows out of the formation, along with any water from the condensation of injected steam. The basis of the process is that the injected steam forms a "steam chamber" that grows vertically and horizontally in the formation. The heat from the steam reduces the viscosity of the heavy crude oil or bitumen which allows it to flow down into the lower wellbore. The steam and gases rise because of their low density compared to the heavy crude oil below, ensuring that steam is not produced at the lower production well. The gases released, which include methane, carbon dioxide, and usually some hydrogen sulfide, tend to rise in the steam chamber, filling the void space left by the oil and, to a certain extent, forming an insulating heat blanket above the steam. Oil and water flow is by a countercurrent, gravity driven drainage into the lower well bore. The condensed water and crude oil or bitumen is recovered to the surface by pumps such as progressive cavity pumps that work well for moving high-viscosity fluids with suspended solids.

Operating the injection and production wells at approximately reservoir pressure eliminates the instability problems that plague all high-pressure steam processes and SAGD produces a smooth, even production that can be as high as 70% to 80% of oil in place in suitable reservoirs. The process is relatively insensitive to shale streaks and other vertical barriers to steam and fluid flow because, as the rock is heated, differential thermal expansion causes fractures in it, allowing steam and fluids to flow through. This allows recovery rates of 60% to 70% of oil in place, even in formations with many thin shale barriers. Thermally, SAGD is twice as efficient as the older cyclic steam stimulation (CSS) process, and it results in far fewer wells being damaged by high pressure. Combined with the higher oil recovery rates achieved, this means that SAGD is much more economic than pressure-driven steam process where the reservoir is reasonably thick. With the low cost of drilling horizontal well pairs, and the very high recovery rates of the SAGD process (up to 60% of the oil in place), SAGD is economically attractive to oil companies.

Thermally enhanced oil recovery methods (TEOR) are tertiary recovery techniques that heat the oil, thus reducing its viscosity and making it easier to extract. Steam injection is the most common form of TEOR, and is often done with a cogeneration plant. In this type of cogeneration plant, a gas turbine is used to generate electricity and the waste heat is used to produce steam, which is then injected into the reservoir. This form of recovery is used extensively to increase oil production. In-situ burning is another form of TEOR, but instead of steam, some of the oil is burned to heat the surrounding oil.

Occasionally, surfactants (detergents) are injected to alter the surface tension between the water and oil in the reservoir, mobilizing oil which would otherwise remain in the reservoir as residual oil. Another method to reduce viscosity is carbon dioxide flooding. Tertiary recovery allows another 5% to 15% of the reservoir's oil to be recovered.

5.3.2 Chemical flooding

Chemical flooding processes can be divided into three main categories: surfactant flooding, polymer flooding and caustic flooding. Fig. 5.10 illustrates polymer flooding process.

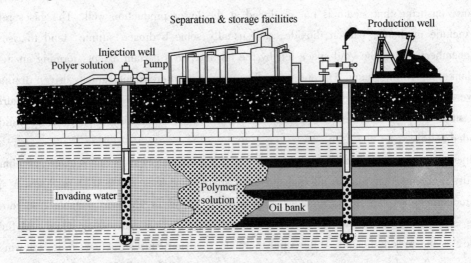

Fig. 5.10 Polymer flooding process

This process can either reduce the crude's viscosity or increase the viscosity of water which has also been injected to force the crude out of the stratum. Detergent-like surfactants such as rhamnolipids are injected to lower the capillary pressure that impedes oil droplets from moving through a reservoir. This can also be done by injection of surfactant followed by polymer flooding, results in controlling the mobility which in turn enhances oil recovery. Caustic injected into the petroleum reservoir reacts chemically with the fatty acids present in the petroleum derivatives and forms in situ sodium salts of fatty acids. The formation of these surfactants results in ultra-low interfacial tension.

Microbial treatments is another tertiary recovery method. Special blends of the microbes are used to treat and break down the hydrocarbon chain in oil thus making the oil easy to recover as well as being more economic versus other conventional methods.

5.3.3 Miscible flooding

Key Words miscible flooding

Miscible flooding involves the injection of a solvent such as alcohol, refined hydrocarbons, condensed hydrocarbon gases, liquefied petroleum gases, or carbon dioxide, which can dissolve in the reservoir oil. The injected solvent reduce the capillary forces that cause oil retention in the pore spaces of the reservoir rocks. In this process, the injected solvent slug is followed by the infection of a liquid or gas to force the solvent-oil mixture out. The miscible displacement process can be subdivided into the miscible slug process, the enriched gas process, the high-pressure lean gas process, the mutual solvent, and the carbon dioxide processes.

The miscible slug process involves the injection of a slug of liquid hydrocarbons equal to about one half of the pore volume of the reservoir. The liquid hydrocarbon slug is followed by gas or water injection to drive the slug through the reservoir. In the enriched gas process, the injected slug (10% to 20% pore volume) of enriched natural gas is followed by lean gas and water. The high-pressure lean gas process consists of injecting a lean gas at a high pressure in order to cause retrograde evaporation of the crude oil and formation of a miscible phase, which consists of C_2-C_6 components, between the reservoir oil and the gas. The main difference between the enriched gas and the high-pressure lean gas process is that in the enriched gas process the C_2-C_6 components are transferred from the gas to the oil, whereas in the high-pressure lean gas process, the C_2-C_6 components are transferred from the oil to the gas.

The mutual solvent process consists of injecting solvents (e.g. alcohols), which are miscible between the reservoir oil and water. These solvents form a single phase in the petroleum reservoir and improve oil recovery. A very high concentration of these solvents is required to maintain the single phase. In the carbon dioxide process, the mechanism of carbon dioxide miscibility in oil is temperature and reservoir oil composition; carbon dioxide can create a miscible front, which moves as a single liquid phase and efficiently displaces reservoir oil to the producing wells. The carbon dioxide miscibility can be achieved at pressures as low as 1 500 psi at normal reservoir temperatures. The presence of impurities in the carbon dioxide, such as nitrogen and methane, increase the miscibility pressure, whereas impurities such as propane and hydrogen sulfide decrease it.

5.4 Enhanced Oil Recovery (EOR)

Key Words enhanced oil recovery; gas injection; chemical injection; ultrasonic stimulation;

microbial injection

Enhanced oil recovery is a generic term for techniques for increasing the amount of crude oil that can be extracted from an oil field. Using EOR, 30% ~ 60 %, or more, of the reservoir's original oil can be extracted compared with 20% ~ 40% using primary and secondary recovery.

Enhanced oil recovery is also called improved oil recovery or tertiary recovery (as opposed to primary and secondary recovery). Sometimes the term quaternary recovery is used to refer to more advanced, speculative, EOR techniques.

Enhanced oil recovery is achieved by gas injection, chemical injection, ultrasonic stimulation, microbial injection, or thermal recovery (which includes cyclic steam, steamflooding, and fireflooding).

5.4.1 Gas injection

Key Words gas injection

Gas injection is presently the most-commonly used approach to enhanced recovery. A gas is injected into the oil-bearing stratum under high pressure. That pressure pushes the oil into the pipe and up to the surface. In addition to the beneficial effect of the pressure, this method sometimes aids recovery by reducing the viscosity of the crude oil as the gas mixes with it. Gases commonly used include CO_2, natural gas or nitrogen.

Oil displacement by carbon dioxide injection relies on the phase behavior of the mixtures of that gas and the crude, which are strongly dependent on reservoir temperature, pressure and crude oil composition. These mechanisms range from oil swelling and viscosity reduction for injection of immiscible fluids (at low pressures) to completely miscible displacement in high-pressure applications. In these applications, more than half and up to two-thirds of the injected CO_2 returns with the produced oil and is usually re-injected into the reservoir to minimize operating costs. The remainder is trapped in the oil reservoir by various means.

5.4.2 Ultrasonic stimulation

It has been proposed to use high-power ultrasonic vibrations from a piezoelectric vibration unit lowered into the drillhead, to "shake" the oil droplets from the rock matrices, allowing them to move more freely toward the drillhead. This technique is projected to be most effective immediately around the drillhead.

5.4.3 Microbial injection

Microbial injection is part of microbial enhanced oil recovery and is presently rarely used, both because of its higher cost and because the developments in this field are more recent than other techniques. Strains of microbes have been both discovered and developed (using gene mutation) which function either by partially digesting long hydrocarbon molecules, by generating biosurfactants, or by emitting carbon dioxide (which then functions as described in Gas injection above).

Three approaches have been used to achieve microbial injection. In the first approach, bacterial cultures mixed with a food source (a carbohydrate such as molasses is commonly used) are injected into the oil field. In the second approach, used since 1985, nutrients are injected into the ground to nurture existing microbial bodies; these nutrients cause the bacteria to increase production of the natural surfactants they normally use to metabolize crude oil underground. After the injected nutrients are consumed, the microbes go into near-shutdown mode, their exteriors become hydrophilic, and they migrate to the oil-water interface area, where they cause oil droplets to form from the larger oil mass, making the droplets more likely to migrate to the wellhead.

The third approach is used to address the problem of paraffin components of the crude oil, which tend to separate from the crude as it flows to the surface. Since the Earth's surface is considerably cooler than the petroleum deposits (a temperature drop of 13-14 degree F per thousand feet of depth is usual), the paraffin's higher melting point causes it to solidify as it is cooled during the upward flow. Bacteria capable of breaking these paraffin chains into smaller chains (which would then flow more easily) are injected into the wellhead, either near the point of first congealment or in the rock stratum itself.

Wet combustion: in this process, a large amount of heat is left behind in the swap formation as waste heat. The heat utilization and efficiency of the process could be improved by water injection. In this process, water is injected with air. Superheated steam forms in an evaporation front and travels behind the combustion front. The important advantage of this process is that the amount of residual oil left to be burned as fuel by the burning front is considerably decreased, which in turn displaces more oil and less air is required to burn a unit volume of oil in the reservoir.

5.4.4 Alternative methods

Alternative enhanced oil recovery mechanisms include VAPEX (for Vapor Extraction), Electro-Thermal Dynamic Stripping Process (ET-DSP). VAPEX uses solvents instead of steam to displace oil and reduce its viscosity. ET-DSP is a patented process that uses electricity to heat oil sands deposits to mobilize bitumen allowing production using simple vertical wells. ISC uses oxygen to generate heat that diminishes oil viscosity; alongside carbon dioxide generated by heavy crude oil displace oil toward production wells. One ISC approach is called THAI for Toe to Heel Air Injection.

Summary

It is sure to say that it is hard for reservoir exploitation to recover all the oil and gas from underground. Generally speaking, only 10% of the underground energy can be extracted naturally. Even with injection technology, 30% ~ 50% of crude oil can be recovered. That is to say, there are still quite large quantities of resources are stillburied underground.

udes six approaches: Rock and liquid expansion drive, depletion drive, gas cap drive, water drive, gravity drainage drive and combination drive. secondary recovery is the artificial recovery method that consists of gas lift, water flooding. Tertiary recovery is also a kind of enhanced recovery method, which covers: chemical flooding (surfactant, polymer, caustic), thermal recovery (in-situ combustion, steam injection, wet combustion), miscible flooding (miscible slug process, enriched gas process, high pressure lean gas process, mutual solvent process, CO_2 process). The enhanced oil recovery is much complicated: gas injection, chemical injection, ultrasonic stimulation, and microbial injection etc.

The future development of EOR is difficult to predict. Yet as the technology goes further, it will surely become more sufficient and perfect.

Technical English Applications

Anouncement & Notice

Anouncement is usually orally delivered practical writing, while Notice is written one. Broadcasting is one of the oral announcement. Notice is divided into two kinds: bulletin and broadcast announcement. Bulletin is printed on the notice boards, or written on a blackboard or whiteboard to let people know and is often delivered inside the unit. Letter-Like notice is a kind of formal style, generally used in formal occasion, and delivered through post-office or sent by someone.

Anouncement and Notice must be short and brief, use present and future tense. But now the Anouncement and Notice are not so much limited, especially on internet.

The components of the notice:

1. Title
2. Date of issue
3. Salutation
4. Body
5. Unit or person of issue

【Example 1】

Announcement

(1) The Petroleum Engineering program is offerring Petroleum Fluids (PETR 245) as a distance education course this summer. The course is designed for students interested in pursuing a B. S. degree in Petroleum Engineering but have scheduling problems at NMT or are transfer students. See PETR245D-Su2010. pdf for more information.

(2) Wild Well Control School was sponsored by Chevron and Marble (Alumnus).

(3) Senior Design Presentations date: Friday, April 30, 2010. Location and time: MSEC 101 at 1:30 p. m.

(4) Spring 2010 newsletter is available.

【Example 2】

Carnarvon Petroleum Limited
ABN 60 002 688 851
Notice is given that the Annual General Meeting
of Carnarvon Petroleum Limited will be held at
RoyalPerth Yacht Club
Australia II Drive, Crawley
Perth, Western Australia.
at 11. 00am on Friday, 27th November 2009
Carnarvon Petroleum Limited ABN 60 002 688 851
Registered Office: Ground Floor,1322 Hay Street, West Perth, WA 6005
Telephone: +61 8 9321 2665, Facsimile:+61 8 9321 8867
And here is a module of anotice:
NOTICE OF…
Dear Mr. / Madam…,
It is a great pleasure to inform you that, approved by…, … has decided to …. Please come to … in …days for … upon the receipt of this notice.
(Noticed by)…

Excercises

Part 1 Reading comprehension

1. What is the duty of recovery engineering?
2. What is primary recovery? And secondary recovery?
3. How many regular injection patterns are there? What are they?
4. What is tertiary recovery?
5. What does "EOR" stand for? How many EOR techniques are mentioned here?

Part 2 Pair off the following phrases

production well	溶解气驱
bubble-point pressure	驱动机理
depletion drive	油气比
primary recovery	采油树
pore space	活塞气举
aquifer	溶解气
gas-oil ratio	泡点压力
driving mechanism	一次采油
Christmas tree	生产井
solution gas	残油
plunger lift	含水层
residual oil	孔隙空间

Part 3 Fill in the blanks with the following phrases and expressions

be the result of   be bounded on   in general
at some point   be subdivided into   consist of

1. Many reservoirs _____ a portion or all of their peripheries by water bearing rocks called aquifers.

2. Over the lifetime of the well, the pressure will fall, and _____ there will be insufficient underground pressure to force the oil to the surface.

3. _____, the selection of a suitable flooding pattern for the reservoir depends on the number and location of existing wells.

4. Regardless of the source of water, the water drive _____ water moving into the pore spaces originally occupied by oil, replacing the oil and displacing it to the producing wells.

5. The miscible displacement process can _____ the miscible slug process, the enriched gas process, the high-pressure lean gas process, the mutual solvent, and the carbon dioxide

processes.

6. The mutual solvent process _____ injecting solvents (e.g., alcohols), which are miscible between the reservoir oil and water.

Part 4　Translation practice

1. Translate the following phrases into Chinese

1) result in　　　　　　　　2) a broad view of
3) lack of　　　　　　　　　4) a constant ratio
5) compared to　　　　　　　6) On the other hand
7) speak of　　　　　　　　8) as a result of
9) rely on　　　　　　　　　10) because of

2. Translate the following sentences into English

1) 气举是一种被广泛应用的人工举升方法,通过这种方法用注入井注入天然气,降低静液柱的比重,因此降低背压,允许油藏压力将产出流体连同天然气一起推出地表。

2) 在三次采油中,蒸汽被注入到油田内,这里的原油比普通原油更浓、更重。

3) 加热强化采油法(TEOR)是三次采油技术,(用)这种技术将油加热,因而降低其粘度,使其更容易抽取。

4) 在讨论水体流入油藏时,通常要说到边缘水或底水。

Part 5　Writing comprehension

Write a notice.

Reading Material: New Trend of Technology

Using Enzymes to Enhance Oil Recovery

Biofuels are no longer the only beneficiaries of enzyme-assisted energy production. Enhanced-oil-recovery (EOR) techniques are benefiting from enzymatic treatment as well, as technology provider Jumpstart Energy Services recently explained.

Enzymes, the broad class of protein-based catalysts found in all living matter, have been used to accelerate the rate of chemical reactions in various manufacturing industries. Biofuel production has recently generated the most attention for enzymes in terms of energy production, in which the catalysts are used to accelerate the biological breakdown of cellulosic material into sugars suitable for biofuel production. The US Department of Energy recently announced a 4-year, USD33-million investment in projects aimed at improving enzyme systems for this purpose.

But the oilfield is not to be left out, and Jumpstart Energy Services is aiming at EOR techniques for application of its enzyme technologies. "We call our application enzyme-enhanced oil recovery

(EEOR)," said John Gray, President and Founder of Jumpstart. "We focus on combined EOR technologies where enzymes bring benefit to existing secondary or tertiary production."

Jumpstart represents an enzyme fluid technology, sold under the trade name Greenzyme, that is a water-soluble formulation reportedly made from DNA-modified proteins extracted from oil-loving microbes in a batch fermentation process. The enzyme itself is nonliving, which provides EEOR an advantage over microbial EOR techniques that may require a detailed pretreatment involving the injection of a fermentable carbohydrate nutrient base into the reservoir. With the EEOR technique, only a dilution of the enzyme into the injection water is required. No subsequent nutrients are required either, which allows for a broader range of well treatment applications.

Greenzyme is reportedly ideally suited for sandstone, waterdrive formations with <30 API oil, >20% porosity, and >100-md permeability for single well treatments, but can have broader ranges in other applications such as waterfloods. "We've had success in fractured limestone formations as well," Gray said.

Intertek laboratory tests shed light on EEOR mechanism

In order to explain how EEOR works, Jumpstart began laboratory tests at Intertek's Westport Technology Center designed to make an initial determination of the mechanism for any downhole oil-production improvement. These tests included comparing nonenzyme-treated and enzyme-treated 26 API oil samples (a 10% concentration of Greenzyme diluted in water was used) that were both heated under pressure in order to simulate reservoir conditions.

Allan Hartman, Jumpstart's Vice President of Business Development, postulated that the enzymatic treatment may be improving oil recovery by catalyzing the breakdown of larger molecules in the oil into smaller molecules, which might improve the flow characteristics of the oil including heavy oil. A SARA (saturates, aromatics, resins, and asphaltenes) analysis supported the breakdown hypothesis in terms of the saturate content, as the enzyme-treated sample had a 5% lower saturate content than the nonenzyme sample.

Further analysis by means of high-resolution gas chromatography demonstrated that while the nonenzyme-treatment samples had clearly visible hydrocarbon peaks out to at least C_{44} (44 carbon atoms on a molecule, typical for high-carbon content paraffins), the enzyme-treated samples presented much smaller peaks beyond C_{30}, and no visible hydrocarbon peaks past C_{37}. According to Jumpstart, the observed reduction in high-carbon-number paraffins and a corresponding reduction in the molecular size of the waxes point to a positive contribution from the enzyme.

The enzyme's contribution to oil recovery may be a multipronged approach, as further testing indicated. "We commissioned a series of viscosity and interfacial-tension tests on these samples at the same time," Hartman said. "There was a sizable drop in viscosity, from 90.3 cP to 76.1 cP, in the presence of the enzyme treatment."

Interfacial-tension tests, which provide an indirect measure of the relative miscibility between oil and water, were conducted on oil/water samples in the absence of enzyme, oil/water samples in the presence of enzyme but prior to a heating/pressure treatment, and oil/water samples in the presence of enzyme and following a heating/pressure treatment. The Intertek report showed oil/water samples alone had fairly high interfacial tensions, on the order of 20.5 mN/m. For both enzyme-treated samples, there was an order of magnitude decrease in interfacial tension. "We expected to see a reduction of interfacial tension which was confirmed by these tests," Gray said, and noted that the heating/pressure step to simulate reservoir conditions did not influence this behavior.

"This indicated to us that in addition to catalyzing the breakdown of higher molecular-weight paraffins, the enzyme also possesses some biosurfactant properties, helping to release the oil from within the formation in the form of small droplets that are carried with fluids moving to a producing well," Gray continued. "The overall effect appears to improve relative permeability and oil mobility."

By http://www.spe.org/jpt/2008/04/using-enzymes-to-enhance-oil-recovery

GloriOil promises better recovery through biotechnology

U.S.-based GloriOil is successfully applying microbial technology developed in India to improve recovery and reduce operating costs in mature fields in the Texas Panhandle and West Texas. The process, known as Enhanced Oil Recovery by Microbial Consortia (EORMC), reportedly creates a downhole bioreactor in the formation that decreases water cut while also boosting both oil quantity and quality.

The patented process has been in development for ten years by GloriOil's technology provider and co-owner, The Energy and Resources Institute (TERI) of India (GTI Group is the other co-owner). While microbes have been employed for oil recovery purposes for many years, TERI researchers wanted to find more robust microbial biotechnology that could be used in hotter and higher pressure reservoirs.

The ten-year effort has reportedly paid off, as TERI researchers have cultured a set of microbes that can survive temperatures as high as 90℃ and pressures up to 140 kg/cm^2 (~2 000 psi). This is a marked improvement over previous oil recovery microbes that could bear temperatures only up to 65℃.

The microbes used in the EORMC process also work in reservoirs with salinity levels on the order of 4 to 8%.

While the microbes and nutrients are novel, they are applied in a similar manner to previous microbial treatments. Known commonly as the 'huff-puff' method of oil extraction, it involves injecting a microbe-nutrient mixture into the reservoir. Over the course of about two weeks, these microbes incubate in the reservoir, producing carbon dioxide and methane. These gases enter the pores and squeeze out the remaining oil.

At the same time, the microbes produce bio-surfactants that lower the interfacial tension between the oil and the rock face, helping to release the oil from the formation.

The first field application of this technology took place in India for national oil company ONGC's Gujarat fields. TERI reported that by applying this technology to 25 oil wells, 4 500 m^3 (~28 300 bbl) of oil was extracted, translating into revenues of more than USD 675 000.

In addition, TERI reports a potential production cost savings of as much as 35-40% per bbl using this technology.

The success of this and other field trials inIndia has prompted GloriOil to bring TERI's technology to Texas, where several field applications are reportedly planned or under development.

In announcing the Texas field developments, GloriOil CEO Stuart Page expressed a great deal of optimism with how this technology can help producers of mature fields. "With the support we've received from early adopter operators and our investors, we're now ready to deliver affordable well- and field-level enhanced recovery programs that increase production while lowering lifting costs."

By http://www.spe.org/jpt/2007/08/glorioil-promises-better-recovery-through-biotechnology

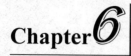

Well Testing

Purpose & Requirements

In order to effectively evaluate a reservoir and ensure well production, we need to know what is happening deeply inside the reservoir by way of well testing. This chapter tends to let reservoir engineers recognize reservoirs, obtaining reservoir parameters and control them through measuring and calculating, using equations established accordingly. Well testing is a technique of evaluating a reservoir and ensuring well production which proceeds a systematic analysis of a well to obtain representative samples of the reservoir fluids and to collect simultaneous measurements of the production rates for individual phase and the corresponding bottom-hole pressure.

Well testing is mainly classified into 6 approaches: Single Well Test, Exploration Well Test, Drill-Stem Test (DST), Production Well Test, Injection Well Test and Multiple Well Test. Transient Well Test is a kind of single well test and is mainly discussed in this chapter.

Key Words single well test; the function of the single-well pressure buildup test run on exploration wells; transient well test

Single Well Test is the technique when the flow rate is changed and the pressure response is recorded in the same well. The function of the single-well pressure buildup test run on exploration wells is that it can provide information on flowing well efficiency, formation transmissibility, and reservoir heterogeneity. Drawdown, buildup, injectivity, falloff etc. are examples of a single-well test. If it is specially designed for long flow and long shut-in period, the test can also provide information on reservoir size, and hydrocarbons in place. When running on a production well, a single-well pressure buildup test generally gives information only on the well's flow efficiency and transmissibility within the well's drainage area.

Transient well test is essentially conducted by creating a pressure disturbance in the reservoir and recording the pressure response at the wellbore, i. e., bottom-hole flowing pressure, P_{wf} as a function of time. Pressure transient test is designed to provide the engineer with a quantitative analysis of the reservoir properties. The pressure transient tests most commonly used in the petroleum industry include:

- pressure drawdown;
- pressure buildup;
- multirate;
- interference;
- pulse;
- drill stem (DST);
- falloff;
- injectivity;
- step rate.

It has long been recognized that the pressure behavior of a reservoir following a rate change directly reflects the geometry and flow properties of the reservoir. Some of the information that can be obtained from a well test includes:

Drawdown tests: Pressure profile, Reservoir behavior, Permeability, Skin, Fracture length, Reservoir limit and shape.

Buildup tests: Reservoir behavior, Permeability, Fracture length, Skin, Reservoir pressure, Boundaries.

DST: Reservoir behavior, Permeability, Skin, Fracture, length, Reservoir limit, Boundaries.

Falloff tests: Mobility in various banks, Skin, Reservoir pressure, Fracture length, Location of front, Boundaries.

Interference and pulse tests: Communication between wells, Reservoir-type behavior, Porosity, Interwell permeability, Vertical permeability.

Layered reservoir tests: Horizontal permeability, Vertical permeability, Skin Average layer pressure, Outer boundaries.

Step-rate tests: Formation parting pressure, Permeability, Skin.

6.1 Drawdown Test

Key Words pressure drawdown test; the fundamental objectives of drawdown testing

A pressure drawdown test is simply a series of bottom-hole pressure measurements made during a period of flow at constant producing rate. Usually the well is shut in prior to the flow test for a period of time sufficient to allow the pressure to equalize throughout the formation, i. e., to reach static pressure. A schematic of the ideal flow rate and pressure history is shown in Fig. 6.1.

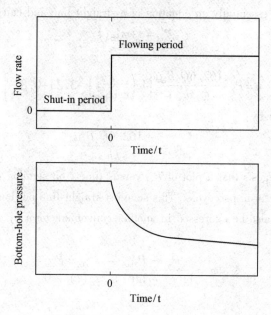

Fig. 6.1 Idealized drawdown test

The fundamental objectives of drawdown testing are to obtain the average permeability, k, of the reservoir rock within the drainage area of the well, and to assess the degree of damage of stimulation induced in the vicinity of the wellbore through drilling and completion practices. Other objectives are to determine the pore volume and to detect reservoir inhomogeneities within the drainage area of the well. When a well is flowing at a constant rate of Q_o under the unsteady-state condition, the pressure behavior of the well will act as if it exists in an infinite-size reservoir. The pressure behavior during this period is described by

Equation as:

$$P_{wf} = P_i - \frac{162.6 Q_o B_o \mu}{kh} \left[\lg\left(\frac{kt}{\phi \mu c_t r_w^2}\right) - 3.23 + 0.87s \right]$$

where k——permeability, mV;

t——time, h;

r_w——wellbore radius, ft;

s——skin factor.

The above expression can be written as:

$$P_{wf} = P_i - \frac{162.6 Q_o B_o \mu}{kh} \times \left[\lg(t) + \lg\left(\frac{k}{\phi \mu c_t r_w^2}\right) - 3.23 + 0.87s \right] \quad (6.1)$$

This relationship is essentially an equation of a straight line and can be expressed as:

$$P_{wf} = a + m\lg(t)$$

where

$$a = P_i - \frac{162.6 Q_o B_o \mu}{kh} \left[\lg\left(\frac{k}{\phi \mu c_t r_w^2}\right) - 3.23 + 0.87s \right]$$

and the slope m is given by:

$$-m = \frac{-162.6 Q_o B_o \mu_o}{kh} \quad (6.2)$$

Equation (6.1) suggests that a plot of P_{wf} versus time t on semilog graph paper would yield a straight line with a slope m in psi/cycle. This semilog straight-line portion of the drawdown data, as shown in Fig. 6.2, can also be expressed in another convenient form by employing the definition of the slope:

$$m = \frac{P_{wf} - P_{1hr}}{\lg(t) - \lg(1)} = \frac{P_{wf} - P_{1hr}}{\lg(t) - 0}$$

or

$$P_{wf} = m\lg(t) + P_{1hr}$$

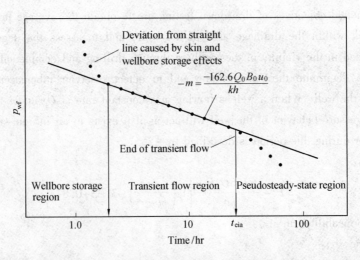

Fig. 6.2 Semilog plot of pressure drawdown data

Notice that Equation (6.2) can also be rearranged to determine the capacity kh of the drainage area of the well. If the thickness is known, then the average permeability is given by:

$$k = \frac{162.6 Q_o B_o \mu_o}{|m|h}$$

where k——average permeability, md;

   $|m|$——absolute value of slope, psi/cycle.

Clearly, kh/μ or k/μ may also be estimated. The skin effect can be obtained by rearranging Equation (6.1) as:

$$s = 1.151 \left[\frac{P_i - P_{wf}}{|m|} - \lg t - \lg\left(\frac{k}{\phi \mu c_t r_w^2}\right) + 3.23 \right]$$

or, more conveniently, if selecting $P_{wf} = P_{1hr}$ which is found on the extension of the straight line at $t = 1$ hr, then:

$$s = 1.151 \left[\frac{P_i - P_{1hr}}{|m|} - \lg\left(\frac{k}{\phi \mu c_t r_w^2}\right) + 3.23 \right] \quad (6.3)$$

where $|m|$ is the absolute value of the slope m.

In Equation:

$$\phi_i = P_i - \left(\frac{\rho}{144}\right) \Delta z_i$$

where ρ is the density in lb/ft^3, P_{1hr} must be obtained from the semilog straight line. If the pressure data measured at 1 hour does not fall on that line, the line must be extrapolated to 1 hour and the extrapolated value of P_{1hr} must be used in Equation (6.3).

This procedure is necessary to avoid calculating an incorrect skin by using a wellbore-storage-influenced pressure. Fig.6.2 illustrates the extrapolation to P_{1hr}. Note that the additional pressure drop due to the skin was expressed previously by Equation

$$\Delta P_{skin} = \left(\frac{Q_o B_o \mu_o}{0.00708 kh}\right) s = 141.2 \left(\frac{Q_o B_o \mu_o}{kh}\right) s$$

as:

$$\Delta P_{skin} = 141.2 \left(\frac{Q_o B_o \mu_o}{kh}\right) s$$

This additional pressure drop can be equivalently written in terms of the semilog straight-line slope m by combining the above expression with that of Equation (6.3) to give:

$$E = \frac{J_{actual}}{J_{ideal}} = \frac{\bar{P} - P_{wf} - \Delta P_{skin}}{\bar{P} - P_{wf}}$$

where $\bar{P}$ is the average pressure in the well drainage area.

If the drawdown test is long enough, the bottom-hole pressure will deviate from the semilog straight line and make the transition from infinite acting to pseudosteady state. The rate of pressure decline during the pseudosteady-state flow is defined as:

$$\frac{dP}{dt} = \frac{0.23396q}{c_t(\pi r_e^2)h\phi} = \frac{-0.23396q}{c_t(A)h\phi} = \frac{-0.23396q}{c_t(\text{pore volume})} \quad (6.4)$$

Under this condition, the pressure will decline at a constant rate at any point in the reservoir including the bottom-hole flowing pressure P_{wf}. That is:

$$\frac{dP_{wf}}{dt} = m' = \frac{-0.23396q}{c_t A h \phi}$$

where m——slope of the Cartesian straight line, during the pseudosteady state, psi/hr;

  q——flow rate, bbl/d;

  A——drainage area, ft^2.

[Example 1]

Estimate the oil permeability and skin factor from the drawdown data of Fig. 6.3. The following reservoir data are available:

$h = 130$ ft, $\quad\quad\quad \varphi = 20\%$, $\quad\quad\quad r_w = 0.25$ ft,
$P_i = 1\,154$ psi, $\quad\quad Q_o = 348$ STB/D, $\quad m = -22$ psi/cycle
$B_o = 1.14$ bbl/STB, $\quad \mu_o = 3.93$ cp, $\quad\quad c_t = 8.74 \times 10^{-6}$ psi-1

Assuming that the wellbore storage effect is not significant, calculate:

· the permeability k;

· the skin factor s;

· the additional pressure drop due to the skin ΔP_{skin}.

Solution

Step 1. From Fig. 6.3, calculate P_{1hr}:

$P_{1hr} = 954$ psi

Step 2. Determine the slope of the transient flow line:

$$m = -22 \text{ psi/cycle}$$

Step 3. Calculate the permeability by applying Equation (6.2):

$$k/\text{md} = \frac{-162.6 Q_o B_o \mu_o}{mh} = \frac{-161.6 \times 348 \times 1.14 \times 3.93}{-22 \times 130} = 89$$

Step 4. Solve for the skin factors by using Equation (6.3):

$$s = 1.151 \left[\frac{P_i - P_{1hr}}{|m|} - \lg\left(\frac{k}{\phi \mu c_t r_w^2}\right) + 3.23 \right] =$$

$$1.151 \left[\left(\frac{1\,154 - 954}{22}\right) - \left(\frac{89}{0.2 \times 3.93 \times 8.74 \times 10^{-6} \times 0.25^2}\right) + 3.2275 \right] = 4.6$$

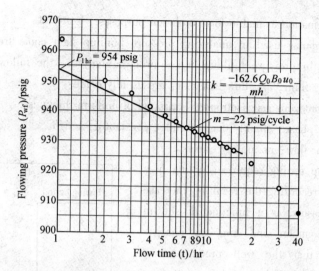

Fig. 6.3 Earlougher's semilog data plot for the drawdown test

Step 5. Calculate the additional pressure drop:
$$\Delta P_{skin}/\text{psi} = 0.87|m|s = 0.87 \times 22 \times 4.6 = 88$$

6.2 Pressure Buildup Test

Key Words   pressure buildup test

The use of pressure buildup data has provided the reservoir engineer with one more useful tool in the determination of reservoir behavior. Pressure buildup test describes the buildup in wellbore pressure with time after a well has been shut in. One of the principal objectives of this analysis is to determine the static reservoir pressure without waiting weeks or months for the pressure in the entire reservoir to stabilize. Because the buildup in wellbore pressure will generally follow some definite trend, it has been possible to extend the pressure buildup analysis to determine:

- the effective reservoir permeability;
- the extent of permeability damage around the wellbore;
- the presence of faults and to some degree the distance to the faults;
- any interference between producing wells;
- the limits of the reservoir where there is not a strong water drive or where the aquifer is no larger than the hydrocarbon reservoir.

Certainly all of this information will probably not be available from any given analysis, and the degree of usefulness of any of this information will depend on the experience in the area and the amount of other information available for correlation purposes.

The general formulas used in analyzing pressure buildup data come from a solution of the diffusivity equation. In pressure buildup and drawdown analyses, the following assumptions, as regards the reservoir, fluid, and flow behavior, are usually made:

- Reservoir: homogeneous; isotropic; horizontal of uniform thickness.
- Fluid: single phase; slightly compressible; constant μ_o and B_o.
- Flow: laminar flow; no gravity effects.

Pressure buildup testing requires shutting in a producing well and recording the resulting increase in the wellbore pressure as a function of shut-in time. The most common and simplest analysis techniques require that the well produce at a constant rate for a flowing time of t_p, either from startup or long enough to establish a stabilized pressure distribution, before shut in. Traditionally, the shut-in time is denoted by the symbol (Δt). Fig. 6.4 schematically shows the stabilized constant flow rate before shut-in and the ideal behavior of the pressure increase during the buildup period. The pressure is measured immediately before shut in and is recorded as a function of time during the shut-in period. The resulting pressure buildup curve is then analyzed to determine reservoir properties and the

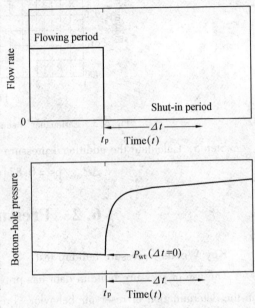

Fig. 6.4 Idealized pressure buildup test

wellbore condition. Stabilizing the well at a constant rate before testing is an important part of a pressure buildup test. If stabilization is overlooked or is impossible, standard data analysis techniques may provide erroneous information about the formation.

Two widely used methods are discussed below, these are:

(1) the Horner plot;
(2) the Miller-Dyes-Hutchinson method.

6.3 Horner Plot

A pressure buildup test is described mathematically by using the principle of superposition. Before the shut-in, the well is allowed to flow at a constant flow rate of Q_o STB/day for t_p days. At the end of the flowing period, the well is shut in with a corresponding change in the flow rate from the "old" rate of Q_o to the "new" flow rate of $Q_{new} = 0$, i.e., $Q_{new} - Q_{old} = -Q_o$.

Calculation of the total pressure change which occurs at the sand face during the shut-in time is basically the sum of the pressure changes that are caused by:

· flowing the well at a stabilized flow rate of Q_{old}, i.e., the flow rate before shut-in Q_o, and is in effect over the entire time of $t_p + \Delta t$;

· the net change in the flow rate from Q_o to 0 and is in effect over Δt.

The composite effect is obtained by adding the individual constant-rate solutions at the specified rate-time sequence, as:

$$P_i - P_{ws} = (\Delta P)_{total} = (\Delta P)_{due\ to(Q_0 - 0)} + (\Delta P)_{due\ to(0 - Q_0)}$$

where P_i——initial reservoir pressure, psi;

P_{ws}——wellbore pressure during shut in, psi.

The above expression indicates that there are two contributions to the total pressure change at the wellbore resulting from the two individual flow rates. The first contribution results from increasing the rate from 0 to Q_o and is in effect over the entire time period $t_p + \Delta t$, thus

$$(\Delta P)_{Q_0 - 0} = \left[\frac{162.6(Q_0 - 0)B_o\mu_o}{kh}\right] \times \left[\lg\left(\frac{k(t_p + \Delta t)}{\phi\mu_o c_t r_w^2}\right) - 3.23 + 0.87s\right]$$

The second contribution results from decreasing the rate from Q_o to 0 at t_p, i.e., shut-in time, thus

$$(\Delta P)_{Q_0 - 0} = \left[\frac{162.6(0 - Q_0)B_o\mu_o}{kh}\right] \times \left[\lg\left(\frac{k\Delta t}{\phi\mu_o c_t r_w^2}\right) - 3.23 + 0.87s\right]$$

The pressure behavior in the well during the shut-in period is then given by:

$$P_i - P_{ws} = \frac{162.6 Q_o \mu_o B_o}{kh}\left[\lg\left(\frac{k(t_p + \Delta t)}{\phi\mu_o c_t r_w^2}\right) - 3.23\right] - \frac{162.6(-Q_o)\mu_o B_o}{kh}\left[\lg\left(\frac{k\Delta t}{\phi\mu_o c_t r_w^2}\right) - 3.23\right]$$

Expanding this equation and canceling terms gives:

$$P_{ws} = P_i - \frac{162.6 Q_o \mu_o B_o}{kh}\left[\lg\left(\frac{t_p + \Delta t}{\Delta t}\right)\right] \tag{6.5}$$

where P_i——initial reservoir pressure, psi;

P_{ws}——sand face pressure during pressure buildup, psi;

t_p——flowing time before shut-in, h;

Q_o——stabilized well flow rate before shut-in, STB/d;

Δt——shut-in time, h.

The pressure buildup equation, i.e., Equation (6.4) was introduced by Horner and is commonly referred to as the Horner equation.

Equation (6.4) is basically an equation of a straight line that can be expressed as:

$$P_{ws} = P_i - m\left[\lg\left(\frac{t_p + \Delta t}{\Delta t}\right)\right] \tag{6.6}$$

This expression suggests that a plot of P_{ws} vs. $(t_p+\Delta t)/\Delta t$ on a semilog scale would produce a straight-line relationship with intercept P_i and slope m, where:

$$m = \frac{162.6Q_o B_o \mu_o}{kh} \tag{6.7}$$

or:

$$k = \frac{162.6Q_o B_o \mu_o}{mh}$$

and where m——slope of straight line, psi/cycle;

k——permeability, md.

This plot, commonly referred to as the Horner plot, is illustrated in Fig. 6.5. Note that on the Horner plot, the scale of time ratio $(t_p+\Delta t)/\Delta t$ increases from right to left. It is observed from Equation (6.4) that $P_{ws} = P_i$ when the time ratio is unity. Graphically this means that the initial reservoir pressure P_i, can be obtained by extrapolating the Horner plot straight line to $(t_p + \Delta t)/\Delta t = 1$. The time corresponding to the point of shut-in, t_p can be estimated from the following equation:

$$t_p = \frac{24N_p}{Q_o}$$

where N_p——well cumulative oil produced before shut in, STB;

Q_o——stabilized well flow rate before shut in, STB/d;

t_p——total production time, h.

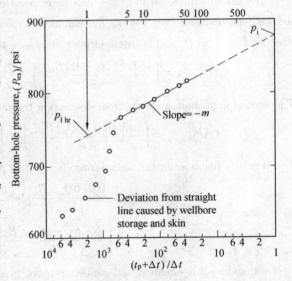

Fig.6.5 Horner plot

Earlougher pointed out that a result of using the superposition principle is that the skin factor, s, does not appear in the general pressure buildup equation, Equation (6.4). That means the Horner-plot slope is not affected by the skin factor; however, the skin factor still does affect the shape of the pressure buildup data. In fact, an early time deviation from the straight line can be caused by the skin factor as well as by wellbore storage, as illustrated in Fig. 6.4. The deviation can be significant for the large negative skins that occur in hydraulically fractured wells. The skin factor does affect flowing pressure before shut-in and its value may be estimated from the buildup test data plus the flowing pressure immediately before the buildup test, as given by:

$$s = 1.151\left[\frac{P_{1hr} - P_{wfat\Delta t=0}}{|m|} - \lg\left(\frac{k}{\phi\mu c_t r_w^2}\right) + 3.23\right] \tag{6.8}$$

with an additional pressure drop across the altered zone of:

$$\Delta P_{skin} = 0.87|m|s$$

where:

$P_{wfat\Delta t=0}$——bottom-hole flowing pressure immediately before shut in, psi;
s——skin factor;
$|m|$——absolute value of the slope in the Horner plot, psi/cycle;
r_w——wellbore radius, ft.

The value of P_{1hr} must be taken from the Horner straight line. Frequently, the pressure data does not fall on the straight line at 1 hour because of wellbore storage effects or large negative skin factors. In that case, the semilog line must be extrapolated to 1 hour and the corresponding pressure is read.

It should be noted that for a multiphase flow, Equations (6.4) and (6.8) become:

$$P_{ws} = P_i - \frac{162.6q_t}{\lambda_t h}\left[\lg\left(\frac{t_p + \Delta t}{\Delta t}\right)\right]$$

$$s = 1.151\left[\frac{P_{1hr} - P_{wfat\Delta t=0}}{|m|} - \lg\left(\frac{\lambda_t}{\phi c_t r_w^2}\right) + 3.23\right]$$

with:

$$\lambda_t = \frac{k_o}{\mu_o} + \frac{k_w}{\mu_w} + \frac{k_g}{\mu_g}$$

$$q_t = Q_o B_o + Q_w B_w + (Q_g - Q_o R_s)B_g$$

or equivalently in terms of GOR as:

$$q_t = Q_o B_o + Q_w B_w + (GOR - R_s)Q_o B_g$$

where q_t——total fluid voidage rate, bbl/d;
Q_o——oil flow rate, STB/d;
Q_w——water flow rate, STB/d;
Q_g——gas flow rate, scf/d;
R_s——gas solubility, scf/STB;
B_g——gas formation volume factor, bbl/scf;

λ_t——total mobility, md/cp;
k_o——effective permeability to oil, md;
k_w——effective permeability to water, md;
k_g——effective permeability to gas, md.

The regular Horner plot would produce a semilog straight line with a slope m that can be used to determine the total mobility λ_t from:

$$\lambda_t = \frac{162.6 q_t}{mh}$$

Perrine showed that the effective permeability of each phase, i.e., k_o, k_w, and k_g, can be determined as:

$$k_o = \frac{162.6 Q_o B_o \mu_o}{mh}$$

$$k_w = \frac{162.6 Q_w B_w \mu_w}{mh}$$

$$k_g = \frac{162.6 (Q_g - Q_o R_s) B_g \mu_g}{mh}$$

For gas systems, a plot of $m(P_{ws})$ or P_{ws}^2 vs. $(t_p + \Delta t)/\Delta t$ on a semilog scale would produce a straight line relationship with a slope of m and apparent skin factor s as defined by:

For pseudopressure approach:

$$m = \frac{1\,637 Q_G T}{kh}$$

$$s' = 1.151 \left[\frac{m(P_{1hr}) - m(P_{wfat\,\Delta t=0})}{|m|} - \lg\left(\frac{k}{\phi \mu_i c_{ti} r_w^2}\right) + 3.23 \right]$$

For pressure-squared approach:

$$m = \frac{1\,637 Q_g \bar{Z} \mu_g}{kh}$$

$$s' = 1.151 \left[\frac{P_{1hr}^2 - P_{wfat\,\Delta t=0}^2}{|m|} - \lg\left(\frac{k}{\phi \mu_i c_{ti} r_w^2}\right) + 3.23 \right]$$

where the gas flow rate Q_g is expressed in mscf/d. It should be pointed out that when a well is shut in for a pressure buildup test, the well is usually closed at the surface rather than the sand face. Even though the well is shut in, the reservoir fluid continues to flow and accumulates in the wellbore until the well fills sufficiently to transmit the effect of shut-in to the formation. This "after flow" behavior is caused by the wellbore storage and it has a significant influence on pressure buildup data. During the period of wellbore storage effects, the pressure data points fall below the semilog straight line. The duration of these effects may be estimated by making the lg-lg data plot described previously of $\lg(P_{ws} - P_{wf})$ vs. $\lg(\Delta t)$ with P_{wf} as the value recorded immediately before shut-in. When wellbore storage dominates, that plot will have a unit-slope straight line; as the semilog straight line is approached, the lg-lg plot bends over to a gently curving line with a low slope.

The wellbore storage coefficient C is, by selecting a point on the lg-lg unit-slope straight line and reading the coordinate of the point in terms of Δt and ΔP:

$$C = \frac{q\Delta t}{24\Delta P} = \frac{QB\Delta t}{24\Delta P}$$

where Δt——shut-in time, h;
ΔP——pressure difference $(P_{ws} - P_{wf})$, psi;
q——flow rate, bbl/d;
Q——flow rate, STB/d;
B——formation volume factor, bbl/STB.

with a dimensionless wellbore storage coefficient as given by Equation

$$C_D = \frac{5.615C}{2\pi h\phi c_t r_w^2} = \frac{0.8936C}{\phi h c_t r_w^2}$$

as:

$$C_D = \frac{0.8936C}{\phi h c_t r_w^2}$$

In all the pressure buildup test analyses, the lg-lg data plot should be made before the straight line is chosen on the semilog data plot. This lg-lg plot is essential to avoid drawing a semilog straight line through the wellbore storage dominated data. The beginning of the semilog line can be estimated by observing when the data points on the lg-lg plot reach the slowly curving low-slope line and adding 1 to $1\frac{1}{2}$ cycles in time after the end of the unit-slope straight line. Alternatively, the time to the beginning of the semilog straight line can be estimated from:

$$\Delta t > \frac{170\,000 C e^{0.14s}}{(kh/\mu)}$$

where c——calculated wellbore storage coefficient, bbl/psi;
k——permeability, md;
s——skin factor;
h——thickness, ft.

【Example 2】

Tab. 6.1 shows the pressure buildup data from an oil well with an estimated drainage radius of

2 640 ft. Before shut-in, the well had produced at a stabilized rate of 4 900 STB/d for 310 h. Known reservoir data is:

dept = 10 476 ft, r_w = 0.354 ft, c_t = 22.6×10^{-6} psi^{-1}, Q_0 = 4 900 STB/D, h = 482 ft, $P_{wf}(\Delta t = 0)$ = 2 761 psig, μ_0 = 0.20 cp, B_0 = 1.55 bbl/STB, ϕ = 0.09, t_p = 310 h, r_e = 2 640 ft.

Tab. 6.1 Earlougher's pressure buildup data

Δt/h	$t_p+\Delta t$/h	$t_p+\Delta t\Delta t$	P_{ws}/psig
0.0	—	—	2761
0.10	310.30	3101	3057
0.21	310.21	1477	3153
0.31	310.31	1001	3234
0.52	310.52	597	3249
0.63	310.63	493	3256
0.73	310.73	426	3260
0.84	310.84	370	3263
0.94	310.94	331	3266
1.05	311.05	296	3267
1.15	311.15	271	3267
1.36	311.36	229	3271
1.68	311.68	186	3274
1.99	311.99	157	3276
2.51	312.51	125	3280
3.04	313.04	103	3283
3.46	313.46	90.6	3286
4.08	314.08	77.0	3289
5.03	315.03	62.6	3293
5.97	315.97	52.9	3297
6.07	316.07	52.1	3297
7.01	317.01	45.2	3300
8.06	318.06	39.5	3303
9.00	319.00	35.4	3305
10.05	320.05	31.8	3306
13.09	323.09	24.7	3310
16.02	326.02	20.4	3313
20.00	330.00	16.5	3317
26.07	336.07	12.9	3320
31.03	341.03	11.0	3322
34.98	344.98	9.9	3323
37.54	347.54	9.3	3323

Calculate:
- the average permeability k;
- the skin factor s;
- the additional pressure drop due to skin ΔP_{skin}.

Solution

Step 1. Plot P_{ws} vs. $(tp+\Delta t)/\Delta t$ on a semilog scale as shown in Fig. 6.5.

Step 2. Identify the correct straight-line portion of the curve and determine the slope$m$: $m = 40$ psi/cycle

Step 3. Calculate the average permeability by using Equation (6.7)

$$k/\text{md} = \frac{162.6 Q_o B_o \mu_o}{mh} = \frac{162.6 \times 4\,900 \times 1.55 \times 0.22}{40 \times 482} = 12.8$$

Step 4. Determine P_{wf} after 1 hour from the straight-line portion of the curve:

$$P_{1hr}/\text{psi} = 3\,266$$

Step 5. Calculate the skin factor by applying Equation (6.8).

$$s = 1.151\left[\frac{P_{1hr}-P_{wf\Delta t=0}}{m} - \lg\left(\frac{k}{\phi\mu c_t r_w^2}\right) + 3.23\right] =$$

$$1.151\left[\frac{3\,266-2\,761}{40} - \lg\left(\frac{12.8}{0.09\times 0.20\times 22.6\times 10^{-6}\times(0.354)^2}\right) + 3.23\right] = 8.6$$

Step 6. Calculate the additional pressure drop by using:

$$\Delta P_{skin}/\text{psi} = 0.87|m|s = 0.87\times 40\times 8.6 = 299.3$$

6.4 Miller-Dyes-Hutchinson Method

As noted previously, the buildup test exhibits a semilog straight line which begins to bend down and become flat at the later shut-in times because of the effect of the boundaries. Matthews et al. proposed a methodology for estimating average pressure from buildup tests in bounded drainage regions. The MBH method is based on theoretical correlations between the extrapolated semilog straight line to the false pressure P^* and current average drainage are a pressure P. The authors point out that the average pressure in the drainage area of each well can be related to P^* if the geometry, shape, and location of the well relative to the drainage boundaries are known. They developed a set of correction charts, as shown in Fig. 6.6 through 6.9, for various drainage geometries. The y axis of these figures represents the MBH dimensionless pressure P_{DMBH} that is defined by:

$$P_{DMBH} = \frac{2.303(P^*-\bar{P})}{|m|}$$

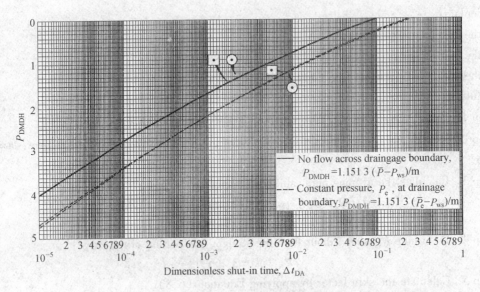

Fig. 6.6 Miller-Dyes-Hutchinson dimensionless pressure for circular and square drainage areas

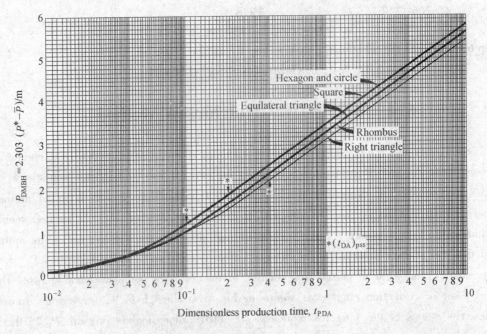

Fig. 6.7 Matthews-Brons-Hazebroek dimensionless pressure for a well in the center of equilateral drainage areas

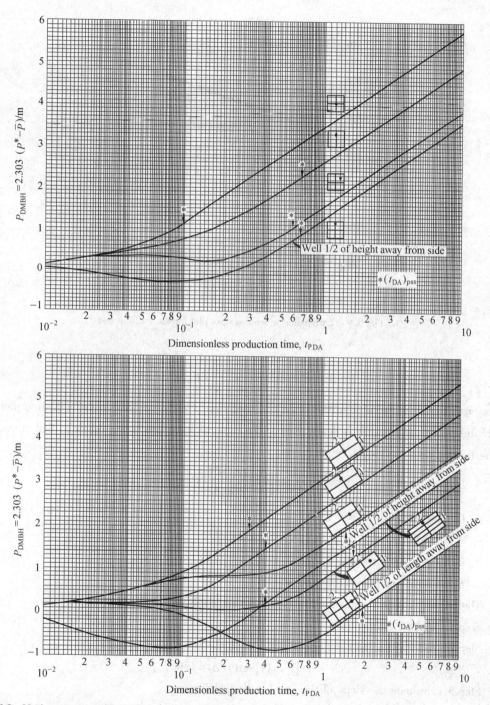

Fig. 6.8 Matthews-Brons-Hazebroek dimensionless pressure for different well locations in a 2:1 rectangular drainage area

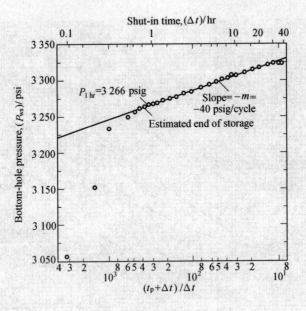

Fig. 6.9 Earlougher's semilog data plot for the buildup test

or

$$\bar{P} = P^* - \left(\frac{|m|}{2.303}\right) P_{DMBH} \qquad (6.9)$$

where m is the absolute value of the slope obtained from the Horner semilog straight-line plot. The MBH dimensionless pressure is determined at the dimensionless producing time t_{PDA} that corresponds to the flowing time t_p. That is:

$$t_{PDA} = \left[\frac{0.0002637k}{\phi \mu c_t A}\right] t_p \qquad (6.10)$$

where t_p——flowing time before shut-in, h;

A——drainage area, ft^2;

k——permeability, md;

c_t——total compressibility, psi^{-1}.

The following steps summarize the procedure for applying the MBH method:

Step 1. Make a Horner plot.

Step 2. Extrapolate the semilog straight line to the value of

$$P^* \text{ at}(t_p + \Delta t)/\Delta t = 1.0$$

Step 3. Evaluate the slope of the semilog straight line m.

Step 4. Calculate the MBH dimensionless producing time t_{PDA} from Equation (6.10):

$$t_{\text{PDA}} = \left[\frac{0.000\ 263\ 7k}{\phi\mu c_t A}\right] t_p$$

Step 5. Find the closest approximation to the shape of the well drainage area in Fig. 6.7 through 6.9 and identify the correction curve.

Step 6. Read the value of P_{DMBH} from the correction curve at t_{PDA}.

Step 7. Calculate the value of $\bar{P}$ from Equation (6.8):

$$\bar{P} = P^* - \left(\frac{|m|}{2.303}\right) P_{\text{DMBH}}$$

As in the normal Horner analysis technique, the producing time t_p is given by:

$$t_p = \frac{24N_p}{Q_o}$$

where N_p is the cumulative volume produced since the last pressure buildup test and Q_o is the constant flow rate just before shut-in. Pinson and Kazemi indicate that t_p should be compared with the time required to reach the pseudosteady state, t_{pss}:

$$t_{\text{pss}} = \left[\frac{\phi\mu c_t A}{0.000\ 236\ 7k}\right](t_{\text{DA}})_{\text{pss}} \qquad (6.11)$$

For a symmetric closed or circular drainage area, $(t_{\text{DA}})_{\text{pss}} = 0.1$ as given in Tab. 6.1 and listed in the fifth column. If $t_p \gg t_{\text{pss}}$, then t_{pss} should ideally replace t_p in both the Horner plot and for use with the MBH dimensionless pressure curves.

The above methodology gives the value of P in the drainage area of one well, e.g., well i. If a number of wells are producing from the reservoir, each well can be analyzed separately to give p for its own drainage area. The reservoir average pressure P_r can be estimated from these individual well average drainage pressures by using one of the relationships given by Equations:

$$\bar{P}_r = \frac{\sum_j [(\bar{P}q)_j / (\partial \bar{P}/\partial t)_j]}{\sum j [q_j / (\partial \bar{P}/\partial t)_j]}$$

and

$$\bar{P}_r = \frac{\sum_j \bar{P}_j \Delta(F)_j / \Delta \bar{P}_j}{\sum_j \Delta(F)_j / \Delta \bar{P}_j}$$

That is:

$$\bar{P}_r = \frac{\sum i(\bar{P}q)_i / (\partial \bar{P}/\partial t)_i}{\sum i q_i / (\partial \bar{P}/\partial t)_i}$$

or:

$$\bar{P}_r = \frac{\sum_i [\bar{P}\Delta(F)/\Delta\bar{P}]_i}{\sum_i [\Delta(F)/\Delta\bar{P}]_i}$$

with:

$$F_t = \int_0^t [Q_0 B_0 + Q_w B_w + (Q_g - Q_0 R_s - Q_w R_{sw})B_g] dt$$

$$F_{t+\Delta t} = \int_0^{t+\Delta t} [Q_0 B_0 + Q_w B_w + (Q_g - Q_0 R_s - Q_w R_{sw})B_g] dt$$

and:

$$\Delta(F) = F_{t+\Delta t} - F_t$$

Similarly, it should be noted that the MBH method and the Fig. 6.6 through 6.9 can be applied for compressible gases by defining P_{DMBH} as:

For the pseudopressure approach

$$P_{DMBH} = \frac{2.303[m(P^*) - m(\bar{P})]}{|m|} \tag{6.12}$$

For the pressure-squared approach

$$P_{DMBH} = \frac{2.303[m(P^*)^2 - m(\bar{P})^2]}{|m|} \tag{6.13}$$

【Example 3】

Using the information given in Example 2 and pressure buildup data listed in Tab. 6.1, calculate the average pressure in the well drainage area and the drainage area by applying Equation:

$$m_{pss} = \frac{(P_{ws2} - P_{ws1})\lg(\Delta t_3/\Delta t_1) - (P_{ws3} - P_{ws1})\lg[\Delta t_2/\Delta t_1]}{(\Delta t_2 - \Delta t_1)\lg(\Delta T_2 \Delta t_1) - (\Delta t_2 - \Delta t_1)\lg(\Delta t_2/\Delta t_1)} \tag{6.14}$$

The data is listed below for convenience:

$r_e = 2\ 640$ ft, $r_w = 0.354$ ft, $c_t = 22.6 \times 10^{-6}$ psi^{-1}, $Q_0 = 4\ 900$ STB/d, $h = 482$ ft, $P_{wfat\Delta t=0} = 2\ 761$ psig, $\mu_0 = 0.20$ cp, $B_0 = 1.55$ bbl/STB, $\phi = 0.09$, $t_p = 310$ h, depth $= 10\ 476$ ft, reported average pressure $= 3\ 323$ psi

Solution

Step 1. Calculate the drainage area of the well:

$$A = \pi r_e^2 = \pi (2\ 640)^2$$

Step 2. Compare the production time t_p, i.e., 310 h, with the time required to reach the pseudosteady state t_{pss} by applying Equation (6.10). Estimate t_{pss} using $(t_{DA})_{pss} = 0.1$ to give:

$$t_{pss}/h = \left[\frac{\phi \mu c_t A}{0.000\ 236\ 7k}\right](t_{DA})_{pss} = \left[\frac{0.09 \times 0.2 \times 22.6 \times 10^{-6} \times \pi \times 2\ 640^2}{0.000\ 263\ 7 \times 12.8}\right] \times 0.1 = 264$$

Thus, we could replace t_p by 264 hours in our analysis because $t_p > t_{pss}$. However, since t_p is only about 1.2 t_{pss}, we use the actual production time of 310 hours in the calculation.

Step 3. Fig. 6.10 does not show P^* since the semilog straight line is not extended to $(t_p+\Delta t)/\Delta t = 1.0$.

However, P^* can be calculated from P_{ws} at $(t_p+\Delta t)/\Delta t = 10.0$ by extrapolating one cycle. That is:

$P^*/\text{psig} = 3\ 325 + (1\ \text{cycle})(40\ \text{psi/cycle}) = 3\ 365$

Step 4. Calculate t_{PDA} by applying Equation (6.14) to give:

$$t_{PDA} = \left[\frac{0.000\ 263\ 7k}{\phi \mu c_t A}\right] t_p = \left[\frac{0.000\ 263\ 7 \times 12.8}{0.09 \times 0.2 \times 22.6 \times 10^{-6} \times \pi \times 2\ 640^2}\right] \times 310 = 0.117$$

Step 5. From the curve of the circle in Fig. 6.7, obtain the value of P_{DMBH} at $t_{PDA} = 0.117$, to give:

$P_{DMBH} = 1.34$

Step 6. Calculate the average pressure from Equation (6.9):

$$\bar{P}/\text{psig} = P^* - \left(\frac{|m|}{2.303}\right) P_{DMBH} = 3\ 365 - \frac{40}{2.303} \times 1.34 = 3\ 342$$

This is 19 psi higher than the maximum pressure recorded of 3 323 psig.

Step 7. Select the coordinates of any three points located on the semilog straight line portion of the Horner plot, to give:

- $(\Delta t_1, P_{ws1}) = (2.52, 3\ 280)$
- $(\Delta t_2, P_{ws2}) = (9.00, 3\ 305)$
- $(\Delta t_3, P_{ws3}) = (20.0, 3\ 317)$

Step 8. Calculate m_{pss} by applying Equation (6.14):

$$m_{pss}/(\text{psi} \cdot \text{h}^{-1}) = \frac{(P_{ws2}-P_{ws1})\lg(\Delta t_3/\Delta t_1) - (P_{ws3}-P_{ws1})\lg(\Delta t_2/\Delta t_1)}{(\Delta t_3-\Delta t_1)\lg(\Delta t_2/\Delta t_1) - (\Delta t_2/\Delta t_1)\lg(\Delta t_3/\Delta t_1)} =$$

$$\frac{(3\ 305-3\ 280)\lg(20/2.51) - (3\ 317-3\ 280)\lg(9/2.51)}{(20-2.51)\lg(9/2.51) - (9-2.51)\lg(20/2.51)} = 0.523\ 39$$

Step 9. The well drainage area can then be calculated from Equation (6.4):

$$A/\text{arces} = \frac{0.233\ 96 Q_o B_o}{c_t m_{pss} h \phi} = \frac{0.233\ 96 \times 4\ 900 \times 1.55}{22.6 \times 10^{-6} \times 0.523\ 39 \times 482 \times 0.09} =$$

$$3\ 462\ 938 \text{ft}^2 = \frac{3\ 363\ 938}{43\ 560} = 80$$

The corresponding drainage radius is 1 050 ft which differs considerably from the given radius of 2 640 ft. Using the calculated drainage radius of 1 050 ft and repeating the MBH calculations gives:

$$t_{pss}/h = \left[\frac{0.09 \times 0.2 \times 22.6 \times 10^{-6} \times \pi \times 1\,050^2}{0.000\,263\,7 \times 12.8}\right] \times 0.1 = 41.7$$

$$t_{PDA} = \left[\frac{0.000\,263\,7 \times 12.8}{0.09 \times 0.2 \times 22.6 \times 10^{-6} \times \pi \times 1\,050^2}\right] \times 310 = 0.743$$

$$p_{DMBH} = 3.15$$

$$\bar{P}/\text{psig} = 3\,365 - \frac{40}{2.303} \times 3.15 = 3\,311$$

The value is 12 psi higher than the reported value of average reservoir pressure.

6.5 Injectivity Well Testing

Key Words   injectivity well testing; the objectives of injection tests

Injectivity well testing is a pressure transient test during injection into a well. Injection well testing and the associated analysis are essentially simple, as long as the mobility ratio between the injected fluid and the reservoir fluid is unity. Earlougher pointed out that the unit-mobility ratio is a reasonable approximation for many reservoirs under water floods. The objectives of injection tests are similar to those of production tests, namely the determination of:

- permeability;
- skin;
- average pressure;
- reservoir heterogeneity;
- front tracking.

Injection well testing involves the application of one or more of the following approaches:

- injectivity test;
- pressure falloff test;
- step-rate injectivity test.

The above three analyses of injection well testing are briefly presented below.

In an injectivity test, the well is shut in until the pressure is stabilized at initial reservoir pressure P_i. At this time, the injection begins at a constant rate q_{inj} as schematically illustrated in Fig. 6.6, while recording the bottom-hole pressure P_{wf}. For a unit-mobility ratio system, the injectivity test would be identical to a pressure drawdown test except that the constant rate is negative with a value of q_{inj}. However, in all the preceding relationships, the injection rate will be treated as a positive value, i.e., $q_{inj} > 0$.

For a constant injection rate, the bottom-hole pressure is given by the linear form of Equation

(6.1) as:

$$P_{wf} = P_{1hr} + m\lg(t)$$

The above relationship indicates that a plot of bottomhole injection pressure versus the logarithm of injection time would produce a straight-line section as shown in Fig. 6.10, with an intercept of P_{1hr} and a slope m as defined by:

$$m = \frac{162.6 q_{inj} B\mu}{kh}$$

where q_{inj}——absolute value of injection rate, STB/d;
m——slope, psi/cycle;
k——permeability, md;
h——thickness, ft.

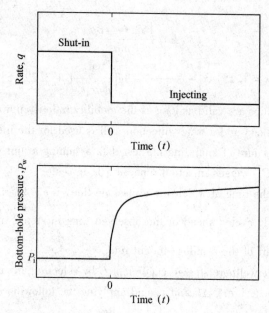

Fig. 6.10 Idealized rate schedule and pressure response for injectivity testing

Sabet pointed out that, depending on whether the density of the injected fluid is higher or lower than the reservoir fluid, the injected fluid will tend to override or underride the reservoir fluid and, therefore the net pay h which should be used in interpreting injectivity tests would not be the same as the net pay which is used in interpreting drawdown tests.

Earlougher pointed out that, as in drawdown testing, the wellbore storage has great effects on the recorded injectivity test data due to the expected large value of the wellbore storage coefficient. Earlougher recommended that all injectivity test analyses must include the lg-lg plot of $(P_{wf} - P_i)$

versus injection time with the objective of determining the duration of the wellbore storage effects. As defined previously, the beginning of the semilog straight line, i.e., the end of the wellbore storage effects, can be estimated from the following expression:

$$t > \frac{(200\,000 + 12\,000s)C}{kh/\mu} \tag{6.15}$$

where t——time that marks the end of wellbore storage effects, h;
k——permeability, md;
s——skin factor;
C——wellbore storage coefficient, bbl/psi;
μ——viscosity, cp.

Once the semilog straight line is identified, the permeability and skin can be determined as outlined previously by:

$$k = \frac{162.6 q_{inj} B \mu}{mh} \tag{6.16}$$

$$s = 1.1513 \left[\frac{P_{1hr} - P_i}{m} - \lg\left(\frac{k}{\phi \mu c_t r_w^2}\right) + 3.2275 \right] \tag{6.17}$$

The above relationships are valid as long as the mobility ratio is approximately equal to 1. If the reservoir is under water flood and a water injection well is used for the injectivity test, the following steps summarize the procedure of analyzing the test data assuming a unit-mobility ratio:

Step 1. Plot $(P_{wf} - P_i)$ versus injection time on a lg-lg scale.

Step 2. Determine the time at which the unit-slope line, i.e., 45° line, ends.

Step 3. Move $1\frac{1}{2}$ lg cycles ahead of the observed time in step 2 and read the corresponding time which marks the start of the semilog straight line.

Step 4. Estimate the wellbore storage coefficient C by selecting any point on the unit-slope line and reading its coordinates, i.e., ΔP and t, and applying the following expression:

$$C = \frac{q_{inj} B t}{24 \Delta P} \tag{6.18}$$

Step 5. Plot P_{wf} vs. t on a semilog scale and determine the slope m of the straight line that represents the transient flow condition.

Step 6. Calculate the permeability k and skin factor from Equations (6.10) and (6.11) respectively.

Step 7. Calculate the radius of investigation r_{inv} at the end of injection time. That is:

$$r_{inv} = 0.0359 \sqrt{\frac{kt}{\phi \mu c_t}} \tag{6.19}$$

Step 8. Estimate the radius to the leading edge of the water bank r_{wb} before the initiation of the injectivity test from:

$$r_{wb} = \sqrt{\frac{5.615 W_{inj}}{\pi h \phi (\bar{S}_w - S_{wi})}} = \sqrt{\frac{5.615 W_{inj}}{\pi h \phi (\Delta S_w)}} \qquad (6.20)$$

where r_{wb}——radius to the water bank, ft;

W_{inj}——cumulative water injected at the start of the test, bbl;

$\bar{S}_w$——average water saturation at the start of the test;

S_{wi}——initial water saturation.

Step 9. Compare r_{wb} with r_{inv}: if $r_{inv} < r_{wb}$, the unit-mobility ratio assumption is justified.

【Example 4】

Fig. 6.6 and 6.7 show pressure response data for a 7 h injectivity test in a water-flooded reservoir in terms of $\lg(P_{wf}-P_i)$ vs. $\lg(t)$ and $\lg(P_{wf})$ vs. $\lg(t)$ respectively. Before the test, the reservoir had been under water flood for 2 years with a constant injection rate of 100 STB/d. The injectivity test was initiated after shutting in all wells for several weeks to stabilize the pressure at P_i. The following data is available:

$c_t = 6.67 \times 10^{-6}$ psi^{-1}, $B = 1.0$ bbl/STB, $\mu = 1.0$ cp, $S_w = 62.4$ lb/ft^3, $\phi = 0.15$, $q_{inj} = 100$ STB/d, $h = 16$ ft, $r_w = 0.25$ ft, $P_i = 194$ psig, $\Delta S_w = 0.4$, depth = 1 002 ft, total test time = 7 h.

The well is completed with 2 inch tubing set on a packer.

Estimate the reservoir permeability and skin factor.

Solution

Step 1. The lg-lg data plot of Fig. 6.11 indicates that the data begins to deviate from the unit-slope line at about 0.55 h. Using the rule of thumb of moving 1 to $1\frac{1}{2}$ cycles in time after the data starts deviating from the unit-slope line, suggests that the start of the semilog straight line begins after 5 to 10 hours of testing. However, Fig. 6.10 and 6.11 clearly show that the wellbore storage effects have ended after 2 to 3 hours.

Step 2. From the unit-slope portion of Fig. 6.11, select the coordinates of a point (i.e., ΔP and t) end calculate the wellbore storage coefficient C by applying Equation (6.12):

$$\Delta P = 408 \text{ psig}$$
$$t = 1 \text{ h}$$
$$C/(\text{bbl} \cdot \text{psi}^{-1}) = \frac{q_{inj} Bt}{24 \Delta P} = \frac{100 \times 1.0 \times 1}{24 \times 408} = 0.010\ 2$$

Step 3. From the semilog plot in Fig. 6.11, determine the slope of the straight line m to give:

$$m = 770 \text{ psig/cycle}$$

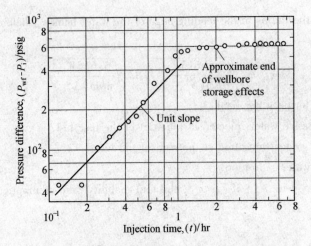

Fig. 6.11　lg-lg data plot for the injectivity test of Example 3
Water injection into a reservoir at static conditions

Step 4. Calculate the permeability and skin factor by using Equations (6.10) and (6.11):

$$k/\text{md} = \frac{162.6 q_{inj} B\mu}{mh} = \frac{162.6 \times 100 \times 1.0 \times 1.0}{80 \times 16} = 12.7$$

$$s = 1.1513 \left[\frac{P_{1hr} - P_i}{m} - \lg\left(\frac{k}{\phi\mu c_t r_w^2}\right) + 3.2275 \right] =$$

$$1.1513 \left[\frac{770 - 194}{80} - \lg\left(\frac{12.7}{0.15 \times 1.0 \times 6.67 \times 10^{-6} \times 0.25^2}\right) + 3.2275 \right] = 2.4$$

Step 5. Calculate the radius of investigation after 7 hours by applying Equation (6.14):

$$r_{inv}/\text{ft} = 0.0359 \sqrt{\frac{kt}{\phi\mu c_t}} = 0.0359 \sqrt{\frac{12.7 \times 7}{0.15 \times 1.0 \times 6.67 \times 10^{-6}}} \approx 338$$

Step 6. Estimate the distance of the leading edge of the water bank before the start of the test from Equation (6.15):

$$W_{inj}/\text{bbl} \approx 2 \times 365 \times 100 \times 1.0 = 73\,000$$

$$r_{wb}/\text{ft} = \sqrt{\frac{5.615 W_{inj}}{\pi h \phi (\Delta S_w)}} = \sqrt{\frac{5.615 \times 73\,000}{\pi \times 16 \times 0.15 \times 0.4}} \approx 369$$

Since $r_{inv} < r_{wb}$, the use of the unit-mobility ratio analysis is justified.

6.6 Pressure Falloff Test

A pressure falloff test is usually preceded by an injectivity test of a long duration. As illustrated schematically in Fig. 6.12, falloff testing is analogous to pressure buildup testing in a production well. After the injectivity test that lasted for a total injection time of t_p at a constant injection rate of

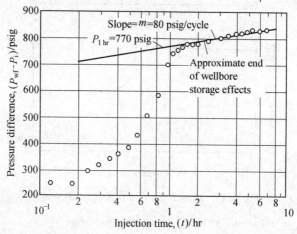

Fig. 6.12 Idealized rate schedule and pressure response for falloff testing

q_{inj}, the well is then shut in. The pressure data taken immediately before and during the shut in period is analyzed by the Horner plot method. The recorded pressure falloff data can be represented by Equation

$$m_{pss} = \frac{(P_{ws2} - P_{ws1})\lg(\Delta t_3/\Delta t_1) - (P_{ws3} - P_{ws1})\lg[\Delta t_2/\Delta t_1]}{(\Delta t_3/\Delta t_1)\lg(\Delta t_2 \Delta t_1) - (\Delta t_2 - \Delta t_1)\lg(\Delta t_3 \Delta t_1)}$$

as:

$$P_{ws} = P^* + m\left[\lg\left(\frac{t_p + \Delta t}{\Delta t}\right)\right]$$

with:

$$m = \left|\frac{162.6 q_{inj} B\mu}{kh}\right|$$

where P^* is the false pressure that is only equal to the initial (original) reservoir pressure in a newly discovered field. As shown in Fig. 6.13, a plot of P_{ws} vs. $\lg[(t_p+\Delta t)/\Delta t]$ would form a straight-line portion with an intercept of P^* at $(t_p+\Delta t)/\Delta t = 1$ and a negative slope of m.

It should be pointed out that the lg-lg data plot should be constructed to identify the end of the wellbore storage effects and beginning of the proper semilog straight line. The permeability and skin

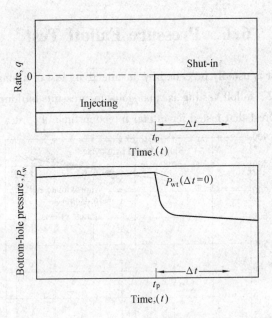

Fig. 6.13 Horner plot of a typical falloff test

factor can be estimated as outlined previously by the expressions:

$$k = \frac{162.6 q_{inj} B \mu}{|m| h}$$

$$s = 1.513 \left[\frac{P_{wfalt\Delta t=0} - P_{1hr}}{|m|} - \lg\left(\frac{k}{\phi \mu c_t r_w^2}\right) + 3.2275 \right]$$

Earlougher indicated that if the injection rate varies before the falloff test, the equivalent injection time may be approximated by:

$$t_p = \frac{24 W_{inj}}{q_{inj}}$$

where W_{inj} is the cumulative volume injected since the last pressure equalization, i.e., last shut-in, and q_{inj} is the injection rate just before shut-in. It is not uncommon for a falloff test to experience a change in wellbore storage after the test begins at the end of the injectivity test. This will occur in any well which goes on vacuum during the test. An injection well will go on vacuum when the bottom-hole pressure decreases to a value which is insufficient to support a column of water to the surface. Prior to going on vacuum, an injection well will experience storage due to water expansion; after going on vacuum, the storage will be due to a falling fluid level. This change in storage will generally exhibit itself as a decrease in the rate of pressure decline.

The falloff data can also be expressed in graphical form by plotting P_{ws} vs. $\lg(\Delta t)$ as proposed by MDH(Miller-Dyes-Hutchinson). The mathematical expression for estimating the false pressure P^* from the MDH analysis is given by Equation:

$$P^* = P_{1hr} + m\lg(t_p + 1)$$

as:

$$P^* = P_{1hr} - |m| \lg(t_p + 1) \tag{6.21}$$

Earlougher pointed out that the MDH plot is more practical to use unless t_p is less than about twice the shut-in time.

The following example, as adopted from the work of McLeod and Coulter and Earlougher, is used to illustrate the methodology of analyzing the falloff pressure data.

【Example 5】

During a stimulation treatment, brine was injected into a well and the falloff data, as reported by McLeod and Coulter, is shown graphically in Fig. 6.14 through 6.16. Other available data includes:

total injection time $t_p = 6.82$ h, total falloff time $= 0.67$ h, $q_{inj} = 807$ STB/d, $B_w = 1.0$ bbl/STB, $c_w = 3.0 \times 10^{-6}$ psi^{-1}, $\phi = 0.25$, $h = 28$ ft, $\mu_w = 1.0$ cp, $c_t = 1.0 \times 10^{-5}$ psi^{-1}, $r_w = 0.4$ ft, $S_w = 67.46$ lb/ft^3, depth $= 4\ 819$ ft, hydrostatic fluid gradient $= 0.468\ 5$ psi/ft.

The recorded shut-in pressures are expressed in terms of wellhead pressures P_{ts} with $P_{tfat\Delta t=0} = 1\ 310$ psig. Calculate:

· the wellbore storage coefficient;
· the permeability;

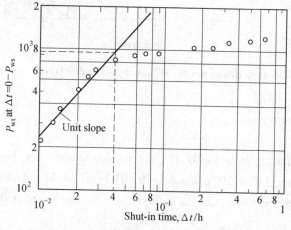

Fig. 6.14 Lg-lg data plot for a falloff test after brine injection, Example 5

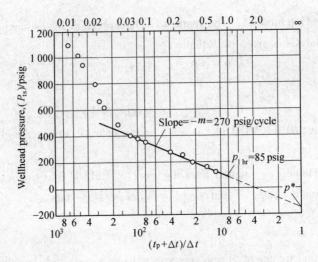

Fig. 6.15 Horner plot of pressure falloff after brine injection, Example 5

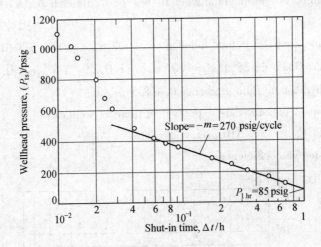

Fig. 6.16 Miller-Dyes-Hutchinson plot of pressure falloff after brine injection, Example 5

- the skin factor;
- the average pressure.

Solution

Step 1. From the lg-lg plot of Fig. 6.15, the semilog straight line begins around 0.1 to 0.2 hours after shut-in. Using $\Delta P = 238$ psi at $\Delta t = 0.01$ hours as the selected coordinates of a point on the unitslope straight line, calculate the wellbore storage coefficient from Equation (6.23), to give:

$$C/(\text{bbl} \cdot \text{psi}^{-1}) = \frac{q_{inj}Bt}{24\Delta P} = \frac{807 \times 1.0 \times 0.01}{24 \times 238} = 0.001\ 4$$

Step 2. Fig. 6.16 and 6.17 show the Horner plot, i.e., wellhead pressures vs. $\lg[(t_p + \Delta t)/\Delta t]$, and the MDH plot, i.e., wellhead pressures vs. $\lg(\Delta t)$, respectively, with both plots giving:

$$m = 270\ \text{psig/cycle}$$
$$P_{1hr} = 85\ \text{psig}$$

Using these two values, calculate k and s:

$$k/\text{md} = \frac{162.6 q_{inj} B\mu}{|m|h} = \frac{162.6 \times 807 \times 1.0 \times 1.0}{270 \times 28} = 17.4$$

$$s = 1.513 \times \left[\frac{P_{wfat\Delta t=0} - P_{1hr}}{|m|} - \lg\left(\frac{k}{\phi \mu c_t r_w^2}\right) + 3.227\ 5\right] =$$

$$1.513 \times \left[\frac{1\ 310 - 85}{270} - \lg\left(\frac{17.4}{0.25 \times 1.0 \times 1.0 \times 10^{-5} \times 0.4^2}\right)\right] + 3.227\ 5 = 0.15$$

Step 3. Determine P^* from the extrapolation of the Horner plot of Fig. 6.16 to $(t_p + \Delta t)/\Delta t = 1$, to give:

$$P_{ts}^* = -151\ \text{psig}$$

Equation (6.15) can be used to approximate P^*:

$$P^* = P_{1hr} - |m|\lg(t_p + 1)$$
$$P_{ts}^* = 85 - (270)\lg(6.82 + 1) = -156\ \text{psig}$$

This is the false pressure at the wellhead, i.e., the surface. Using the hydrostatic gradient of 0.468 5 psi/ft and the depth of 4 819 ft, the reservoir false pressure is:

$$P^*/\text{psig} = 4\ 819 \times 0.468\ 5 - 151 = 2\ 107$$

and since injection time t_p is short compared with the shut-in time, we can assume that:

$$\bar{P} = P^* = 2\ 107\ \text{psig}$$

Pressure falloff analysis in non-unit-mobility ratio systems

Fig. 6.17 shows a plan view of the saturation distribution in the vicinity of an injection well. This figure shows two distinct zones.

Zone 1. represents the water bank with its leading edge at a distance of r_{f1} from the injection well. The mobility λ of the injected fluid in this zone, i.e., zone 1, is defined as the ratio of effective permeability of the injected fluid at its average saturation to its viscosity, or:

$$\lambda_1 = (k/\mu)_1$$

Zone 2. represents the oil bank with the leading edge at a distance of r_{f2} from the injection well. The mobility λ of the oil bank in this zone, i.e., zone 2, is defined as the ratio of oil effective

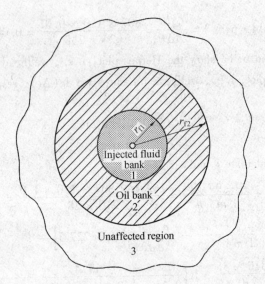

Fig. 6.17 Schematic diagram of fluid distribution around an injection well (composite reservoir)

permeability as evaluated at initial or connate water saturation to its viscosity, or:

The assumption of a two-bank system is applicable if the reservoir is filled with liquid or if the maximum shut-in time of the falloff test is such that the radius of investigation of the test does not exceed the outer radius of the oil bank. The ideal behavior of the falloff test in a two-bank system as expressed in terms of the Horner plot is illustrated in Fig. 6.18.

Fig. 6.18 shows two distinct straight lines with slopes of m_1 and m_2, that intersect at Δt_{fx}. The slope m_1 of the first line is used to estimate the effective permeability to water k_w in the flooded zone

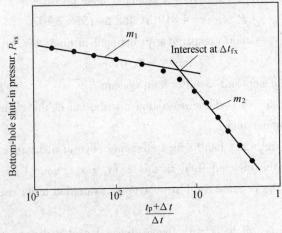

Fig. 6.18 Pressure falloff behavior in a two-bank system

and the skin factor s. It is commonly believed that the slope of the second line m_2 will yield the mobility of the oil bank λ_o. However, Merrill et al. pointed out that the slope m_2 can be used only to determine the oil zone mobility if $r_{f2} > 10 r_{f1}$ and $(\varphi c_t)_1 = (\varphi c_t)_2$, and developed a technique that can be used to determine the distance r_{f1} and mobility of each bank. The technique requires knowing the values of (φc_t) in the first and second zone, i.e., $(\varphi c_t)_1$ and $(\varphi c_t)_2$. The authors proposed the following expression:

$$\lambda = \frac{k}{\mu} = \frac{162.6QB}{m_2 h}$$

The authors also proposed two graphical correlations, as shown in Fig. 6.14 and 6.15, that can be used with the Horner plot to analyze the pressure falloff data.

The proposed technique is summarized by the following:

Step 1. Plot ΔP vs. Δt on a lg-lg scale and determine the end of the wellbore storage effect.

Step 2. Construct the Horner plot or the MDH plot and determine m_1, m_2 and Δt_{fx}.

Step 3. Estimate the effective permeability in the first zone, i.e., injected fluid invaded zone, "zone 1", and the skin factor from:

$$k_1 = \frac{162.6 q_{inj} B \mu}{|m_1| h} \tag{6.22}$$

$$s = 1.513 \left[\frac{P_{wfat\Delta t=0} - P_{1hr}}{|m_1|} - \lg\left(\frac{k_1}{\phi \mu_1 (c_t)_1 r_w^2}\right) + 3.2275 \right]$$

where the subscript "1" denotes zone 1, the injected fluid zone.

Step 4. Calculate the following dimensionless ratios:

$$\frac{m_2}{m_1} \quad \text{and} \quad \frac{(\phi c_t)_1}{(\phi c_t)_2}$$

with the subscripts "1" and "2" denoting zone 1 and zone 2 respectively.

Step 5. Use Fig. 6.19 with the two dimensionless ratios of step 4 and read the mobility ratio λ_1 / λ_2.

Step 6. Estimate the effective permeability in the second zone from the following expression:

$$k_2 = \left(\frac{\mu_2}{\mu_1}\right) \frac{k_1}{\lambda_1 / \lambda_2} \tag{6.23}$$

Step 7. Obtain the dimensionless time Δt_{Dfx} from Fig. 6.21.

Step 8. Calculate the distance to the leading edge of the injected fluid bank r_{f1} from:

$$r_{f1} = \sqrt{\left[\frac{0.0002637(k/\mu)_1}{(\phi c_t)_1}\right]\left(\frac{\Delta t_{fx}}{\Delta t_{Dfx}}\right)} \tag{6.24}$$

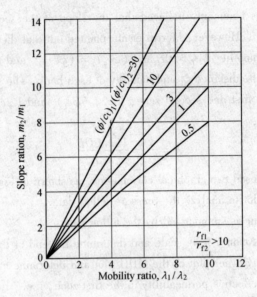

Fig. 6.19 Relationship between mobility ratio, slope ratio, and storage ratio

Summary

Testing is one of the important measures for reservoir engineers to recognize reservoirs, obtain reservoir parameters, and control production rates. Through testing, engineers can judge whether the formation is injured, if there are some faults and confirm the position of the faults, localizes the barriers of the reservoir, and calculate the flow parameter, such as permeability, flow transmissibility, as well as conductivity, etc.

The categorization of testing is much complicated. By type, there are oil and gas testing; by the position of test point, there are surface and underground well testing; for objective, they are pressure, temperature and flow rate testing; for flow state, they are systematic well testing and transient well testing; according to the change of pressure direction, pressure buildup and drawdown testing are measured.

Technical English Applications

Laboratory Report

A laboratory report is a written document of the principle of an experiment, process and result. As it must describe objectively the procedure and the consequence of an experiment, the report must be true, with no subjective inference and little analysis.

The format and style of the laboratory report is similar with that of a professional paper, including:

A. Title

Write a title which can show the content of the report.

B. Introduction

In the introduction, two points are listed:

1. the purpose of the report and,
2. the main arrangement.

C. Procedures

1. State the object, method(s), and control proup.
2. List the apparatus, instruments used, including specifications, types and makers, etc.

D. Results & discussion

List the results with tables, figures, indicating the experiment results, data, etc. The discussion must answer the problems and/or questions listed in the introduction.

E. Conclusion

Give clear conclusion(s) with criteria.

【Example】

Lab Report XRF 83
S2 RANGER

Determination of LowSulphur in Automotive Fuels and Petroleum Products

This report describes the analytical precision of the S2 RANGER with XFlash® for low sulphur detection in automotive fuels and other petroleum products exceeding the actual international standards for EDXRF.

Introduction

Sulphur is present in crude oil in concentrations up to about 5% by weight. It is therefore commonly found in derivative petroleum products from the % levels in lubricating oils down to trace levels in automotive fuels. Sulphur concentrations in petrochemical products, like automotive fuels and lubricants, are of primary concern in the hydrocarbon processing industry. Harmful effects of sulphur on engine parts or machines and hazardous air pollution caused by sulphur oxides are driving regulations that require the reduction and accurate reporting of sulphur content. It has therefore become essential that sulphur concentrations be closely monitored and controlled in all petrochemical products.

In the refining process, sulphur concentrations are reduced from several percent in crude oil to low ppm levels in gasoline. This reduction requires close process control.

To ensure and control petroleum product quality, sulphur analysis is also critical along the supply chain at pipelines, tank farms and customs.

Today energy-dispersive X-ray fluorescence (EDXRF) spectrometry is well established for the analysis of sulphur, as well as additives and impurities, down to the trace level in products derived from petroleum. The development of silicon drifts detectors (SDDs), which provide very good spectral resolution at high count rates and low cost of ownership, has made EDXRF the method of choice at refineries and chemical plants worldwide. Analysis requirements are regulated in international standards like ASTM 4294 and DIN/EN 20847.

This report demonstrates the analytical performance of the S2 RANGER with XFlash® SDD technology for the determination of low sulphur concentrations in automotive fuels and other petroleum products. Measurement reproducibility and long term stability data are presented, showing how the S2 RANGER exceeds international standards for sulphur control.

Instrumentation

The S2 RANGER is distinguished from conventional EDXRF instruments by its innovative design. With direct sample excitation geometry and a maximum excitation power of 50 W, the S2 RANGER's beam path results in high detection sensitivity for all elements. The SDD technology of the XFlash® detector offers excellent resolution, even at high input count rates. This combination of direct excitation beam path and high resolution leads to the outstanding analytical performance of the S2 RANGER.

The easy and intuitive touch screen operation of the S2 RANGER makes the instrument especially useful in industrial settings. The TouchControl™ interface is easy to learn and failsafe to operate even for new or inexperienced users.

Sample preparation

System calibration was performed using eight standards prepared with blank iso-octane and dinbuthyl sulphide covering the concentration range from 0 to 0.1%. The calibration range of ASTM 4294/DIN EN ISO 20847 was expanded with two additional standards of 5 and 10 ppm.

For the measurements, 5 g of the sample or standard were poured into a liquid cup with 5 μm polycarbonate film support.

Measurement parameters

The measurements were performed on the S2 RANGER with XFlash detector using Pd Lα1 excitation at 10 kV and 2 000 μA in a helium atmosphere. The total measurement time was 300 s.

Results

The calibration curve was calculated from the intensity of the standard samples with multiple regression. The absolute standard deviation of the calibration was 0.78 ppm, indicating very good correlation between certified and measured concentrations of the standards. With less than 1 ppm absolute deviation, the calibration was suitable for the reliable analysis of sulphur concentrations down to about 10 ppm. The calibration curve is shown in Fig. 6.20.

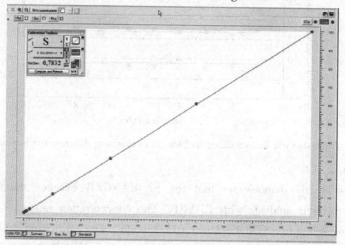

Fig. 6.20 Calibration curve for sulphur in fuel-concentration range 0 ~ 1 000 ppm

The detection limit for sulphur in fuel samples is 1 ppm (3σ, 300s).

The analytical precision was tested with two diesel fuel samples: sample one with a concentration of 10 ppm and sample two with 17 ppm sulphur. The results of the test are shown in Tab. 6.2 and Fig. 6.21.

Tab. 6.2 Precision test results for two diesel fuel samples containing different sulphur concentrations

Sample Number	Diesel 1 (10 ppm)	Diesel 2 (17 ppm)
1	9.9	17.4
2	8.7	15.8
3	8.4	17.1
4	10.5	17.0
5	9.0	17.6
6	8.8	17.4
7	9.3	16.2
8	9.8	17.5
9	9.1	16.3
Average	9.3	16.9
Abs. Std. Dev.	0.7	0.7
Rel. Std. Dev.	7.2	3.9

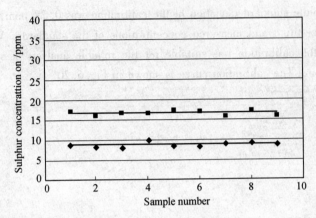

Fig. 6.21 Precision test for two diesel fuel samples containing different sulphur concentrations

Conclusions

These results clearly demonstrate that the S2 RANGER exceeds the actual international standards for low sulphur analysis with EDXRF. The concentration range of sulphur analysis in automotive fuels according to ASTM 4294 is 0.015%~5%. The calibration data achieved a sulphur detection limit of 1 ppm. The analytical precisions shown at two very low sulphur concentrations are proof of the high analytical performance of the S2 RANGER with XFlash® detector.

The S2 RANGER's analytical precision and accuracy satisfy all demands for reliable quality and process control. The instrument's flexibility for other analytical tasks, such as the determination of additives in lubricants or residual catalysts, in combination with its easy, intuitive TouchControl™ make the S2 RANGER the instrument of choice for the petrochemical industry.

Precision

Authors

Dr. Kai Behrens

Dr. Heiko Roland Reβ

Alexander Seyfarth, Dipl. Min.

Bruker AXS

Excercises

Part 1 Reading comprehension

1. What is Well Test?
2. What is the difference between Single Well Test and Transient Well Test?
3. What are pressure drawdown test and pressure build-up test?
4. What is MBH (Matthews-Brons-Hazebroek) method based on?

5. What are the fundamental objectives of drawdown testing?

6. What are the objectives of injection tests?

Part 2 Fill in the blanks with the following phrases and expressions

under this condition   at the end of   as a function of
in terms of   shut in   due to

1. This additional pressure drop can be equivalently written _____ the semilog straight-line slope m by combining the above expression with that of Equation (6.3).

2. _____ the pressure will decline at a constant rate at any point in the reservoir including the bottom-hole flowing pressure P_{wf}.

3. As in drawdown testing, the wellbore storage has great effects on the recorded injectivity test data _____ the expected large value of the wellbore storage coefficient.

4. Pressure buildup testing requires shutting in a producing well and recording the resulting increase in the wellbore pressure _____ shut-in time.

5. Calculate the radius of investigation r_{inv} _____ injection time.

6. The pressure data taken immediately before and during the _____ period is analyzed by the Horner plot method.

Part 3 Pair off the following phrases

unit-mobility ratio	井底
systematic analysis	流动性
Transient Well Test	压力分布图
bottom-hole	压力恢复
pressure behavior	将……与……相比较
flow properties	流度比
Pressure profile	系统分析
vertical permeability	恒定流量
constant rate of	泄油面积
pressure buildup	不稳定试井
drainage area	压力动态
compare… with…	垂向渗透率

Part 4 Translation practice

1. Translate the following phrases into Chinese:

1) as a function of   2) wellbore radius
3) be defined as   4) provide … with …
5) build up   6) be obtained by

7) point out 8) be based on
9) be similar to 10) in time

2. Translate the following sentences into English：

1）此阶段的压力动态（pressure behavior）由方程式表示为……。

2）上述表达式（expression）可以写成……。

3）如果选择 $t = 1$ h 时在直线延长线上找出的 $P_{wf} = P_{1hr}$，则……。

4）拟稳定流期间的压力下降率被定义为……。

5）图 4 勾画出了关井前的保持的恒定产量以及压力恢复期间压力增大的理想特性曲线。

Part 5 Writing comprehension

Suppose you've finished an experiment, and write a Laboratory Report.

Reading Material: New Trend of Technology

New Well Test Separator Unveiled

In a move promising to deliver more accurate and safer well performance monitoring, Schlumberger has released its new CleanPhase well test separator. The three-phase separator system reportedly enables optimum retention of fluids, allowing for cleaner phases and better measurements.

Conventional well test separation systems have relied on a higher degree of manual intervention to divert initial cleaned-up fluid into a low-pressure tank, which increases both safety risks to the operator and overall cleanup times. Schlumberger states that its new separator incorporates two pieces of equipment that help alleviate these concerns.

The first is Schlumberger's SmartWeir technology, which uses radar to unobtrusively monitor liquid levels and adjust the weir to accommodate the most challenging well effluents. The technology allows the CleanPhase separator to optimize retention times to the appropriate phases during the entire job, from the beginning of well cleanup to the end of the well test. The separator uses this technology to manage effluent phase levels inside the vessel, thus making it a true three-phase separator. The CleanPhase well test separator.

Coriolis meters are the second technology upgrade to the new separator. These nonintrusive meters measure each phase individually with a high degree of accuracy and remain online during the entire monitoring operation. The meters operate independently of fluid properties and eliminate the need to vent gas to the atmosphere. The use of these meters while a well is flowing lowers the need for manual intervention, which reduces risks to both personnel and the environment.

The company states that the separator allows the first reservoir fluids to be identified sooner than with traditional methods, allowing well testing to begin earlier. It also allows faster cleanups by flowing the well to a higher-pressure vessel than is possible with conventional setups, which eliminates the need for and risk of pressurized storage tanks.

The new separator can handle high water cut and fluctuating flow rates without slowing down the process, which leads to the efficient isolation and measurement of purer single-phase fluids. The speed with which separation information is delivered from the CleanPhase separator allows decisions to be made more accurately and essentially in real time.

"The CleanPhase separator is a rejuvenated approach to phase isolation during the separation process," said Eugene Francois Kleyn, CleanPhase product champion, Schlumberger. "Phase isolation limits the uncertainty inherent during reservoir characterization and significantly aids in the efficient disposal of the individual phases. The new generation well test separator allows flowback activities to be conducted confidently by increasing safety, reducing manual intervention, and providing seamless operations."

For more information, visit www.slb.com/CleanPhase.

Ted Moon is the Technology Editor of JPT Online. He brings information on emerging technologies, R&D successes, new field applications, updates from SPE papers about recent innovations, and more. If you have a question or suggestion for future article topics, email Ted at teched@spe.org.

By http://www.spe.org/jpt/2008/11/new-well-test-separator-unveiled

Chapter 7

Oil Production Engineering

Purpose & Requirements

Key Words   production system; the responsibility of production engineers

After wells are drilled and logged, maps are revised, and the reservoir begins to take shape as a volume having certain dimensions, they then become part of a dynamic production system. Once production begins, the reservoir is considered as a part of a larger production system that includes the reservoir, wellbore, tubing string, artificial lift equipment, surface control devices, gathering lines, separators, treaters, tanks, and metering devices.

All of these elements behave according to their own specific performance relationships, but each, in turn, also depends upon and influences the other elements. The responsibility of production engineers are the interaction of these performance relationships as production occurs over time, anticipating performance changes and designing the system to maximize recovery of oil and gas economically.

In this chapter, production system equipments are typically listed, starting with the downhole components, surface flow control equipment, pumping system, as well as surface production facilities, then finally to sales lines.

7.1 Downhole Components

Key Words   downhole components; functions

Together with the cement sheath holding them in place, casings are the main downhole components. There are kinds of casings, the functions of which are:

- supporting the sides of the hole;
- preventing communication of fluids and pressures between shallow and deep formations;

- allowing for control of pressures;
- providing a base for surface and subsurface equipment.

7.1.1 Casing components

Key Words strings and their sizes

Strings and their sizes: There are a number of concentric "strings", whose relative sizes and strengths, the setting depths, and cementing techniques vary according to the depth and drilling program for the well. See Fig. 7.1. The conductor, with diameter 20", setting depth 36 m, prevents the surface hole from caving in and it also prevents lost circulation. Surface casing, diameter 143/4", setting depth 150 m, provides protection for shallow freshwater formations, and the production casing, 7", about 2 450 m, is set to or through the productive zones, to isolate them and allow for selective completions. There may be intermediate casing strings between surface and production casing if the depth of the well requires it. Each casing string is cemented in place and the production string is perforated across the productive zone.

7.1.2 Tubing components

Key Words primary reasons for utilizing production tubing; packer; multistring packer; sliding sleeve; tubing anchor; blast joint; safety joint; landing nipple; gas-lift mandrels; subsurface safety valve

The central downhole component of a completed well is the production tubing See Figure 7.2. There are five primary reasons for utilizing production tubing as a conduit for producing fluids:
- It is relatively easy to remove if problems develop.
- It isolates producing fluids from the casing and makes control of the fluids easier.
- It facilitates circulation of heavy fluids into the wellbore to control the well.
- Its smaller diameter allows for safety devices and artificial lift equipment to be included in the completion design.
- It allows for more efficient producing rates from lower productivity wells.

Tubing is suspended from a tubing hanger within the wellhead at the surface, and the producing zone(s) may be isolated by production packers in the tubing string. A well may be completed with several strings of tubing (dual completion, triple completion, etc.), each carrying production from a different zone. Some extremely productive wells produce through casing without tubing, or through both tubing and the casing-tubing annulus.

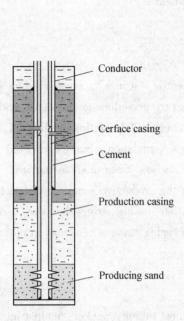 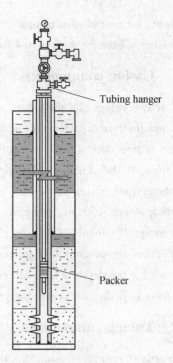

Fig. 7.1　Schematic of a basic casing installation　　Fig. 7.2　Schematic of a basic tubing installation

Packer: A packer seals the casing-tubing annulus with a rubber packing element, thus preventing flow and pressure communication between tubing and annulus. Packers are designed either to remain in the well permanently or to be retrieved if future downhole work is required. Mechanically set packers rely on tubing or drillpipe movement to force grooved "slips" to grip the casing and to expand the sealing element during the setting procedure. Hydraulically set packers are engaged by fluid pressure. Some packers can also be set with an explosive charge triggered from the surface by an electrical cable (electric line), or wireline. There are a wide variety of packers available to meet the requirements of specific completion designs.

Multistring Packer: The multistring packer seals the casing-tubing annulus where more than one tubing string is involved. Up to five-string packers are available, but more than a triple completion is rare because of the difficulty of retrieval if problems develop.

Sliding Sleeve: the sliding sleeve component is a wireline-operated sleeve, which will open or close ports in the tubing to allow fluid in or out. This feature is useful for circulating annular fluid out of the hole after a packer is set, or for opening a selective completion at a future date. This type of component is also called a circulating sleeve.

Tubing Anchor: The tubing anchor is essentially a packer without the sealing element and is designed to prevent tubing but not fluid movement. It also allows partial removal of the tubing string.

Blast Joint: A blast joint is a section of heavy-duty tubing located opposite production perforations in a multistring completion. It prevents erosion of the tubing by high-velocity flow (especially with sand production).

Safety Joint: The safety joint allows for the parting of an auxiliary tubing string beneath a multiple string packer when the packer is being retrieved. Usually it consists of a sleeve-type arrangement with shear pins that part after a certain tension is reached.

Landing Nipple (Fig. 7.3): Landing nipples are a variety of short tubing components with interior profiles that allow for the wireline setting of plugs, safety valves, chokes, pressure gauges, etc., within the tubing by using the appropriate locking device. Using a wireline to set and retrieve production tubing equipment is common practice in areas where pulling the entire tubing string is difficult or expensive, for example, offshore. A flow coupling is a short, heavy-duty tubing joint run above and below tubing restrictions (safety valves, chokes, etc.) that minimize abrasive effects of turbulent flow caused by the restrictions.

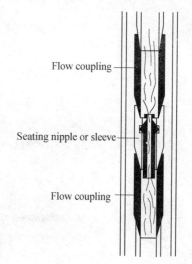

Fig. 7.3 Landing nipple and flow coupling installation. Courtesy Baker Packers, a Baker Oil Tools Company

Gas-Lift Mandrels: A gas-lift mandrel is a tubing component that holds a gas-lift valve which, in turn, allows the passage of gas-lift gas between annulus and tubing. Side-pocket mandrels allow for wireline placement and retrieval of gas-lift valves within the tubing string.

Subsurface Safety Valve (Fig. 7.4): This component is a valve assembly within the tubing string, which is designed to close in case of emergency. The valve can be an integral part of the tubing string (tubing retrievable or set inside the tubing with wireline (wireline retrievable). These valves can be surface controlled by means of hydraulic pressure or designed to close at a certain predetermined flow rate.

Tubing string components are expensive, and so is the cost of pulling the string out of the hole should future problems arise. A good completion design anticipates future performance problems and provides the flexibility to handle them, while balancing completion costs against the risk of future remedial work.

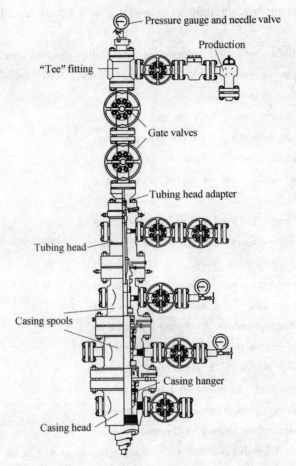

Fig. 7.4 Surface flow control installation for a single tubing string, multiple casing string, flowing well

7.2 Surface Flow Control Equipment

Key Words wellhead; Christmas tree; The functions of the wellhead; reason to maintain a certain flow rate

The valves and connections at the top of the well are often referred to collectively as the "wellhead" or "Christmas tree". Actually these terms refer to separate sections of the entire arrangement of surface flow control equipment. The functions of the wellhead are the safely controlling of the flow of fluids under pressure and sealing the annular openings between concentric casing and tubing strings, and providing a base for blowout control equipment during drilling operations.

The design of the entire arrangement depends on several factors:
- the expected maximum and operating pressures;
- the number and sizes of casing strings;
- the number and sizes of tubing strings;
- the need for auxiliary equipment, such as subsurface safety valves, electrical conduits for submersible pumps, and chemical injection equipment;
- the outside environment, onshore, offshore, or subsea;
- the inside environment: CO_2 and H_2S content of produced fluids or corrosive formation water;
- the operator's safety policy and the prevailing safety regulations;
- the operator's equipment inventory and preference for a given manufacturer.

Fig. 7.5 shows a typical surface flow control installation for a multiple casing string, single tubing string, flowing well. The casinghead (Fig. 7.6) is screwed, or welder to the outermost casing stub. The inside of the casinghead provides a shouldered sealing surface for the casing hanger. Which grips the hanging casing and usually allows the weight of the casing string to provide the force necessary to seal off the annulus between the outer and inner casing strings. A casing pack off, or similar sealing element, is sometimes used to provide additional pressure sealing for the annulus. Casing spools allow for additional casing strings to be hung and sealed off above the casinghead. During the drilling operation, the inside of the casinghead or spool, is protected with a temporary bushing to prevent damage from drillpipe rotation. Normally, the casinghead and casing spools have at least one additional connection designed to allow fluid access and pressure monitoring of the concentric annular spaces during production.

The tubing head performs a function similar to the casinghead, in that it accommodates a tubing hanger (Fig. 7.4), which usually screws onto the top of the tubing string(s) and seals off the casing-tubing annulus with metal-to-metal and/or rubber sealing elements. Often the tubing hanger is further secured by a series of set screws. An adapter (also called a tubing "bonnet") provides a transition from the tubing head to the arrangement of valves and fittings above the casing and tubing head, used to control flow (the "Christmas tree").

In the Christmas tree, the bottom valve, often called the master valve, is the primary means for completely shutting in the well. This and other valves used in the tree are normally gate valves that operate by moving a metal barrier to block the flow stream. Often, safety regulations require that one valve be pressure-actuated to automatically shut off flow in case of operating problem or natural disasters. Offshore wells usually require a downhole safety valve in addition to this surface safety system. The tree allows for vertical entry into the tubing by removal of the top adapter. A "tee"-type

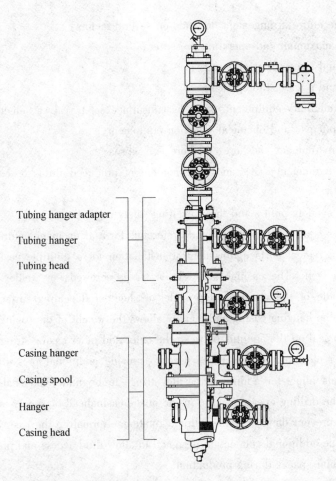

Fig. 7.5 Casinghead and casing hanger installation and tubing head and tubing hanger installation

fitting allows for redirection of the vertical flow stream to a horizontal flow line.

The produced fluids in the flowing well, before entering the surface flow-line, must pass through the smallest restriction in the surface flow equipment—the choke. Chokes, located in the Christmas tree, provide a means for controlling production rate by restricting the area available for flow. This restriction is normally a bean or orifice of a specified diameter, and must be inserted into the choke body. The reason to maintain a certain flow rate are:

- to prevent sand production;
- to control water or gas production;
- to maintain the most efficient production rate for a particular reservoir producing mechanism;
- to produce the well at a fixed allowable production rate designated by a governmental regulatory agency.

Chapter 7 Oil Production Engineering

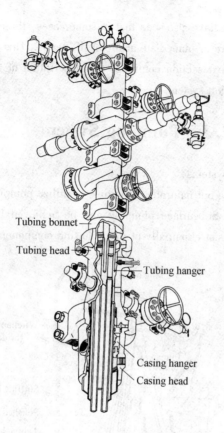

Fig. 7.6 Wellhead and Christmas tree for a dual tubing completion utilizing clamp-type connection

In the case of a positive choke, the flow is controlled by alternately inserting various beans with appropriately sized orifices. With an adjustable choke we may vary the flow restriction mechanically without changing the bean. Tubing pressure is measured upstream from the choke (toward the well).

Fig. 7.6 show examples of surface flow control equipment for a variety of completions. While most manufacturers make components with bolted flange connections, some companies also manufacture wellhead and Christmas tree equipment with clamp connections to allow speedy assembly. Wellhead and Christmas tree components are available for all types of specific design situations. Most equipment can be adapted to allow that different manufacturers' components be combined in a single installation.

The downhole and wellhead components of a completed well can vary, depending on the complexity of the completion design. Generally, the most important completion components are the tubing string and the surface choke, because these components usually have the greatest effect on the flowing performance of a well. We have also seen that in some cases, the original completion should be designed in anticipation of future or immediate artificial lift needs. This is an important point that needs to be kept in mind. The next section continues the description of the equipment that exists further downstream in the production system.

7.3 Pumping System

Key Words   rod pumping systems

When oil and gas stop flowing out naturally, it is time to utilize pumping system to force oil and gas up deeply from underground. Subsurface pumping can be achieved by various methods. Rod pumping systems (Fig. 7.7) consist essentially of the following components:

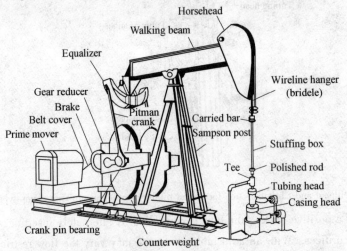

Fig. 7.7   Rod pumping component

- the subsurface pump, which displaces the fluid at the bottom of the well and thereby reduces bottomhole pressure;
- the rod string, which transmits power to the pump from the surface;
- the surface unit, which transfers rotating motion to a linear oscillation of the rod string;
- the gear reducer, which controls the speed of the motor or engine that is the prime mover.

7.3.1   Rod pump

Key Words   different types of API pump designations; typical designs of pumps

The subsurface pump (Fig. 7.8) is essentially a plunger and valve arrangement within a tube or barrel. When the close-fitting plunger is lifted within the barrel, it creates a low-pressure region below the plunger, which is filled by fluid from the formation. Simultaneously, the plunger and rods lift fluid up the tubing. The valves are designed to open and close so that they allow fluids to enter the pump on the upstroke and be displaced above the traveling valve on the downstroke. The fluid above the traveling valve moves one full stroke upward on the upstroke. There is a wide variety of pumps designed for many different applications. The different types of API pump designations are given in Fig. 7.9. The API (American Petroleum Institute) has designed a classification system using the criteria listed in the following.

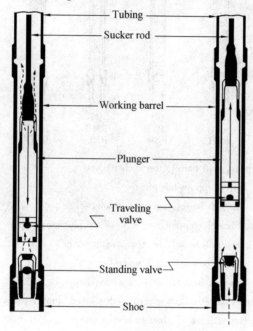

Fig. 7.8 Subsurface pump portion of a rod pump

- tubing size
- pump bore size
- rod or tubing pump
- barrel-type
- plunger-type
- pump seating assembly location
- traveling or stationary barrel
- type of seating assembly
- barrel length
- plunger length

· extensions

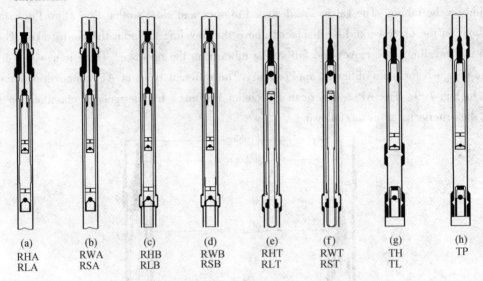

(a) RHA; RLA (b) RWA; RSA (c) RHB; RLB (d) RWB; RSB (e) RHT; RLT (f) RWT; RST (g) TH; TL (h) TP

(a) RHA: Rod, stationary heavy wall barrel, top anchor pump

RLA: Rod, stationary liner barrel, top anchor pump

(b) RWA: Rod, stationary thin wall barrel, top anchor pump

RSA: Rod stationary thin wall barrel, top anchor, soft-packed plunger pump

(c) RHB: Rod, stationary heavy wall barrel, boeeom anchor pump

RLB: Rod, stationary liner barrel, bottom anchor pump

(d) RWB: Rod, stationary thin wall barrel, bottom anchor pump

RSB: Rod, stationary thin wall barrel bottom anchor, soft-packed plunger pump

(e) RHT: Rod, traveling heavy wall barrel, bottom anchor pump

RLT: Rod, traveling liner barrel, bottom anchor pump

(f) RWT: Rod, traveling thin wall barrel, bottom anchor pump

RST: Rod, traveling thin wall barrel, bottom anchor, soft-pcked plunger pump

(g) TH: Tubing, heavy wall barrel pump

TL: Tubing, liner barrel pump

(h) TP: Tbing, heavy wall barrel soft-packed plunger pump

Fig. 7.9 API pump classification shcematic

The sucker rods are usually about 25 ft (7.62 m) long and are connected with threaded couplings. In deep wells, a tapered string of rods, decreasing in diameter with depth, can be run to maximize strength at the point of maximum load—the top of the string (Fig. 7.10, Fig. 7.11).

Chapter 7 Oil Production Engineering

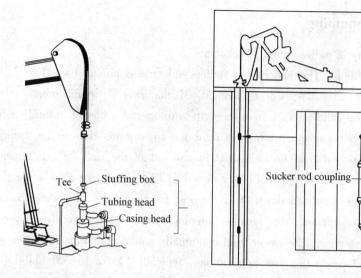

Fig. 7.10 Surface control equipment for low pressure pumping well installation

Fig. 7.11 Sucker rod

The surface unit also varies in design and size. Typical designs of pumps are the conventional (Class 1) and the Mark II or air balanced units (Class III units) (Fig. 7.12). Unit sizes are designated by torque rating, peak load, and stroke length. They can range from a unit with a 16 in (0.406 m) stroke and a maximum load of 3 200 lb (1 451 kg), to one with a 300 in (7.62 m) stroke and a maximum load of 47 000 lb (21 319 kg). The torque rating for the gear reducer of these two units varies by a factor of 570. Prime movers are either internal combustion engines or electric motors. For any given pumping unit, the pump rate maybe changed within a limited range by changing the pump rate or stroke length. Rod pumping meets a wide range of artificial lift needs with typical producing rates from 5 to 600 bbl/d (0.795 to 95.4 m^3/d)

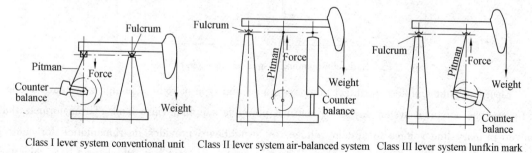

Class I lever system conventional unit   Class II lever system air-balanced system   Class III lever system lunfkin mark

Fig. 7.12 Beam pumping classification

7.3.2 Rodless pumping

Key Words category of rodless pump; mechanism

Category of rodless pump: The majority of rodless subsurface pumps (see Fig. 7.13) are mainly hydraulic and electrical submersible centrifugal. Mechanism: Hydraulic pumps rely on the use of a high-pressure power fluid pumped from the surface to operate a downhole fluid engine. The engine, in turn, drives a piston to pump formation fluid and spent power fluid to the surface (Fig. 7.14). Most engine/pump units can be circulated in and out of the well for maintenance. The power fluid system can be either opened (OPF) or closed (CPF) depending on whether the power fluid is commingled with the produced fluids or is returned to the surface in a closed conduit. In addition to the downhole equipment, this type of pumping system requires a surface power fluid pump and a power fluid reservoir. The power fluid is normally crude oil or water. Hydraulic pumps have a fairly wide range of production rate applications, typically 135 to 15 000 bbl/d (21.5 to 2 385 m^3/d).

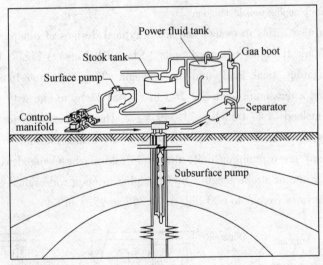

Fig. 7.13 Hydraulic pumping system for open power fluid system

Electrical submersible centrifugal pumps are a second type of rodless pumping system. In Fig. 7.14, we see a typical system layout. Electrical power is supplied via a bank of transformers that convert primary line voltage to system voltage. A switchboard provides instrumentation for control and overload protection. The junction box. acts as a vent to prevent gas, which may have migrated up the power cable, from reaching the electrical switch-board. Power is transmitted through the power cable to an electric motor at the bottom of the tubing string. The motor is isolated from well

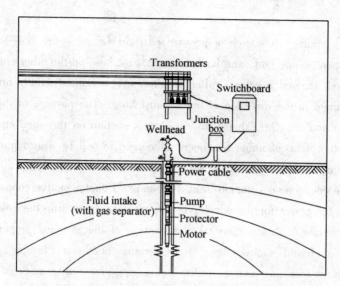

Fig. 7.14 Electrical submersible pump system

fluids by a protector. Above that is a gas separator and the motor driven pump, which normally is a multistage centrifugal pump. These pumps can handle a wide range of rates from 200 to 60 000 bbl/d (31.8 to 9 540 m^3/d).

7.3.3 Plunger pumping

Rod and rodless pumping systems achieve a reduction in bottomhole pressure by mechanical displacement of fluid up the tubing. A third artificial lift process involves the use of gas to power a plunger the length of the tubing string—in effect, a gas-lift powered pump that utilizes the entire tubing string as the barrel. Plunger lift is typically an intermediate artificial lift method for wells that ultimately must be pumped but have a low productivity index (PI) and a high enough gas-oil ratio to operate the plunger.

7.3.4 Hydraulic pumping

Key Words   jet pump; mechanism of jet pump

Jet pump is a type of hydraulic pump where the energy from one fluid (liquid or gas) is transferred to another fluid via the Venturi effect. As the fluid passes through a tapered jet, kinetic energy increases and pressure decreases drawing fluid from the suction into the flow stream.

Jet pumps can be used for draining areas which may contain combustible fluids (which could ignite if exposed to the workings of a standard electric or internal combustion powered pump) or high levels of debris (for example water eductor) which could damage screws or blades in conventional pump designs.

Mechanism of jet pump: A source of pressurized fluid (e.g. a fire hose) is connected to a chamber which is open on one end, and leads to an exhaust hose on the other end. The pressurized fluid is forced through tapered nozzles (called eductor jets) mounted axially on the inside of the pump chamber, pointed in the direction of the exhaust hose. The passage of the pressurized fluid through the chamber and into the exhaust hose creates a suction on the open end of the chamber, such that any fluid the pump chamber has been submerged in will be drawn into the chamber and thence into the exhaust hose along with the fluid from the eductor jet nozzles.

There are three connections common to all jet pumps. Eductor motive connection (left): This connection is where the power for the eductor is generated by increasing the velocity of the motive fluid. The eductor nozzle in this section takes advantage of the physical properties of the motive fluid. Eductors with liquid motives use a converging nozzle as liquids are not generally compressible. Eductors with gas motives utilize converging-diverging nozzles to achieve maximum benefit from the compressibility of the gas. Preferably, eductor nozzles have smooth flow paths manufactured and controlled to the tightest economical tolerances. Flow paths with sudden steps or roughness on these high velocity surfaces cause turbulence, which makes the flawed eductor nozzle operate less efficiently.

Suction connection (bottom): This connection of the eductor is where the pumping action of the eductor takes place. The motive fluid passes through the suction chamber, entraining the suction fluid as it passes. The friction between the fluids causes the chamber to be evacuated. This allows pressure in the suction vessel to push additional fluid into the suction connection of the eductor. The high velocity of the motive stream in this section of the eductor directs the combined fluids toward the outlet section of the eductor.

Discharge connection (right): As the motive fluid entrains the suction fluid, part of the kinetic energy of the motive fluid is imparted to the suction fluid. This allows the resulting mixture to discharge at an intermediate pressure. The percentage of the motive pressure that can be recovered is dependent upon the ratio of motive flow to suction flow and the amount of suction pressure pulled on the suction port. The mixture then passes through the diverging taper that converts the kinetic energy back to pressure. The combined fluid then leaves the outlet.

7.3.5 Progressive cavity pumping (PC Pump)

Key Words　the progressive cavity pumping (PC Pump) system

The progressive cavity pumping (PC Pump) system (see Fig. 7.15, 7.16) typically consists of a surface driving device, sucker rod string and downhole PC pump. The PC pump is comprised of a single helical-shaped rotor that turns inside a double helical elastomer-lined stator. The stator is attached to the production tubing string and remains stationary during pumping. The rotor is attached to a sucker rod string which is suspended and rotated by the surface drive. As the rotor turns eccentrically in the stator, a series of sealed cavities form and progress from the inlet to the discharge end of the pump.

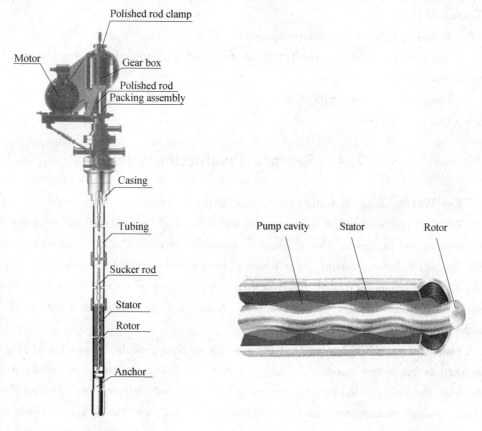

Fig. 7.15　PC Pump block diagram　　　Fig. 7.16　PC (Progressive Cavity) Pump system

With a few moving parts, PC pump has no valve and complicated flowing passage, little hydraulic loss, continuous suction and drainage of medium, and no gas lock and sand plug. It can pump various fluid including high viscosity crude oil and mixed fluid with oil content or high water content.

The surface driving device is mechanically driving device and is fitted with a self-aligning radial thrust spherical roller bearing which can share the axial load of the pump and is driven by belts and gear reducer. The driving speed can be regulated by changing belts or by the variable speed drive (VSD). It is simple and reliable in operation.

Features

· Widely suitable fluid range: pumping sand-laden heavy crude oil and bitumen

· No internal valves to clog or gas lock

· High system efficiency

· Low capital investment and low power consumption, simple installation with minimal maintenance costs

· Portable, light weight surface equipment

· Surface driving device fitted with an advanced hydraulic reverse rotation-proof system to prevent the backspin

· Pumps oil and water with solids

· Quiet operation

7.4 Surface Production Facilities

Key Words usage of surface production facilities

The fluid produced from a well is usually a mixture of oil, gas, water, and sediment at elevated temperatures and pressures. The oil alone is a complex mixture of many hydrocarbon compounds, and oils from different reservoirs have different physical and chemical characteristics. All crude oils have a certain amount of gas dissolved in them. A gas phase may exist in the production stream, having come out of solution with the drop in pressure up the tubing, or it may exist in and be produced from the reservoir as free gas.

Formation water may be carried in the gas state as vapor, emulsified as a liquid with the oil, or produced as free water. Sand, silt, and clay from the formation can be carried by the produced fluids into the wellbore and be produced along with scale and corrosion products from the casing or tubing. Various contaminants can be present in the oil, gas, and water. These include CO_2, H_2S, and dissolved salts.

The usage of surface production facilities: Surface production facilities are designed to turn this mixture into separate streams of clean, dehydrated oil and gas and safely disposable water. Only then can the oil and gas be metered and sold, or sent for further processing to a plant or refinery.

7.4.1 Separation

The produced fluids leave the Christmas tree via a flow Line—usually a 2- or 3-in (5- to 8-cm) pipe, which may be below or above ground at onshore installations, or perhaps on the seafloor for a subsea completion. Subsea completions are often equipped with TFL (through-flow-line)

connections whereby the flow line connects to the Christmas tree in a smooth loop. The flow line (gathering line) generally travels by the shortest route to the surface production facilities. If the production facilities are shared by a group of wells, as is often the case, the flow line will probably connect to a production manifold which is an assembly of valves that allows each well's flow stream to be shut in or diverted to a particular portion of the production facilities.

Normally, a separator is the first piece of production processing equipment the fluid stream encounters. Separators are usually classified by physical shape, and Fig. 7.17 shows the basic vertical, horizontal and spherical separator configurations.

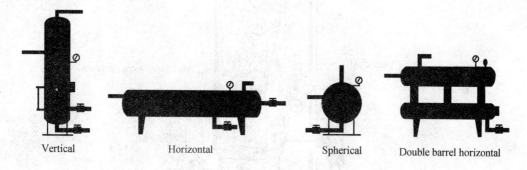

Fig. 7.17 Separator configurations

The operation of a typical vertical, two-phase, gas-liquid separator (shown schematically in Fig. 7.18): the oil-gas-water mixture enters through an inlet on the side of the tank-shaped vessel. The fluid stream immediately strikes a metal plate, which diverts the flow around the inner surface of the cylindrical separator, imparting a centrifugal motion. This motion throws the liquid to the outer edge of the cylinder and allows the gas to remain near its center. The lighter gas portion of the fluid stream, now separated, rises through the center of the vessel while the liquid falls. Some separators have an arrangement of metal fins at the inlet, which abruptly changes the fluids flow direction and velocity. In this case, the liquid's higher inertia carries it away from the gas and downward, while the gas rises to the top of the separator. Still another feature of some separators is the presence of a system of baffles, which spread the liquid out as it drops to the bottom of the vessel. This allows any gas bubbles, carried in the liquid, to easily escape. The amount of time the oil is allowed to settle in the separator prior to being dumped at the outlet is termed retention time. Normal retention time is usually 30 to 90 seconds. For a given liquid flow rate through the separator, an increase in retention time will require an increase in vessel size or liquid depth. The added cost of a larger separator may not be justified by the additional separation of gas that a longer retention time allows. Our surface design, then, must be based on economical considerations as well as system performance.

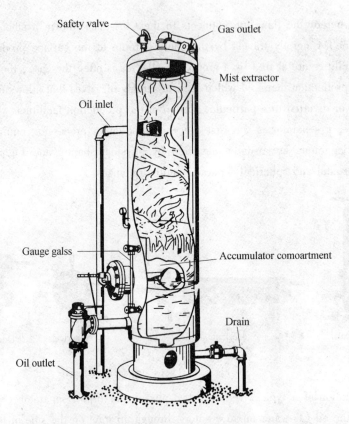

Fig. 7.18 Conventional vertical separator

The gas phase, which is directed to the upper portion of the vessel, is usually passed through a mist extractor to remove minute liquid droplets entrained in the gas. Here, three processes act to separate liquid from the gas: flow velocity changes; direction changes; and impingement, or the adherence and coalescence of liquid mist on a surface. A combination of these three processes is incorporated into a coalescing pack-type mist extractor made of knitted wire mesh or layers of inert particles with shapes designed for maximum surface area. Centrifugal-type mist extractors (Fig. 7.19) used in vertical separators have a set of vanes that cause the circular motion of gas, throwing the heavier liquid droplets to the wall of the vessel to drain to the bottom. Its efficiency increases as the velocity of the gas stream increases.

The gas flow rate through the separator is controlled by a back pressure valve, which maintains the desired pressure in the vessel. A liquid level controller causes oil to be discharged from the separator when the appropriate level is reached, and prevents gas from escaping through the liquid outlet. The control is usually pneumatic (gas pressure-operated), but in low-pressure applications,

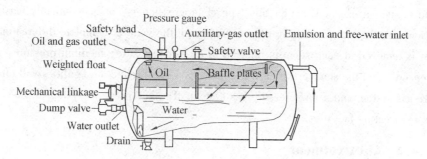

Fig. 7.19 Schematic of a low pressure free-water knockout

an internal, float-operated lever valve is employed.

Vertical separators are often used on low to intermediate gas-liquid ratio well streams. They are more readily cleaned if sand or paraffin are produced, and occupy less floor space on offshore platforms. However, a vertical separator can be more expensive than a horizontal separator with the same separation capacity. Horizontal separators, therefore, are usually more cost-efficient, especially for high to medium gas-liquid ratio streams, for liquid-liquid separation, and in applications where foaming oil is a problem.

Horizontal separators often have closely spaced horizontal baffle plates that extract liquids. A double barrel horizontal separator has a higher liquid capacity because incoming free liquid is immediately drained away from the upper section into the lower. This allows a higher velocity gas flow through the upper baffled section. Spherical separators are much less common than vertical or horizontal types. They tend to have lower installation and maintenance costs. They are more compact, but lack the capacity for high gas rates or liquid surges.

Separators are sized according to the expected oil and gas production rates, the necessary operating pressure and temperature, and the oil and gas properties. For example, a vertical separator about 2 ft (0.61 m) in diameter and 10 ft (3.05m) high, with a retention time of one minute, will handle about 1 300 bbl/d (207 m^3/d) of typical crude oil. A single barrel horizontal separator 2 ft (0.61m) in diameter and 10 ft (3.05 m) long will handle about 2 000 bbl/d (318 m^3/d) and a 3 ft (0.91m) diameter spherical separator about 1 100 bbl/d (175 m^3/d). For comparison, 100 to 200 bbl/d (16 to 32 m^3/d) is about the output of a normal garden hose.

When gas is removed from contact with the liquid as it is separated, the process is called differential separation. This process results in the highest volume of oil being recovered where the oil contains a relatively small amount of gas. Because most operators are concerned with maximizing the oil volume, this approach is preferred. A long series of separators, each operating at a slightly lower pressure and allowing for the removal of the liberated gas from each stage, would provide the highest oil yield in such a case. Although this type of progression is not economically feasible, multistage separation with three or four separators can approach the yield of complete differential recovery. The gas that is removed at each stage is referred to as high-pressure, medium-pressure, or low-pressure gas, depending on the stage at which it is removed. Field production facilities will often have a high-pressure gas system and a low-pressure gas system. The low-pressure system is often used for fuel to operate the treating facilities.

7.4.2 Oil treatment

Key Words　　water cut; chemical treatment ; heat treatment ; gunbarrel treater; heater-treaters; electrostatic treaters

In many oil fields, following the initial gas-oil separation process, the oil must be treated to remove water, salt, or H_2S. Most pipeline quality oil must have its water content reduced to the 0.2 to 2 by volume range. Because salt water is generally associated with oil in the reservoir, its production along with the oil is not unusual. Almost all well streams contain water droplets of various sizes. If, because of their higher density, they collect together and settle out within a reasonably short time they are called free water. The water cut measured on one or several samples of the well stream normally refers to free water, and is expressed as the volume of water relative to the total volume of liquid.

$$100 \times \frac{\text{volume of free-water}}{\text{total volume of production liquid}} = \% \text{ water cut}$$

The sample is assumed to be representative. A free-water knockout is a simple separation vessel located along the flow stream at a point of minimum turbulence, where the oil and water mixture is allowed sufficient time for its density differences to act to separate the phases.

A more difficult separation problem arises when the oil and water are produced as an emulsion. Most oilfield emulsions are the water-in-oil type, where individual water particles are dispersed in a continuous body of oil. An inverted, or oil-in-water, emulsion can also occur, especially when the ratio of water to oil is very high. Two things are necessary to produce an emulsion of water and oil: agitation and an emulsifying agent. As well fluids move through the formation, through the perforations and completion equipment, up the tubing and through a choke, turbulence and mechanical mixing provide the agitation necessary to disperse the droplets of water throughout the oil phase, or droplets of oil throughout the water phase. Many crude oils also contain carbonates, sulfates, and finely divided solids, which may act as emulsifying agents. These agents increase the stability of the interfacial films separating the dispersed and continuous phases.

In order to "break" the emulsion and separate the oil from the water, a variety of processes have been developed. Treating vessels, which utilize more than one treating process to attack particularly stable or "tight" emulsions, are common. Chemical treatment uses chemical action to rupture the tough film surrounding the dispersed droplets. The selection of the most effective chemical demulsifier for a given crude oil-water emulsion is usually a trial-and-error process. Chemicals are normally added continuously to the produced fluids, as far upstream from the treating or separation facilities as possible. Heat treatment is used to reduce the viscosity of the emulsion and promote gravity segregation. In direct heaters, the crude oil emulsion is passed through a coil of pipe that is exposed to a direct flame. In indirect heaters the pipe carrying the emulsion passes through a water bath, which obtains its heat from a fire-tube. Sometimes an internal heater is used in a "gunbarrel" treater —an older but still useful treating method (shown in Fig. 7.20). In the gunbarrel treater, the emulsion flows into the central flume and enters the tank at the bottom, rising through a water layer heated by internals coils. Heater-treaters (Fig. 7.20) are used to heat the emulsion and separate the oil and water in the same processing vessel. The raw emulsion is preheated by the warm, clean oil leaving the vessel, and the water level is controlled by a siphon. Collision and coalescence of dispersed water droplets in an emulsion can be accomplished by inducing electrical charges in the particles through the application of an electric field. Electrostatic treaters are normally horizontal vessels, such as those shown in Fig. 7.21. The emulsion enters the electrostatic treaters and passes through an initial separating section where it is heated and must pass upward through a water layer. Any emulsion not yet broken then rises through an electrically charged grid. The salt water droplets then become dipoles with oppositely charged ends. The droplets are attracted to one another. They collide, coalesce, and form larger drops until they are heavy enough to settle to the water section of the vessel and be drained. Electrostatic forces can be hundreds of times greater than the gravitational forces acting to separate oil and water in a conventional treater.

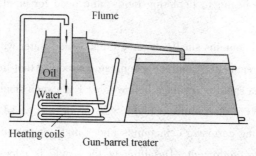

Fig. 7.20 Heater-treaters

The simplest and least expensive method for breaking an emulsion is generally the most practical. Chemical treatment is usually the preferred method if it will suffice. The addition of heat

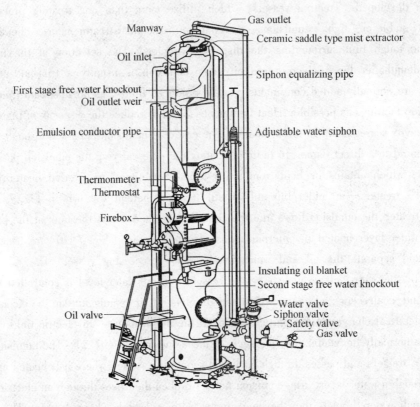

Fig. 7.21 Schematic of a heater-treater

and/or electrostatic coalescence is necessary and economically attractive when emulsions are particularly stubborn. As older fields begin to produce increasingly higher water cuts, and when water injection projects are begun in depleting fields, the need for emulsion treating processes can increase.

Most produced oil still contains small amounts of emulsified water with solids dispersed within it even after separation and treatment. Contract specifications require that this BS&W (Basic Sediment and Water) be reduced to a small percentage before sale. Even such small amounts of water can still cause problems, particularly if the salinity is high. Salty crude will cause severe problems during the refining process by producing corrosive compounds under high temperatures and depositing mineral residues within the refining equipment. Desalting of the crude is necessary if the salt content is greater than 15 to 25 lb (6.8 to 11.3 kg) of salt per 1 000 bbl (159 m^3) of crude. The procedure is relatively simple: the crude oil is first separated and treated, and free water is removed; the remaining oil and oil-water with small amounts of emulsified water-solids is mixed through a nozzle with fresh water; the intimate mixing of fresh water and salty water in the emulsion forms a new emulsion with a lower salt concentration. This new stable emulsion is broken, usually using electrical dehydrators, and the processed crude oil has a salt content below the required limit(See Fig. 7.22).

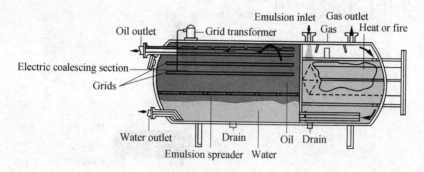

Fig. 7.22 Schematic of an electrostatic treater

Hydrogen sulfide is usually removed from the oil by means of stripping. In stripping a stream of low hydrogen sulfide content gas is mixed with the oil in a stripping tower. This results in the separation of "sweetened" oil and hydrogen sulfide-laden gas.

The various oil treating elements are shown in a flow chart in Fig. 7.23, which outlines the production system components discussed thus far. Several of these oil treatment components may be utilized, depending on the specific processing needs of a given fluid stream. The variations depend on the particular fluid stream and the processing needed. The final component in the oil handling portion of the production system is the metering equipment.

7.4.3 Gas treatment

Key Words a scrubber; dry-type gas scrubbers; wet-type gas scrubbers; low-temperature extraction; low temperature separator; gas sweetening; the amine process

As mentioned earlier, gas can be separated from the production stream in several stages at several pressures. The low-pressure gas is often used for lease fuel requirements. It may also be compressed to a higher pressure and mixed with the high-pressure separator gas, or perhaps with high-pressure gas from producing gas wells nearby. Before gas may be sold it must be brought to pipeline quality and be delivered to the pipeline at an appropriate pressure. The major quality control requirements are met by the removal of liquid condensate water vapor, and any hydrogen sulfide.

There are several types of gas treating vessels that remove condensate from the gas stream. A

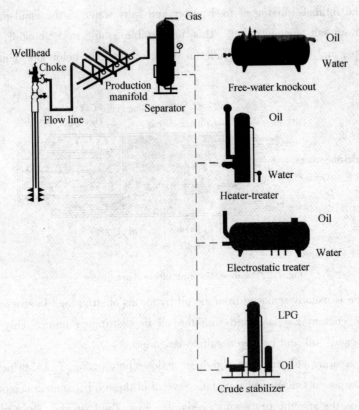

Fig. 7.23 Production system flow charts showing several oil treatment alternatives

scrubber is a separator designed to handle streams with high gas-to-liquid ratios. Often a scrubber is used in gas gathering systems to handle a rather homogeneous production stream, as opposed to conventional oil and gas separators, which might have to handle slugs of liquids. Dry-type gas scrubbers use internal vanes or woven wire mesh mist extractors to coalesce the small droplets of liquid from the gas stream. Wet-type gas scrubbers allow the gas stream to pass through an oil (or similar liquid) bath that removes dust, scale, rust, etc., before it passes through the mist extractor. Extremely small ($<5 \mu$) contaminant particles may be removed by passing the gas stream through a fine high-quality filtering medium such as fiberglass in a filter-separator. If the gas stream contains substantial liquids, a combination of filtering and mist extraction may take place within the filter separator vessel. Passage through filter elements causes a pressure drop in the flow stream, which must be monitored to determine when the elements need changing.

  Another method of separating liquids from a gas stream is by low-temperature extraction. This process is an efficient method for separating high-pressure gas and condensate well streams. Essentially, low-temperature extraction causes the pressure on the gas stream to be reduced by having it flow though a restriction (choke). Throttling the gas in this manner leads to a sharp reduction in temperature and the condensation of water and liquid hydrocarbons. Hydrates (water-hydrocarbon compounds that resemble ice) would normally form in a conventional separator under these conditions and prevent its operation. The low temperature separator, however, is designed to use heat from the warm fluid upstream of the choke to melt any hydrates that form. This type of separation simultaneously removes both condensate and water from the gas.

Removing water vapor or dehydrating natural gas can also be accomplished by two other practical methods:
- absorption with liquid desiccants, such as glycol or methanol; and
- adsorption with solid desiccants, such as alumina, silica gel, or calcium chloride.

The difference in these two methods is that liquid desiccants, such as glycol, react chemically with water molecules and hold them (absorb them) until heated. Dry desiccants, on the other hand, such as activated alumina or silica gel, adsorb the water molecules on their surface rather than absorb.

In the absorption process, a lean glycol-water solution (95% to 99% glycol) enters at the top of the absorber column and is first cooled by the previously dehydrated gas leaving the unit. Wet gas enters the column from the bottom. The glycol falls through a series of bubble-cap trays where the "dry" glycol and ascending wet gas are intimately mixed and the water vapor is absorbed. As the glycol descends, it becomes more-water-rich. To remove the water vapor, the water-rich glycol solution is delivered to a reboiler, where it is heated and the water is separated from the glycol by fractional distillation in a stripper column. The glycol is then ready to be reused and the water can be disposed (see Fig. 7.24).

Solid desiccant dehydrators are not as common as liquid desiccant dehydrators. In such separation, the wet gas passes through a separator, which removes as much free liquid as possible. The gas is then passed downward through the contactor column that is packed with adsorbing desiccant. After a period of usage, the desiccant becomes saturated with water, and a portion of the main gas-stream is heated and used to drive the adsorbed water from the desiccant so that it may be reused. A solid desiccant may be used in this way for one to four years before it loses effective surface area through plugging. Removal of acid gases, also called gas sweetening, is achieved primarily through one of two processes:
- the amine process, which removes both CO_2 and H_2S; or
- the iron oxide process, which removes H_2S selectively.

The amine process is based on the chemical reaction of weak organic bases with weak acids (H_2S or CO_2) to produce a water-soluble salt. The natural gas is contacted with the amine solution in a series of bubble-cap trays in a contactor tower (similar to a liquid dehydrator). In the iron

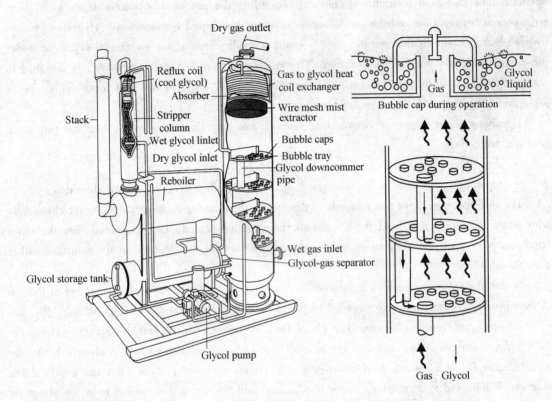

Fig. 7.24 Schematic of glycol dehydration unit showing operation of bubble-cap absorber

oxide process (also called iron sponge) a chemical reaction between iron oxide and hydrogen sulfide produces iron sulfide and water. As the sour gas flows through a bed of iron-oxide-impregnated wood chips, the iron sulfide remains in the bed. When the ability of the bed to remove H_2S is exhausted, the wood chips are replaced or regenerated. A similar process uses zinc oxide powder in a slurry solution.

After being sweetened and before being dehydrated, the gas stream may need to be compressed to enable it to enter the sales pipeline. The size capacities and inlet and outlet pressures for compressors vary over a wide range. As a rule of thumb, the compression ratio for a single stage of compression should not exceed 4∶1. Thus, it is possible to raise the pressure from 100 psi to 400 psi in a single stage, but two stages would be needed to go from 50 psi to 400 psi. Compressors may be found at other points in the field, whenever it is necessary to increase the pressure of a gas stream.

Gas compressors are usually either:

· reciprocating compressors, which rely on an arrangement of inlet and outlet values combined with a piston and cylinder to compress the gas; or

· centrifugal compressors, which rely on a series of rotating impellers to supply centrifugal force to the gas, increasing its pressure.

Reciprocating compressors come in a wide range of sizes and are often operated by internal combustion engines, usually powered by natural gas. Centrifugal compressors are driven by steam turbines and generally require more sophisticated maintenance. The various gas treating elements are shown in a flow chart in Fig. 7.25. When gas has been separated, sweetened, compressed, and if necessary, dehydrated, it is then metered and sold.

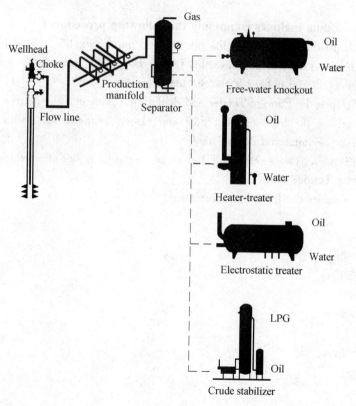

Fig. 7.25 Production system flow charts showing several gas treatment alternatives

The various gas treating elements are shown in a flow chart in Fig. 7.25. Several of these oil treatment components may be utilized, depending on the specific processing needs of a given fluid stream. The variations depend on the particular fluid stream and the processing needed. The final component in the oil handling portion of the production system is the metering equipment.

Technical English Applications

Invitation to Bid and Bidding

Invitation to Bid and Bidding are respectively named international bidding and international submission of tender. The specialty is that, under the same condition of subject matter, let bidders compete freely. Invitation to Bid and Bidding are two aspects of trading. Submission of tenders is that the tenderer present real quotation to bidders prior to the Closing Date according to the bidding conditions.

1. Advertised bidding includes commonly the following procedures

Call for bid: Advertise the bidding on the internet and inquire qualification of bidders.

Submission of tenders: Bidders purchase the Tender Document, provide their business details for effective communication and deliver it back to tenderer.

Opening of bid: Open the Form of Tender and declare the price and the deliver date only, with all bidders presenting, on the legal opening time and place. Tenderer can, with the promise of presider, amend the price value and deliver date.

Getting of bid: Tenderer chooses the only bidder and signs the letter of acceptance.

2. How to write Tender Notice

Tender Notice includes the following information:

A. Title

B. Organizaion

C. Tender details

D. Tender location

E. Tender type

F. Tender category

G. Products

H. Tender document file

Important dates:

I. Publish date

J. Bid opening date

Contact details:

K. Adress

L. Country

M. Company website

Other information:

N. Tender notice number

O. Tender scope

P. Publication detail

Examples of writing Tender Notice

【Example 1】

Supply of Heating Oil

Organization: Conseil General De La Somme
Tender Name: Supply of heating oil
Tender Details: Contract award notice for supply of heating oil.
Tender Location: Amiens
Tender Type: Contract awards
Tender Category: Oils, greases & lubricants
Products: Oil
Tender Document File:
Important Dates:
Publish Date: November 20, 2009
Bid Opening Date: January 05, 2010 Time: 5:00 p.m.
Contact Details:
Address: 53 Rue DeLa Republique
Country: France
Company Website: http://somme.fr
Other Information:
Tender Notice Number: 2009/S 224-321498
Tender Scope: International
Publish Detail: Internet: November 20, 2009

【Example 2】

Oil and Gas Development Company Limited
(Supply Chain Management Department)
Tender Notice

(1) Oil & Gas Development Company Limited (OGDCL), the largest exploration and production listed company of Pakistan having operations at 48 locations and fields in all the four Provinces, intends to procure material for its operations. The details about the company can be obtained from http://www.ogdcl.com.

(2) Sealed bids, along with earnest money equivalent to 2% of the quoted value, are invited

under two envelops bidding procedure (Financial & Technical) from bonafide manufacturers/ importers/ suppliers/ sole agents & stockiest registered with Sales Tax. Department for supply of the following material on F. O. R. basis, (Detailed specifications of the under mentioned material are available in the Tender Documents with bid submission details):

S. #	TENDER NO.	DESCRIPTION	TENDER COST (Rs.)	TENDER-SALE CLOSING DATE	BID SUB-MISSION DATE	BID OPENING DATE
01	PROC-L(A)/PT/ P&P/UCH/ 13262/09	PIPES & FITTINGS MATERIAL	500.00	23-11-09	02-12-09	02-12-09
02	PROC-L(A) PT/WS/ 13373/09	MICA (FINE & COARSE)	500.00	23-11-09	02-12-09	02-12-09
03	PROC-L(B) PT/EXPL/ 13329/09	AIR CONDITIONE COMPRESSORS	500.00	23-11-09	03-12-09	03-12-09
04	PROC-L(B) PT/WS/13351/09	TARPAULIN	500.00	23-11-09	03-12-09	03-12-09
05	PROC-L(A)PT/ G&R/13295/09	CENTRIFUGE MACHINE	500.00	23-11-09	03-12-09	03-12-09
06	PROC-L(A)PT/ ADMN/ 13348/09	WATER TREATMENT CHEMICALS	500.00	23-11-09	04-12-09	04-12-09
07	PROC-L(C)PT/ ADMN/ 13361/09	PVC FILLS FOR COOLING TOWER (HVAC) BAC MODEL 3803-2 & BEARINGS KIT	500.00	23-11-09	04-12-09	04-12-09
08	PROC-L(A)PT/ MUDLOG/ 13350/09	CALIBRATION GASES	500.00	23-11-09	07-12-09	07-12-09
09	PROC-L(A)PT/ SS/13378/09	BRANDED ASSEMBLED COMPUTERS	500.00	23-11-09	08-12-09	08-12-09

(3) Separate Tender Document of each Tender can be obtained from the Reception of OGDCL

House, Jinnah Avenue, Islamabad against above mentioned Tender cost (non-refundable) in shape of Bank Draft/Demand Draft/ Pay Order/Call Deposit in favour of Oil & Gas Development Company Limited on any working day between 1 000 h to 1 200 h. Firms/Suppliers of other cities may send their request along with PO/DD/CD to GM (SCM) for dispatch of Tender Document through mail/courier.

(4) The sealed bids must be dropped in the Tender Box till 1 030 h on the date. Bids will be opened publicly at 1 100 h on the due date.

(5) The above advertised Tenders and their Annexure(s) can also be reviewed on our website www.ogdcl.com under the title bar to Tenders. All bidders are recommended to visit the online tenders before purchasing the Tender Document.

(6) Bidders must provide their business details at the time of tender purchase including address, Phone & Fax Numbers, E-mail (if any) for effective communication. OGDCL will not be responsible for intimation of queries/ information in case subject detail is not provided.

(7) Without prejudice to other right of the Company, tenderers, their subcontractors and other suppliers shall be disqualified from participating in the bidding process if:

they are or have been at any time during the past five years, involved in litigation, arbitration or any other dispute or event that may in the opinion of the Company, have material adverse effect on the Tenderer's ability to perform the Contract;

its involvement in litigation is chronic;

its past conduct or execution of works under contract has been poor.

(8) The Purchaser reserves the right to accept or reject any Bid and to annul the bidding process and reject all the Bids at any time prior to award of Purchase Order. OGDCL shall communicate to those suppliers or contractors who have not been pre-qualified the reasons for not pre-qualifying them.

General Manager
(Supply Chain Management)
OGDCL House, Jinnah Avenue,
Islamabad, Pakistan.
Ph#+92-051-2623033
Fax#+92-051-9209859 & 9218048

Exercises

Part 1 Reading comprehension

1. Answer the following questions:

1) What are the functions of Christmas tree?
2) What are the typical designs of pumps?
3) How many types of API pump designations are there? And what are they?
4) What does PC Pump system typically consist of and what are the features of it?
5) How many kinds of separators are there and what are they?

2. Summarize the following:
1) The operation of a typical vertical, two-phase, gas-liquid separator.
2) Process of producing oil from wellhead to sales pipelines.

Part 2 Fill in the blanks with the following phrases and expressions

in place   by means of   in that
in turn   act as   be contacted with

1. Each casing string is cemented _____ and the production string is perforated across the productive zone.

2. These valves can be surface controlled _____ hydraulic pressure or designed to close at a certain predetermined flow rate.

3. The tubing head performs a function similar to the casinghead, _____ it accommodates a tubing hanger, which usually screws onto the top of the tubing string(s) and seals off the casing-tubing annulus with metal-to-metal and/or rubber sealing elements.

4. Many crude oils also contain carbonates, sulfates, and finely divided solids, which may _____ emulsifying agents.

5. All of these elements behave according to their own specific performance relationships, but each, _____, also depends upon and influences the other elements.

6. The natural gas _____ the amine solution in a series of bubble-cap trays in a contactor tower.

Part 3 Pair off the following phrases

artificial lift	产油带
downhole component	滑套
producing zone	浮箍
rubber packing element	齿轮减速器
sliding sleeve	连接盒
tubing anchor	抽油杆
blast joint	工作筒
flow coupling	防磨接头
gear reducer	井下装置

junction box   油管锚
sucker rod   人工举升
working barrel   封隔器胶皮筒

Part 4   Translation practice

1. Translate the following phrases into Chinese:

1) rely on   2) seal off
3) consist of   4) be protected with
5) refer to   6) pass through
7) be achieved by   8) be comprised of
9) be attached to   10) wide variety of

2. Translate the following sentences into Chinese:

1) Mechanically set packers rely on tubing or drillpipe movement to force grooved "slips" to grip the casing and to expand the sealing element during the setting procedure.

2) Normally, the casinghead and casing spools have at least one additional connection designed to allow fluid access and pressure monitoring of the concentric annular spaces during production.

3) A gas phase may exist in the production stream, having come out of solution with the drop in pressure up the tubing, or it may exist in and be produced from the reservoir as free gas.

4) It is important to remember that the physical and chemical characteristics of the crude oil and gas entering the separator help determine the degree of separation possible at a given operating temperature and pressure.

5) Surface casing provides protection for shallow freshwater formations, and the producing string of casing is set to or through the productive zones, to isolate them and allow for selective completions.

Part 5   Writing Comprehension

Write a Tender Notice.

Reading Material: New Technoloy

Deliquification Technology Maximizes Gas Well Production

Liquid loading in gas wells is a well known phenomenon in mature reservoirs. At depletion stage, the energy of the reservoir is not high enough to transport liquid droplets to the surface. They begin accumulating at the bottom of the well bore and cause backpressure on the reservoir, reducing gas production and eventually killing the well.

It is estimated there are around 775 000 active gas wells globally — excluding Russia and

China — with 43 000 new wells drilled annually. With approximately 90% of wells suffering from liquid loading, there is an increasing demand for reliable, cost-effective deliquification solutions.

Caledyne has produced the first complete deliquification system suitable for offshore applications. The first installations are due in several locations over the coming months, including the southern North Sea, mainland Europe, and offshore Indonesia.

Challenges in different environments

Various artificial lift technologies are used to mitigate the consequences of liquid loading and to extend the production life of mature gas reservoirs. Most systems have been developed and used successfully in onshore environments. Approaches range from lowering wellhead pressures by using compressors or eductors to downhole artificial lift using plunger lift, surfactant technology, or pumping technologies. Depending on the individual well/field characteristics, these technologies have proven highly successful in mitigating losses caused by liquid loading.

Challenges range from offshore environmental considerations and field characteristics, such as liquid loading with hydrocarbon condensate, to cost pressures. In the main, the industry tries to address these challenges through the evolution of deliquification technologies from onshore to offshore.

Offshore environments technical challenges

The main challenges in offshore environments occur when legislation requires sub-surface-safety valves (SSSV). SSSVs need to be able to shut in wells in case of an emergency, which is done with a flapper-type arrangement valve. Hydraulic pressure is taken off of the control line, and the flapper of the SSSV closes and shuts in the well. The dilemma with the traditional SSSVs is that by definition nothing can be run through the flapper-valve when it is closed in emergency. Most artificial lift technologies (surfactant injection lines, rods, power cables) need to be run through the SSSV when being retrofitted to wells. Several operating and service companies have addressed this by developing enhanced SSSVs, although a reduction in the effective flow area is often the result.

Another challenge is wellhead penetration. Most forms of artificial lift technology such as surfactant injection lines, coiled tubing for gas lift applications, and power cables need to penetrate the wellhead. This can be a technically challenging exercise if no spools can be changed out or a very costly exercise if — as a consequence of wellhead modifications — flowline heights need to be changed.

Reservoir, cost challenges

Some of the fields experiencing liquid loading have been characterized as retrograde gas condensate fields. This causes two factors that can potentially impact production in such fields:

(1) The drop-out of hydrocarbon condensate from gas in the reservoir causes a reduction of

relative permeability to gas, leading to less inflow of gas into the wellbore, known as condensate banking.

(2) Liquid loading with hydrocarbon condensate can lower the success of surfactant injection, one of the most widely and successfully used deliquification technologies, as hydrocarbon is technically very different from foam than it is to water. Several condensate foamers have been developed, but their operating range is narrow.

Potential economic deliquification benefits are significant. And the number of wells in need of these technologies is high — in part because wells subject to liquid loading are mostly mature and were not originally completed with the purpose of deliquification in mind. Because the remaining lifespan of these wells is relatively short, there is an added reluctance to invest significant amounts of money as there is increased risk of not recouping the original investment.

Many mature offshore wells produce to unmanned installations or platforms with limited crane capacities and deck space, which makes any type of workover activity a costly exercise.

Deliquification technologies have to be cost-effective in the long run, i. e., run with the minimum requirement for intervention, monitoring, and optimization.

Complete solution

Caledyne has produced the first complete deliquification system including its balance pump, Torus Valve, and pin hole injection (PHI) system.

The patented Caledyne Torus Safety Valve was developed in response to industry demand for an "enabling solution" to retrofit artificial lift technologies into existing wells, previously restricted due to the flapper-type SSSV.

Development of the 41/2-in. size was facilitated through a joint industry collaborative project by the Industry Technology Facilitator (ITF), with contributions from major operators BP, Chevron, ConocoPhillips, and Total. The Torus SSSV allows any artificial lift solution to be installed in offshore operations. It is a fail-safe closed insert safety valve, offering a permanent conduit through the center of the valve. It is installed in the safety valve nipple profile and operated by the existing hydraulic control line, using a sliding sleeve mechanism to shut in production. The sleeve is operated via a power spring and piston arrangement akin to industry standard flapper-type safety valves. Using the sliding sleeve mechanism results in a far greater flow area than that made available by flapper valves using a bypass mechanism for umbilicals. During API 14A qualification, the valve has proven to be a zero leakage valve even at low pressures.

The Caledyne balance pump, which can be installed through the Torus Safety Valve, provides a cost-effective, reliable deliquification method for operators of both onshore and offshore wells suffering from liquid loading. It is a retrofit solution that allows operators to avoid costly workovers.

The hydraulically actuated reciprocating low-volume pump is operated by two hydraulic lines, one filled with oil, the other with water. The differential hydrostatic pressure between the water and oil acts to move the internal piston downward. Applying pressure to the oil line drives the piston upward, lifting the water trapped above the traveling check valve and drawing water into the lower chamber. Removing the pressure from the hydraulic line allows the water line to return the piston, after which pressure is reapplied to the hydraulic line.

The pump is designed for maximum reliability and increased run-life. All metal work is constructed from AISI 420 80 ksi stainless steel for increased corrosion resistance to H_2S and CO_2.

The PHI is a retrofit surface termination system that minimizes disruption at the surface when umbilicals are fed through the wellhead and avoids the insertion of spool pieces or flow line modifications. It has been designed for all semi-permanent deliquification installations, both onshore and offshore.

The PHI system provides communication via a hollow tubing hanger tie bolt through a sub landed in the tubing hanger profile. Should a tie-down bolt not be available, an alternative entry point can be created above the tubing hanger. For offshore applications, the system is generally used in conjunction with the Torus Insert Safety Valve configured for capillary installations.

This allows communication into the well with the following advantages — no disturbance to topside infrastructure, no compromise on safety or well integrity, no significant downtime, and no need to kill the well.

By http://www.epmag.com/

Chapter 8

Instrumentation & Computerization

Purpose & Requirements

With further development of computerization, more and more petroleum utilized instruments has been sequenced. The purpose of instrumentation and computerization is to speed up the process of drilling, cementing, completion, testing etc, measure and control production data precisely, shorten calculating time, save man power, as well as reduce consumption of materials. As a petroleum engineer, it is extremely important to know in detail the mechanism of instrumentation and computerization, learn to utilize new computerized instruments. Computerization of petroleum industry is now proceeding and will be spreading with no time all over the world.

This chapter mainly introduces the utilization of instrumentation on processing and controlling on almost every cite in petroleum industry. Here parts of instruments on drilling and mud system are listed.

8.1 Instruments on Drilling

The ultrasonic inspection equipment for drill pipe joints and drill collars that can be completed in 1 minute of the pipe flaw 12 m, using unique arrested water film technology, may be utilized to the different diameter of pipe wall thickness and different type automatically. The operator is very convenient, simple use of pipe fittings. The same automatic equipment can also be used for drill string conversion joint. On the weld burnish can accomplish automatic positioning, fixed, one-time, and scanning. The main testing equipment operation and evaluation system has computer integrated access and self-checking function test data, high sensitivity, accurate and reliable.

8.1.1 Portable ultrasonic flow detector MFD500

MFD500 portable ultrasonic flow detector adopte the international advanced IC technique and new-style color TFT LCD display (see Fig. 8.1). Its each performance index all arrive or even beyond international excellence. The instrument use the artificial intelligence technology. It has very strong function and can be used very convenient. MFD500 can test, orient, evaluate and diagnose various flaws such as crack, lard, air hole in work pieces interior swiftly and accurately without any destruction. It can not only be used in lab but also can be used on engineering site. Also, it can be widely used for safety checking and life evaluating in fields of aeronautics, rail transportation and boiler pressure vessel.

Fig. 8.1 ultrasonic flow detector MFD500

KEY FEATURES

With Chinese display, master-slave menu, shortcut key and digital swiftly knob, it's designed with leading technology and can be used very conveniently.

With digital color TFT LCD display, it can choose the background colour and wave color acoording to the environment. And the LCD brightness also can be set freely by yourself.

Designed with high performance security-guarantee battery module, it's easy for disassembly and assembly. And it can charge independent with offline. And the large capacity and high performance Lithium-ion battery module make the instrument continously working time to above 8 hours.

With small size and light weight, the instrument can be hold by one hand. Its durable in use and lead industry trend.

RANGE: 0 ~ 9 999 mm (at steel velocity); range selectable in fixed steps or continuously variable.

PULSER: Spike excitation with low, middle and high choices of the pulse energy.

Pulse Repetition Rate: manually adjustable from 10 to 1 000 Hz.

Pulse width: Adjustable in a certain range to match different probes.

Damping: 100, 200, 400 selectable to meet different resolution and sensitivity need.

Probe work mode: Single element, dual element and through transmission.

RECEIVER

Real-time sampling at 160 MHz high speed enough to record the defect information.

Rectification: Positive half wave, negative halfwave, full wave, and RF.

DB Step: 0 dB, 0.1 dB, 2 dB, 6 dB step value as well as auto-gain mode.

ALARM: Alarm with sound and light.

MERMORY

Total 100 configuration channels store all instrument operating parameters plus DAC/AVG curve; stored configuration data can be easily previewed and recalled for quick, repeatable instrument setup. Total 1 000 datasets store all instrument operating parameters plus A-scan. All the configuration channels and datasets can be transferred to PC via USB port.

FUNCTIONS

Peak Hold: Automatically searching the peak wave inside the gate and hold it on the display.

Equivalent diameter calculation: find out the peak echo and calculate its equivalent diameter.

Continuous Record: Record the display continuously and save it to the memory inside the instrument.

Defect Localization: Localize the defect position, including the distance, the depth and its plane projection distance.

Defect Sizing: calculate the defect size.

Defect Evaluation: Evaluate the defect by echo envelope.

DAC: Distance Amplitude Correction.

AVG: Distance Gain Size curve function.

Crack measure: Measure and calculate the crack depth.

B-SCAN: Display the cross-section of the test block.

8.1.2 NDJ series rotational viscometer

NDJ series rotational viscometer (see Fig. 8.2) is designed for the determination of viscosity and rheological behavior of fluid and semi-fluid. It is used to indicate the plastic viscosity of the mud (Tab. 8.1).

Fig. 8.2 rotational viscometer NDJ Series

Tab. 8.1 Rotational Viscometer NDJ Series Characteristics

Model	NDJ-1	NDJ-4	NDJ-7
Measurement Range	$0.1 \sim 1 \times 10^5$ mPa·s	$10 \sim 2 \times 10^6$ mPa·s	$1 \sim 1 \times 10^6$ mPa·s
Rotor Speed/rpm	6/12/30/60	0.3/0.6/1.5/3/6/12/30/60	7.7/75/750
Accuracy	±5% Newtonian Fluid		
Overall Dimensions	445 mm ×235 mm ×380 mm		185 mm ×165 mm × 450 mm
Net Weight	8 kg		12 kg

8.1.3 K34715 BV5000 programmable brookfield viscosity liquid bath

Fig. 8.3 illustrates K34715 BV5000 programmable brookfield viscosity liquid bath.

Fig. 8.3　K34715 BV5000 programmable brookfield viscosity liquidBath

1. Test method

Determines the low temperature, low shear rate viscosities of gear oils, automatic transmission fluids, hydraulic oils and other fluid lubricants by use of the Brookfield viscometer.

2. Features and benefits

- Sample soaking and testing in a single bath, eliminating the need for an air bath and the risk of sample temperature rise during transfer
- Redesigned for improved control of sample movement and handling during testing
- Microprocessor PID temperature control duplicates the sample cooling rates in ASTM D2983
- Up to 40 cooling/testing temperature profiles can be stored in memory

3. Programmable brookfield viscosity liquid bath

Redesigned programmable baths with improved features for sample handling and testing. Bath accommodates 10 samples for Brookfield Viscosity testing. Sample cells are immersed in a liquid bath for the entire soaking and testing period, eliminating the need to transfer cells from an air bath to a liquid bath with insulated balsa wood carriers. Also eliminated is the inherent risk of sample temperature rise during transfer. The programmable microprocessor PID controller stores up to 40 temperature profiles that duplicate the sample cooling rates found in ASTM D2983. Steady state temperature accuracy and uniformity exceed ASTM requirements throughout the operating range from ambient to $-55℃$. Air-cooled hermetic compressors provide efficient operation with the use of CFC-free refrigerants.

The mounting position for the Brookfield Viscometer has been changed to permit easier access to the samples and viscometer controls. Cabinet has a front window and glare-free fluorescent lighting for distortion free viewing of the sample cells. Cabinet construction is polyester-epoxy finished steel with a chemical-resistant composite top surface. A removable insulated cover with handle is included. Bath rests on adjustable leveling feet. Safety features include a probe fault detection circuit in the primary temperature controller and a redundant latching controller and probe for temperature fault protection.

4. Specifications

Conforms to the specifications of:

ASTM D2983 – Note 1 and Appendix X3; IP 267; CEC L18A-30; ISO 9262

Sample capacity: 10 samples

Temperature control: Microprocessor PID digital-indicating programmable controller with ±0.05℃ steady state stability

Operating Range: Ambient to -55℃

5. Electrical requirements

220–240V, 50 Hz, Single Phase, 12.6A

220–240V, 60 Hz, Single Phase, 12.6A

6. Dimensions $L \times W \times H$, in. (cm)

41×34×38 (104×86.5×96.5)

Net Weight: 327 lbs (148.5 kg)

7. Shipping information

Shipping Weight: 497 lbs (226 kg)

Dimensions: 41.5 Cu. ft.

8.1.4 DIS-500H digital inclinometer system

Model: DIS-500H (see Fig. 8.4)

Source area: Canada, Roctest

Use: The DIS-500H inclinometer probe is designed for accurate measurement of vertical heave or settlement in embankments, dams and foundations. The inclinometer probe operates in inclinometer casing which is placed in trenches during fill operations or installed in boreholes.

The Roctest Telemac biaxial inclinometer system comprises a probe, cable reel and PDA. The probe is fitted with guide wheels and contains two MEMS accelerometers measuring in A and B planes. It is connected by a graduated cable to the cable reel. The "read" button on the PDA or a remote handheld activator allow for the saving of readings from the accelerometers. These are transmitted cable free to the PDA

Fig. 8.4 DIS–500H Digital inclinometer probe

and saved via Bluetooth transmission.

Features

- Digital from probe to PDA overcoming cable electrical resistance and noise issues.
- No field connections required, avoids water ingress and connection failures.
- Solid state electronics ensure long, trouble free use in a site environment
- Light, easily portable by one person
- PDA allows easy interface with most office systems and applications.
- Enhanced PDA Sofware provides a range of presentations with built in "current borehole" back up facility.

8.2 Mud Instruments

8.2.1 HKCX-DZ series wired drilling electronic inclinometer

1. Usage

HKCX-DZ series wired drilling electronic inclinometer (see Fig. 8.5) is for real-time orientation control by controlling the tool face. Directional operation could be finished and the borehole's trail could be controlled

Fig. 8.5 HKCX-DZ series wired drilling electronic inclinometer

2. Characteristics

(1) Simplify survey process and reduce labor intensity: the survey could be done by only one person without winch and throwing off kelly.

(2) Time saving: there is no need to adjust mud circularly, then the drilling time is saved and process is simplified.

(3) More secure: Drilling tool could be lifted at any time even in the process of survey.

(4) The deeper well could be taken survey: the instrument could withstand high temperature, high external pressure and could work at deeper depth.

(5) Save cost, prevent accident and risk effectively.

8.2.2 Multi-shot electronic inclinometer

Fig. 8.6 illustrates Multi-shot electronic inclinometer.

Chapter 8 Instrumentation & Computerization

Fig. 8.6 Multi-shot electronic inclinometer

1. Characteristics

Consecutive collecting time: ≥12 hours.

Extensional time: 2 ~ 720 minutes.

Interval time of collection shots: 20 ~ 3 600 seconds, minimum collecting interval time is 1 second.

Capability: 1 800 shots (22 series) and 2 000 shots (03 series).

Temperature: −40 ℃ ~ 125 ℃.

High accuracy and stability.

Multiple anti-shock buffer system effectively increases the instrument's ability of anti-shock and anti-vibration.

The power-off protection.

Intelligent judging system.

Rechargeable battery could be used over 800 times.

Operation Software with different language version.

2. Products Series

Products series see Tab. 8.2

Tab. 8.2 Products Series of Multi-shot electronic inclinometer

Max. outside diamter mm	Max. pressure-proof MPa	Max. working temperature	Inclination		Azimuth		Product No.
			Range	Accuracy	Range	Accuracy	
φ45	90	125℃	0° ~ 180°	±0.2°	0° ~ 360°	±15°	HKCX-DZ-AAA
φ			0° ~ 55°				HKCX-DZ-AAB
	125	250℃	0° ~ 180°				HKCX-DZ-AAG
			0° ~ 55°				HKCX-DZ-AAH

8.2.3 Thermocups

Thermocups and cup heaters (see Fig. 8.7) are designed for controlling the temperature of a mud sample while taking readings with a rheometer or viscometer. Normal heat-up time is 30 minutes and the pilot light turns on when the well reaches the set temperature. Drilling fluid has a low thermal conductivity, so it must be agitated in order to reach a uniform temperature within a reasonable length of time.

For safety considerations, the fluid should never be heated above 200 ℉ (93℃). The rotor and bob should not be immersed for long periods in the fluid as vapors will rise up into the bearings and condense, causing corrosion. The holes in the stage of the RIGCHINA Viscometers have been positioned to hold the heated cups at a 45° angle to the line of the instrument for better accommodation of thermometers and power cables. Description: Cup Heater with removable stainless steel cup, 220 Volt, Rated power: 300 W. For regulated temperatures up to 200 ℉ (93℃) Size: 168×125×114 mm. Weight: 2 kg.

8.2.4 Xym-2 mud balance

1. Product details of Xym-2 mud balance:

The Rigchina mud balance provides a simple, practical method for the accurate determination of fluid density (see Fig. 8.8). The durable construction of the Rigchina mud balance makes it ideal for field use. Despite its sensitivity, it contains no easily broken parts. Principally, the balance consists of a base and graduated arm with cup, lid, knife-edge, rider, built-in spirit level, and a counter weight.

Fig. 8.7　thermocups　　　　　　Fig. 8.8　Xym-2 mud balance

A plastic carrying case is provided to hold the balance intact and in its working position.

2. Specifications:

Type: XYM-2

Configuration: Engineering plastics/metal

Overall size: 500×60×120

Chapter 8 Instrumentation & Computerization

Technical Parameters

Item	TYPE	Measurement range	Accuracy	Mud capacity
1	XYM-1	0.96 ~ 2.0 g/cm³/(8.0 ~ 171 b/gal)	0.01 g/cm³	140 cm³
2	XYM-2	0.96 ~ 2.5 g/cm³/(8.0 ~ 211 b/gal)		
3	XYM-3	0.96 ~ 3.0 g/cm³/(8.0 ~ 251 b/gal)		
4	XYM-5	0.7 ~ 2.4 g/cm³/(5.8 ~ 201 b/gal)		
5	XYM-7	0.1 ~ 1.5 g/cm³/(0.8 ~ 131 b/gal)		

8.2.5 Shearometer kit

The Shearometer is used for determining the gel strength of drilling muds(see Fig.8.9). The results are read directly from a calibrated scale, and give gel strength in pounds of shear per 100 square feet of area. The Rigchina Shearometer kit includes a Shearometer cup with graduated scale, two 5-gram Shearometer tubes and instructions.

Fig.8.9 Shearometer

When left under static conditions in normal to high temperatures at the bottom of an open borehole, some fluids tend to thicken and, in some cases, may solidify. Rigchina Aging Cells have been designed to aid in predicting the performance of drilling fluids under static, high temperature conditions.

SHEAROMETER KIT

Weights and Dimensions:

Part No	Description	Dimensions (Inches)	Dimensions (Centimeters)	Weights (gm)
24000	Shearometer Kit	10×10×8	25.4×25.4×20.3	791.0
24102	Shearometer cup with Scale	10×10×8	25.4×25.4×20.3	772.0
24200	Shearometer Tube, 5-gram	2.5×2.5×6	6.35×6.35×15.2	103.9
25500	Weight set, 1 to 200 grams	5.75×2.5×2.25	14.6×6.35×5.7	745.8

8.3 Computerizing scheme for Drilling Data Management

This computer program gives out build-in information, quickly customize and update morning reports, manage and find well data, visualize downhole data, analyze drilling data and performance, produce work orders from WellView cost information, analyze time data.

Fig. 8.10 ~ 8.16 illustrate the computer program which is well designed and modified to fullfill the demand of the users.

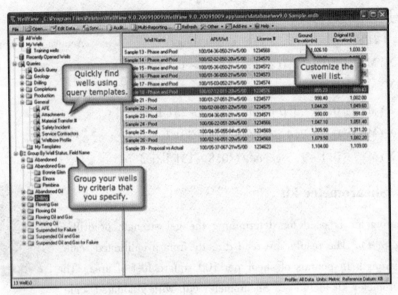

Fig. 8.10 The Well Explorer provides powerful group, search, and display capabilities to identify offsets quickly and to manage well work operations

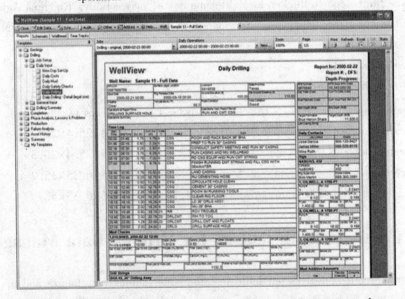

Fig. 8.11 WellView's flexible reporting provides interactive report templates that are specific to your company's workflow. Field staff can review the data specific to their job function and double-click an area of the report to quickly update that data

Chapter 8 Instrumentation & Computerization

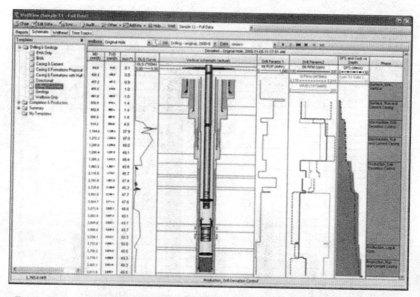

Fig. 8.12 Use schematics to view detailed drilling information to improve data quality, gain insight, and increase collaboration

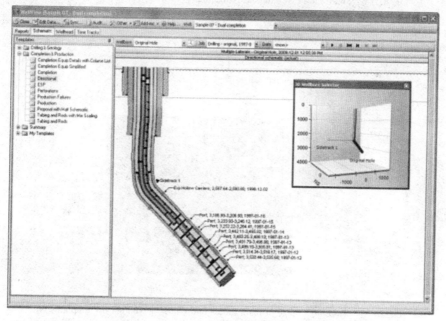

Fig. 8.13 View directional tracks (actual and proposed), drawn from actual survey data. A 3D graph displays all the wellbores in the well file

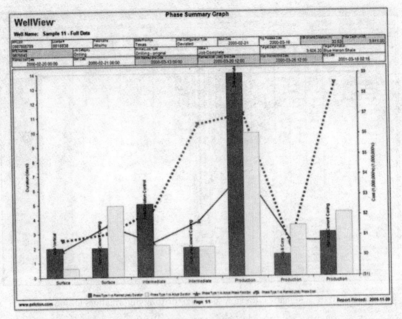

Fig. 8.14 WellView's database continually evolves so you can capture, manage, and analyze more data. Examples include phase analysis, lessons learned, cost, and performance

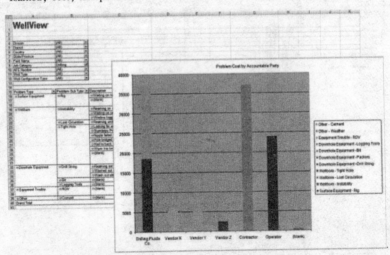

Fig. 8.15 Take advantage of pivot tables and charts as you set up templates for exporting multi well data to Excel

Chapter 8 Instrumentation & Computerization

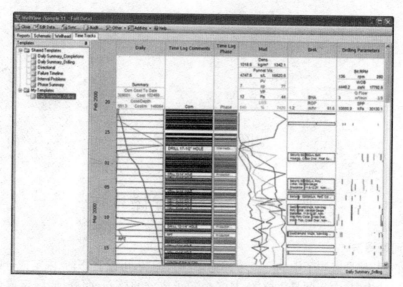

Fig. 8.16 Use Time Tracks to see trends in your WellView time-series data. Time Tracks looks from the beginning to the end of your data, starting with its earliest date. Monitor your drilling operations, such as fluid properties, drill strings, problems, and lessons. Zoom in to see the details. Zoom out to get the big picture

Summary

Computerization has brought complicated calculating and performing work much easier and more convenient, and no other power can take place of the power of computer. It is predicted that in no more than a few decades, the global petroleum industry will be completely computerized. So, don't hesitate using computer programming as the advanced processing measure and make better and better use of it.

Exercises

Part 1 Translatation
Translate Text 8.1.1 into Chinese with the help of the dictionary.
Part 2 Programming practice
Try to write a simple program accordingly if you are familiar with computer programming.

附　　录

附录 I　中英文互译技巧

1. 中心词翻译法

所谓中心词,就是以句子中的一个单词为中心,其前后可以有修饰、限定成分的语法结构。在这样的语法结构中,中心词是主要的,是各个句子成分的核心,而修饰、限定成分是次要的,只是起进一步的修饰及限定作用。所以,翻译时抓住句子中各个句子成分中的中心词是把握准确翻译的关键。

中心词的分类:

(1)名词做中心词,其他修饰词或限定词放在前面或后面,修饰、限定、说明或者描述这个中心词。修饰、限定、说明或者描述的词有:形容词、冠词、名词、数词、介词短语、动词不定式、-ing 形式,以及-ed 形式。除冠词只能放在中心词之前、动词不定式只能放在中心词之后以外,其他的词既可放在中心词之前,也可以放在之后。其修饰、描述从句有:定语从句;其说明、限定从句有:同位语从句,表语从句。

eg. (sedimentary) basin

译文:　沉积盆地

这里的中心词是 basin,修饰词是 sedimentary。

(three)(layers of) fluids(in that deposition basin)

译文:那个沉积盆地中三个层面的流体

中心词是 fluids,限定词是 three,表示数量,修饰词是 layers of,in that deposition basin 是介词短语,后置修饰 fluids。

eg. (braided)(steel) cable (about 1 1/8 inches in diameter)

直径大约为 $1\frac{1}{8}$ 英寸的辫状钢丝绳

这里的中心词是 cable,steel 是名词,说明 cable,braided 表示被动及完成,前置修饰 steel cable, about $1\frac{1}{8}$ inches in diameter 是介词短语,后置修饰 cable。

eg. (the)(new)(difficult) problem (to solve)

译文:有待于解决的新难题

这里的中心词是 problem,限定词是 the,修饰词是 difficult 及 to solve 。特别要提到的是,非谓语前、后置修饰中心词时,总是和中心词之间有逻辑上的主谓关系或动宾关系,一定要特别注意。上面的短语中的动词不定式 to solve 就与中心词 problem 有逻辑上的动宾关系:solve the problem 。

eg. (the)(hoisting) system (used)(to raise and lower and to suspend equipment in the well)

用于提起、下落及悬停井中设备的提升系统

这里的中心词是 system, hoisting 就是-ing 形式,表示常规动作,修饰 system, used 是-ed 形式,表示被动,描述 system,其后的几个动词不定式都表示目的。

eg. (several)(assigned) workers (to work)

译文:几位被派去工作的工人

这里的中心词是 workers,后面的动词不定式 to work 就与中心词 workers 有逻辑上的主谓关系:

workers work

中心词 workers 前面的过去分词(即-ed 形式) assigned 与中心词 workers 就有逻辑上的被动及完成关系:

workers have been assigned

eg. (depressed) area (of the earth's crust)

译文: 地壳沉陷区域

这里的中心词是 area,修饰词分别是前置-ed 形式和后置介词短语。

(depressed) area (of the earth's crust)(where tiny plats and animals lived)

译文:动植物生存过的地壳沉陷区域

同上句,这里多了一个定语从句,表示地点,修饰中心词 area 。

The principle (that rod pumping unit works) is of complications.

译文:有杆泵工作原理是复杂的。

that rod pumping unit works 就是同位语从句,说明中心词 the principle 。

The diagram shows what happens at the piston.

译文:工作原理图说明活塞的运行状况。

what happens at the piston 是表语从句,起说明作用,用于说明中心词 The diagram 。

(2)动词做中心词,其修饰词有:副词、介词短语、动词不定式、-ing、-ed 形式。其修饰从句有状语从句。

eg. [In order to control subsurface fluid pressure], engineer adjusts the weight of the drilling mud [to exert a greater pressure on the bottom of the well].

译文:为了达到控制地下流体压力的目的,工程师调节钻井液的比重,以期对井底施加更大的压力。

这里 In order to control subsurface fluid pressure 修饰中心词 adjusts,表示调节的目的,to exert a greater pressure on the bottom of the well 也用于修饰 adjusts,表示调节的结果。

eg. Completion engineers use the screen and gravel pack [in wire-wrapped screen completion], [minimizing the entry of sand into the wellbore], [preventing problems caused by sand].

译文:完井工程师们在绕丝筛管完井中使用了筛网及砾石充填,最大限度地减少了流入井眼的沙石量,防止了沙石引发出来的问题。

这句话中连续出现了三个状语,都修饰谓语中心词 use, in wire-wrapped screen completion 是介词短语,表示"使用"的范围,minimizing the entry of sand into the wellbore 和 preventing problems caused by sand 都是-ing 短语,表示"使用"后产生的效果。

eg. While drilling, the pressure exerts on the formation [excessively] [that the fluids inside could not flow into the well hole easily].

译文:钻井过程中向地层施加过压,以使其内的流体不能挤入井眼。

that the fluids inside could not flow into the well hole easily 就是状语从句,表示 exerts 的目的。

(3)形容词做中心词,其修饰词有:副词、动词不定式、-ing、-ed 形式。其修饰从句有:状语从句。

eg. Oil-grades of cement are [nearly] [all] sulphate-resistant, [since water containing sulphates has a deleterious effect on set cement].

译文:固井水泥几乎都必须防酸,因为含水硫酸盐对固化水泥十分有害。

这里,副词 nearly all 以及从句 since water containing sulphates has a deleterious effect on set cement 都修饰中心词 sulphate-resistant。

(4)副词做中心词,其修饰词有:副词,动词不定式,-ing, -ed 形式。其修饰从句有:状语从句。

eg. The new well is [extremely] [far] away [from the old one].

译文:新井离老井相当地远。

中心词是 away,修饰词有 extremely, far 以及 from the old one。

总结:将上述中心词分别充当一句话的句子成分,那么一句话中就有可能出现两个或以上的中心词。抓住复杂句中的中心词,就可以抓住句子的精髓,进而流畅地翻译。此法不仅适用于英译汉,也同样适用于汉译英。

2. 对比排序翻译法

对比排序翻译法即按照英汉句式的排列顺序规律——对照进行翻译的方法。英语和汉语的句子结构极为相似,基本上都是主谓结构。只是英汉句中的状语排列顺序略有不同。抓住这种规律,就能非常容易地进行英汉互译了。现将英汉句子成分的排列顺序分别对照如下:

英语　　　　　　　　　　　　　　　汉语

动态句型:

(1)主谓句:状语(从句)+主语+状语+谓语+状语(从句);　　状语(从句)+主语+状语+谓语

(2)动宾句:状语(从句)+主语+状语+谓语+宾语+状语(从句);　　状语(从句)+主语+状语+谓语+宾语

静态句型:

(1)系表句:状语(从句)+主语+be+状语+表语+状语(从句));　　状语(从句)+主语+状语+谓语(是)+表语

(2)存在句:状语(从句)+there+状语+be+主语+状语(从句);　　状语(从句)+谓语(有)+主语

由上述英汉句子成分的排列顺序对比来看,英汉句式的排列不同点是:

a. 英语句尾的状语(从句)居多,而汉语句尾通常没有状语。所以在将英语译成汉语时,除表示目的的状语以外,几乎都把句尾的状语翻译到谓语之前。

eg. The drilling fluid enters the swivel [by way of the "gooseneck"].

译文:钻井液[通过"鹅颈管"]流进旋转接头(水龙头)。

We will stop the pump immediately after circulation.

译文:我们[在循环后][马上]停泵。

Please help me [to connect the sensor to the standpipe].

译文:请帮我[把传感器上到立管上]。

to connect the sensor to the standpipe 是目的,翻译到谓语之后。

b. 主从复合句中英语的从句既可在主句之前,也可以在主句之后;而汉语除结果从句在主句之后以外,都把从句翻译到句首。

eg. [After the tool joint has been "broken" with the tongs], the pipe may be unscrewed [further] [by turning the rotary or by using a spinning wrench].

译文:[钻杆接头[用大钳]松扣以后],钻杆即可[通过转动转盘或使用旋转扳手]卸扣。

We can get the best effect [if the pressure is kept from 0.2 to 0.3 MPa].

译文:[保持0.2~0.3 MPa压力时]除泥效果最佳。

Other devices are [also] used [to clean the drilling mud] [before it flows back into the mud pits].

译文:[在钻井泥浆返回到泥浆池之前],也使用其他设备清除泥浆中的杂质。

c. 英语系表句中的状语在 be 和表语之间及句尾,存在句中的状语在句首及句尾,而汉语的状语则除了表示目的或结果的状语以外,几乎都把句尾的状语翻译到句首或谓语之前,并且基本不译出 be。

eg. This well is [extremely] deep.

译文:这口井[特别地]深。

There are (additional) pressure losses [in the flow line].

译文:[在出油管线]有(额外的)压力损失。

There are (a wide variety of) packers (available) [to meet the requirements of specific completion designs].

译文:有(各种类型的)封隔器[以满足特种完井设计的要求]。

to meet the requirements of specific completion designs 表示目的,翻译到句尾。

eg. (As we know), [while drilling], there are two fluid pressures [at the bottom of the well].

译文:(正如我们所知),[钻井时],[井底]有(两种)(流体)压力。

句尾的 at the bottom of the well 就翻译到了谓语之前。

3. 被动变主动翻译法

被动变主动翻译法即将原英文被动句翻译成汉语的主动句。这有时需要将汉译部分人为地加上主语,但常常翻译成祈使句为好。

eg. In order to control subsurface fluid pressure, the weight of the drilling mud is adjusted to exert a greater pressure on the bottom of the well.

译文:为了达到控制井底流体压力的目的,必须调节钻井液的比重,以期向井底施加更大的压力。

这里将 the drilling mud is adjusted 翻译成了主动结构,并且将谓语改成祈使结构。

This is called overbalance, and the drilling mud is then forced into the surrounding rocks.

译文:这就叫做"过平衡"钻井,以强迫钻井液进入周围的岩石。

并列句的前一句翻译成主动句,后一句省略了主语。

4. 拆分翻译法

拆分翻译法即打乱现有句子的语言顺序,按其原始的意义进行重新翻译的方法。这种方法要求我们能看出原句的拆分部位,并将其还原。

eg. A good understanding has been obtained of the world's first coal bed methane (CBM) which is tapped from coal seams by removing water to reduce pressure will be produced for liquefied natural gas (LNG).

译文:我们已经很清楚地知道,世界上开始通过除水处理以降低压力的方法从煤层中提取煤层甲烷液化天然气。

上句中 of the world's first coal bed methane (CBM) which is tapped from coal seams by removing water to reduce pressure will be produced for liquefied natural gas（LNG）整体做 understanding 的后置修饰成分，只是为了紧凑理解句子，将这个修饰成分拆分到了句尾。

The underground petroleum is very likely to have dissolved in it water that obviously may help to increase the pressure in it.

译文：地下的石油非常有可能含有已经溶解在其中的水分，这显然就会增大石油在地下的压力。

这句话乍看起来好像 to have dissolved 是动词不定式的完成式，但后面的 it 不可能和 water 同时做 in 的宾语。仔细分析后就知道 dissolved in it 是过去分词短语作前置定语修饰中心词 water。于是本句经过这样拆分，就容易翻译了。

还有下面的一句：

As we know, a good understanding has been obtained of petroleum which is a combination of several fractions.

这里的句子为了修饰的方便，把 understanding 后面的 of petroleum 放到了本句谓语的后面，目的是能方便地用定语从句加以修饰。句子本来的结构是：

As we know, a good understanding of petroleum has been obtained which is a combination of several fractions.

这样经过拆分后，句子结构就明显化，便于翻译了。

译文：众所周知，石油是由几种馏分组成的。

以上的英译汉过程完全是可逆的，即完全可以用同样的方法将汉语翻译成英语。

5. 主题词翻译法

汉语一句话中若连续出现几个词，其中的一个起主导作用，这里称之为主题词。例如主题词为动词时，就要将这个动词作为谓语，其他动词是次要的，这里称之为辅助动词，就作为非谓语进行翻译。

eg. 一般地，分步骤钻一口井，开始打表层，进深 60～400 m，依据最后的井深而定，然后再钻至所需深度 1 000～2 500 m。

译文：A well is drilled in stages, starting with a surface hole, ranging from 60 to 400 m depending on the final depth conditions, then drilling to the depth required from 1 000 to 2 500 m.

这里"钻"是主题动词，用做谓语进行翻译，其他动词如"打表层"、"进深"、"依据"、"钻进"等均是从属动词，按非谓语进行翻译。

6. 并列句翻译法

汉语的一句话中若出现三个以上的连续性动作或行为，翻译成英语时，将前几个动作或行为之间直接用逗号隔开，而在最后两个动作或行为之间用 and 连接，这样的行文显得流畅、自然，且有很强的逻辑性。

eg. 地质学家勘探油气，地质化学家和古生物学家研究地下岩石样本，钻探人员实施钻井,生产人员将油气泵送、储存起来。

译文:The petroleum geologists explore oil and gas, the geochemists and paleontologists analyze the samples from underground, the drillers drill the well and, the pumpers transfer oil and gas into field storage tanks.

如果多个谓语拥有同一个主语,则翻译时第二个谓语开始即省略主语。

eg. 将钻井液泵出泥浆池,经过立管,再通过鹅颈管进入旋转接头,穿过钻井管线,最后到达钻头。

译文:The drilling mud comes out of the mud pits, goes up to the stand pipe, enters the swivel by the way of the goose neck, travels through drilling strings, and reaches the drilling bit.

附录Ⅱ 专业英语常用时态及非谓语表达法

1. 时态

谓语中动作执行时间和动作状态的有机结合,就构成了时态。首先,英语的时态是仅对于谓语而言的,即,只有谓语才能有时态的变化。谓语的时态变化离不开动作执行时间和动作状态这两个有关的概念。抓住这两个概念,并弄清楚它们之间的逻辑关系,是正确使用时态的关键。

首先要弄清楚英语的动作执行时间概念。英语的时间概念与汉语的不同,汉语有"现在"、"过去"、"将来",而英语的动作执行时间除了有"现在"、"过去"、"将来"以外,还有"过去将来"之说,就是从"过去"算起"将来"的时间。

再弄清楚英语的动作状态概念。英语共有四个动作状态(高级英语语法中称之为英语的四个"体"),即"一般"、"完成"、"进行"和"完成进行"。"一般"是指非固定的、多次、反复的动作或行为状态;"完成"是指有了结果或影响的动作或行为状态;"进行"是指具体的、一次性的动作或行为状态;"完成进行"是指当时还没有形成最终结果或影响的动作或行为状态,还要继续下去。

这样,用这四个时间分别和四个状态进行排列、组合,就构成了英语的16个时态。

动作状态的具体表达式为时间状语,具体表现为:A.时间范围状语,B.时间界限状语,C.具体时间状语。所谓"时间范围"是指动作或行为执行时所在的时间范围区段。它们通常是:today, yesterday, tomorrow, this month/year, last month/year, next month/year 等。这一类状语都是用于表示笼统、大概的时间范围的状语。频率副词做状语也属于时间范围状语的范畴。典型的有:every day/month/year, always(总是), frequently, usually, often, sometimes, ever, never 等。因为这些状语都是非固定的、反复、频繁出现的,所以我们在这里把它们归类为"一般时态"的状语,也称之为"一般时态"标识词,即它们在一般时态中作为标识词出现在句子中。时间界限状语是以某一时间作为动作或行为的持续终点,或动作与时间界限状语产生时间差。这样前后就形成了界限,用于表示动作或行为的结果或影响。典型的时间界限状语有:so far, by now, by the time, by the end of, before, since, after, already, (not) yet, recently 等,我们在这里给它们归类为"完成时态"的标识词。具体时间状语指的是正在进行的,一次性固定时间的状语,这样的状语可能不是正在进行的动作,而是具体的动作。典型的有:now, just now, at the moment, always(一直在),when 等。这些状语都是固定、具体的时间状语,我们在这里把它们归类为"进行时态"的标识词。

抓住动作或行为的执行时间和时间状语之间的关系是应用时态的关键,其中时间状语起最终决定时态的作用。

(1)时间概念的判定

①一句话中没有或不需要时间状语时,通常用"现在"表示。

eg. We learn Petroleum English. (没有时间状语)
　　Petroleum is powerful. (不需要时间状语)

②当将来的动作肯定发生时,用现在代替将来。

eg. Spud in, please. (肯定要发生的动作,用祈使句)
　　Our tool pusher is 30 next year. (明年肯定 30 岁)

③当回忆过去的动作或行为时,用"过去"表示。

eg. Most crude oil and natural gas originate from plant and animal life that thrived millions of years ago. (回忆 millions of years ago 所发生的事)

④当期望或预料某个动作或行为时,用"将来"表示。

eg. Mr. Smith said he would visit the oil field the following year. (期望)
　　This child will be a geologist. (预料)

⑤当时间状语可以选择(既可以是现在,也可以是过去或将来)时,用"现在"表示。

eg. Every time you check the equipment, don't forget to cut off the power. ("每一次"既可以是现在,又可以是将来)

理解时态的关键是,一定要清楚动作执行时间和时间状语之间的逻辑关系。一般地,科技英语经常使用一般时态,完成时态和将来时态次之。下面就对这几种时态进行详细解析。

(2)时态判定关键

①一般时态判定关键

a. 动作执行时间不固定,时间状语也不固定,为"一般"。

b. 动作执行时间包含在时间范围状语范围内,永远小于时间状语,并且有活动余地。

例如:Petroleum plays an important role in industry.

这里动作执行时间和时间状语均未固定,所以是一般现在时态。

注意,如果一句话中没有或不缺时间状语,则需根据语言环境决定时态,通常为一般现在时态。

Tiny plants and animals lived and deposited with mud and silt millions of years ago.

这里有时间状语 millions of years ago,是对过去的回忆,所以用一般过去时态。

如果以"过去"作为起点,"将来"要发生的动作或行为就是"一般过去将来时"了。

eg. After they had pumped the cementing plug, they would pull 3 stands out of the hole slowly and make up the kelly for circulation.

②完成时态判定关键

a. 动作执行时间和时间状语均不固定;时间状语只表示界限,不表示范围。

b. 动作执行时间在前,界限时间状语在后,两者产生了时间上的差异(时间差),进而体现出了动作或行为的结果或影响。

eg. Conventional beam units have proven to be reliable [so far].

过去就证实可靠,直到现在为止还证实可靠,有时间差。

[By this time next week], we'll have drilled another well.

说话时钻井的动作早就开始了,动作在前;By this time next week 是表示将来界限的时间状语,动作在后。两者产生时间差,所以是将来完成时态。

Has the cement plug been drilled out?

钻取动作发生在过去,但到现在还不知道结果。两者产生时间差,所以是现在完成时态。

③进行时态判定关键

a. 动作执行时间和时间状语均固定,即均为"具体"时间。

b. 动作执行时间等于时间状语,没有活动余地,是一次性行为。

eg. We are running casing [now].

判定:"正在"属于"具体"时间状语,动作或行为的执行时间固定在"现在",是现在一次性行为,故时态为"现在进行时"。

同理,如果动作或行为的具体执行时间是在过去或将来,就一定用过去进行时态或将来进行时态。

eg. The driller was taking out the wear bushing [just now].

请注意以下两点:

①有的动作或行为虽然不是正在进行的,但却是具体的,一次性的,也必须用进行时态表示,换句话说,这样的动作或行为的执行时间和时间状语均固定了,是事实,不能再选择、更改了。

eg. I am working in the well site office.

乍一看,这句话好像应该是一般现在时态。但仔细一分析就不难发现,"工作"这个动作的执行时间是具体事实,是固定的;时间状语是"现在",只不过被省略了,也是固定的,所以一定是"现在进行时态"。

②因为一般将来时态只表示将来可能发生,也可能不发生的动作或行为(不固定),所以

当要表示将来肯定要发生的动作或行为时,就一定用将来进行时态表示(固定)。

eg. We shall be doing the leak-off test [in a few minutes].

2. 非谓语动词表达法

不能用做谓语,又在句子中充当除谓语以外其他句子成分的动词就是非谓语动词。

非谓语动词是以谓语为参照点进行判定的。正确确定谓语和非谓语这两个动作之间的关系及正确判定非谓语动词动作与其所修饰的中心词(非谓语动词动作的执行者或承受者)之间的关系是正确理解非谓语动词的关键。

判定非谓语动词的方法有以下几种。

(1)动词不定式

以谓语为参照点,如果非谓语动词的动作的执行者是主语、宾语或表语(中心词是本句的主语、宾语或表语),并且动作和谓语同时发生或发生在谓语之后,还没有成为事实,或还没有结果,就用动词不定式表示;动作在谓语之前发生,是对过去的回忆(指向谓语的过去,产生逆向时间差),就一定用动词不定式的完成式表示;如果非谓语动词的动作的承受者是中心词,就一定用动词不定式的被动式表示。

eg. The sediments eventually hardened [to form sedimentary rock].

这里中心词是 The sediments,是本句的主语,谓语是 hardened,非谓语动词是 to form sedimentary rock,做状语,加方括号。显然 to form sedimentary rock 发生在 hardened 之后,所以用动词不定式表示。

eg. Many contractors today use the mechanical vibroseis method [to send energy waves] from a heavy, vibrating vehicle into the earth.

这里谓语和非谓语同时发生,并且以谓语为参照点时,非谓语还没有成为事实,或还没有结果,故用动词不定式表示。

eg. The rig is said [to have been erected yesterday].

中心词 The rig 是非谓语动词动作的承受者,并且安装的动作的时间状语是昨天,在谓语(现在说)之前,是回忆,故用动词不定式的完成被动式。

(2)-ing 形式

以谓语为参照点,如果非谓语动词的动作的执行者就是本句的主语、宾语或表语,并且动作发生在谓语之前,并且谓语发生时,这个动作还在进行,就一定用-ing 形式表示;如果非谓语动词的动作的承受者是主语、宾语或表语,就一定用-ing 形式的被动式表示;按如上条件,动作和谓语同时发生(有时也同时结束),并且是事实,也用-ing 形式表示;动作在谓语之前发生(指向谓语,是顺接关系),并且强调和谓语之间的时间差(必须先于谓语发生)时,就用-ing 的完成式 having -ed 表示,如果不强调时间差(可以和谓语同时发生),就用-ed 表示;此外,如果非谓语动词的动作的执行时间不固定(多次的、重复发生的动作)或既找不出动作的执行者又找不出承受者时,就一律用-ing 表示(属于"悬垂结构")。

eg. We saw a driller [preparing a drilling tool].

这里中心词是 a driller，是本句的宾语，谓语是 saw，非谓语动词是 preparing a drilling tool，做状语。preparing a drilling tool 发生在 saw 之前，并且 preparing a drilling tool 的发出者是本句的宾语 a driller。谓语发生时，这个动作还在进行，所以用-ing 形式表示。

[Not knowing the result], the driller asked the supervisor.

首先，Not knowing the result 的动作发出者是 the driller，和谓语 ask 的发出者是同一人。这两个动作既可以先后发生，也可以同时发生，这时判定为同时发生（没有产生时间差），并且 Not knowing the result 是事实，于是就用-ing 形式。

eg. [Having prepared the fishing tools], the driller began [to fish junks].

谓语 began 和非谓语 Having prepared the fishing tools 的动作执行者是同一个主语，即 the driller，所以动作是主动的。并且两个动作存在时间差，即准备完了打捞工具，才开始打捞。

(3) -ed 形式

非谓语的-ed 表达形式有：

①动作发生在谓语动作之前，其状态持续到谓语发生并且将继续持续下去，即不强调两个动作的时间差，所以用一般式。

eg. We may notice the tubing head [seated] on the casing head.

这里的宾语 tubing head 是中心词，seated 是一种状态，在谓语 notice 发生之前就已经存在，是一种结果，故用-ed 表示。

②当表示被动的动作，即中心词是动作的承受者时。

eg. Cylindrical rock samples (called cores) can be cut using a special coring bit.

这里的中心词是 samples，called 的动作不是由 samples 发出的，是被动的。

③当强调动作和谓语产生时间差时，即-ed 的动作在前，谓语的动作在后时，-ed 用 having been -ed 替换，表示完成被动。

eg. [Having been tested for many times], this instrument is proved to be reliable.

仪表的功能测试在前，证实的结果在后，两者产生了时间差。

VOCABULARY

Chapter 1

a film of ……一层(油)膜
a function of ……的函数
a long-term process 一个长期的过程
a tank of 一潭
a variety of 各种各样的
ability 能力
absent 不存在
absolute permeability 绝对渗透率
absolute porosity 绝对孔隙度(率)
according to 按照
accordingly 因此
account for 说明
accumulate 累积
accumulated production 累计产量
accuracy 精度
accurate 准确的
achieve significance as 精准地表达
adequate 充足的
adhere to 粘附在
adhesion tension 胶粘张力
adjacent to 和……相毗连的
adjacent 毗邻
adopted 采用
aim at 瞄准
alkaline 碱性物
allow 允许

along with 共存于
analysis 分析
ancient 远古的
angle of contact 接触角
anticline 背斜(层)
anticlinic traps 背斜圈闭
apart from 相离
appear 看起来
application 应用(程序)
apply 应用
applied mathematics 应用数学
appraise 评估
appropriate 适当的
approximately 接近于
areal heterogeneity 平面非均质性
arise 产生
artificial 人工的
as a function of… and… 是……与……的函数
as a result of 由于……的结果
as for 至于
assist 有帮助
associated 相关的
assume 假定
assumption 假设
assumptions 假定值
at a velocity of 以……的速度
at commercial rate 以生产规模的速度
atm/cm 大气压/厘米
attractive force 吸引力

attribute 属性，分布
available data 现有数据
available porosity 现有孔隙(度)
base on 基于
basic laws 基本定律
be adapted from 源于
be associated with 与……有关
beat stake 处于决断状态
be capable of 有……的能力
be characterized by 以……为标志
be closely related to 与……紧密相关
be conductive to 有助于
be critical to 对……起决定的作用
be defined as 定义为
be dependent upon 与……有关
be derived by 由……导出
be determined by 由……来确定
be divided into 划分为
be equal to 等于
be equally applicable to 同样应用于
be evidenced by 通过……证明
be expressed as 表达为
be expressed by 用……表达
be expressed for 表示为
be independent of 与……关
be laid down 形成
be limited to 局限于
be rearranged accordingly 做相应地调整

be referred to as 指的就是
be specific for 专用于
be structured to 列出
be subjected to 受……的制约
be surrounded by 被……包围
be termed as 被绘制成
become isolated from 隔离于
become less favourable to 不利于
bedding 地层
behavior 特性；动态
belong to 属于
beneath 在……之下
black waxy shale 黑蜡质页岩
block 阻挡
body of water 水体
boost 增加
both laterally and vertically 横向及纵向
bound technical policy 相关技术法规
bound water 束缚水
boundary condition 极限条件
boundary 边缘
branch 分支
brevity 简式
broad 宽广
bubble-point pressure 泡点压力
buckling 卷曲
building and maintaining a robust 建模
bulk volume 容积
buried depth 埋深
bury 埋藏
bypass 旁通
calcium carbide 碳化钙
calculation 计算
cap rock 盖岩
capacity 产量，性能
capillary 毛细管
capillary forces 毛管张力
carbonate sands 碳酸砂岩
carry out 实现
categories 分类

catenary pores 连通孔隙
cause 导致
cementation 胶结（作用）
centipoise 厘泊
centre 中心
central role 中心角色
channel 通道
characteristic (of) 有……的特性
characteristics 特性（曲线）
characterize 表示为……的特征
chemical compositions 化学组分
chemical flooding 化学剂驱
chemical reaction 化学反应
chemistry 化学
choose 选定
classification 分类
clays 粘土
closed pores 闭合孔隙
cm/s 厘米/秒
coalbed methane (CBM) 煤层甲烷气
coat 覆盖在……的表面
coefficient 系数
combination 混合物
combined effect 联合作用
commercialized oilfields 工业油田
commission 调试
commonly 一般
communicate 相通
compaction 压实
company 公司
comparing with 与……相比
completely 完全地
compressibility 可压缩性
comprise 包含
computer contouring and girding 计算机界定井网
concave 凹状
concept 概念
conceptually 从概念上讲
condition 条件
conductivity 传导率

conform 遵守
connate water saturation 原生水饱和度
considerable 相当大的
consist of 包含
constancy 稳定性
constant 常量
constant value 恒量
constitute 构成
construction 建设
contact angle 接触角
contain 包含
conveniently 方便地
converted to 转化成
convex 凸状
coordinate 坐标
coral reef 珊瑚礁
core 岩心
core analysis 岩心分析
correspond value 对应值
cost 费用
cost effective 经济实效的
create 生成
crest 背斜嵴
critical temperature 临界温度
cross point of two lineal curves 两条线性曲线的交叉点
cross-cut 切断
crude oil 原油
crust 地壳
crystal faces 晶体表面
cul-de-sac pores 单通孔隙
cumulative water influx 累积水侵量
cumulative water injected 累积注水量
current cumulative oil production 当前累积产油量
curve 特性曲线
cut off 切断
Darcy 达西
data set value 数据组

VOCABULARY

dead-end pore 闭合孔隙
decimal 小数
decrease 减小
define...as... 将……定义为……
define 解释
deformation 变形
degree 程度
degree of reserve recovery 采出程度
dehydration 脱水作用
demonstration 论证，表明
denote 表达出
density of formation crude oil 地层原油密度
density of formation water 地层水密度
density 密度
departure 偏差
depend upon 依据……而定
deposite 沉积
depositional environments 沉积环境
depth of interface of oil and water 油水界面深度
deriving 导出
description 描述
design 设计
designation 设计
detailed 详细的
develop 开发，形成
developed fields 已开发油田
development 开发
devise 设计出
diffusion coefficient 扩散系数
diminish 递减
direction 方向
directly 直接地
discontinuous droplets 不连续微滴
displacement of oil 驱油
Dissolved Gas Drive Reservoir 溶解气驱油藏
distinct type 不同的类型
distribution 分布

distribution type 分布类型
dolomite 白云岩
dolomitization 白云石化
dome 圆丘
drainage problem 排驱问题
drill stem tester (DST) 中途测试器
drive mechanism 驱动机理
drive out 排出
drop 液滴
dry gas 干气
due to 由于
dynamics 动态
economic 经济的
economic effect 经济效益
economic limit 经济极限
economic target 经济指标
edge water / boundary water 边水
edge water 边(缘)水
effect 作用
effective porosity 有效孔隙度
effective 有效
Elastic Drive Reservoir (EDR) 弹性驱动油藏
elastic expansion 弹性膨胀
element 要素
emerge 露出
encounter 碰到
engineer 工程师
enhanced oil and gas recovery 增加油气采收率
enhanced oil recovery (EOR) 提高采收率方法采油
entrap 俘获
equation 方程式
escape 逃逸
especially 尤其是
essentially 本质上
establish 建立
estimate 估算
ethyne 乙炔
evaluation well 评价井

evaluation 评价
even ground temperature annually 年平均地温
evidence 证实
except 除非
exceptions 异常
excessive 过度的
exhibit 显示
expansion 膨胀
expel 排出
exploitation 开发
exploiting procedure 开发步骤(过程)
expression 表达式
extensively 广泛地
extraction ratio 采收率
extrapolating 用外推法求得
extreme variability 极端变异性
extremes 极值
fabric selective 选择性组构
factor 因素
fault traps 断层圈闭
fault 断层
fenestral pores 网格孔隙
field development planning 油田开发计划
field model 油田模型
fill 充满
fissured 裂开的
flank bed 侧翼层
flood front 驱替前缘
fluid displacement 流体驱替
fluid phase 流体相
fluid 流体
fluids distribution profile 流体分布断面图
fluorinated surface 氟化物质表面
flush out 冲刷出来
fold 折叠
following 随后的
for this reason 由于这个原因

force 作用力
forecast 预告
form 形成
formation (rock) compressibility 岩层压缩率(系数)
formation liquid density 地层流体密度
formation 地层
formula 公式
fracture 裂缝
fracture pores 裂缝孔隙
fractured (fissured) formation data 断裂地层数据
future reservoir performance 未来油层动态
gas condensate 凝析油
gas desorption 气体解析
gas formation volume factor 天然气地层体积系数
gas production 气产量
gas solubility 气体溶解度
gas top portion 气顶部分
gas-cap drive 气驱
gas-cap reservoir 气顶油藏
general 综合的,一般的
generalized MBE 广义物质平衡方程
generalized relationship 简化的关系式
generally speaking 总的来讲
generate rock properties data 生成岩石性质数据
geologic characteristic 地质特征
geological terms 地质术语
geological times 地质时代
geostatistical estimation techniques 地质统计鉴定技术
geostatistical methods 地质统计方法
given amount of 给定……量
goniometer 测角仪
govern 支配

gradually 逐渐地
grain 颗粒
gravity 重力
hardly 几乎不能
have a bearing on 与……有关
heterogeneity 非均质性
hemispherical shape 半球形
high temperature 高温
hole pattern 布井方式
homogeneous 均质的
horizontal 水平的
hydraulic fracturing 水利压裂
hydrocarbon pore volume 烃类孔隙体积
hydrocarbon 碳水化合物
hydrolyze 水解
hydrophilic 亲水的
hydrophobic 疏水的
ideally 理想地
identify 识别
identify opportunities 寻找机会
illustrate 图示
imbibe...into... 将……吸入……
imbibitional trapping 吸入圈闭
immiscible fluids 不能混溶的流体
immobile 静止
impede 阻挡
impenetrable barrier 非渗透阻层
impermeable barrier 不渗透阻层
impose 利用
improved oil recovery 提高石油采收率
improvements 改进
in addition to 除……以外
in an attempt to 设法
in contrast to 与……相对照
in details 详细地
in direct proportion 成正比
in effect 在效果上
in general 通常
in mathematical terms 用极精确的术语

in order to 为了
in other words 换句话说
in percentage 以百分比计
in place 就地
in quantitative terms 用定量术语
in some cases 在某些情况下
in terms of 根据
in that 因为
in the order of 大约
in the presence of 在……存在的条件下
in the range of 在……范围内
increase 增大
indication 指示方法
industrial oil and gas 工业油气
inert gas 惰性气体
influence 影响
initial 原始
initial formation pressure 原始地层压力
initial gas cap gas reservoir volume 原始气顶气地层体积
initial hydrocarbon volumes in place 原烃储量
initial oil saturation 原始油饱和度
initial oil volume 原油体积
initial oil-in-place 原油地质储量
initial production 初始产量
initial reservoir oil volume 原始油地层体积
initial reservoir pressure 原始油藏压力
initial water saturation 初始水饱和度
initial water saturation 原始水饱和度
injection strategy 注水方案
instantaneous oil/gas ratio 瞬时油气比
instantaneous 瞬间的

VOCABULARY

intensive properties 强度性质
interactions 交互作用
intercept value 截距值
interconnected pore space 连通孔隙空间
interconnect 连通的
intercrystalline pores 晶间孔隙
interface point 临界点
interface 界面
interfacial tension 表面张力
intermediate wettability 中等湿润性
intermediate 中间的
intermingle 混合
interparticle（intergranular）粒间的
interpolating 用内推法求得
interpret 解释
interval 时间间隔
intraparticle（intragranular）粒内的
invade 侵入
inventory 存储清单
investment 投资
irreducible water saturation 残余水饱和度
isolate 隔绝
It is important to recognize that 必须认识到
It is obvious that 显而易见
joints 接合圈闭
judge 判定
label 标记为
laboratory 实验室
lack of 缺少
lagoon 泻湖
lamina 岩石薄片
large amount of data
lateral direction 水平方向
lateral faults 横(向)断层
later 随后
law(s) 定律
layering 分层
lead to 导致

lens trap 环形圈闭
letter 字母
level 水平
liquid and vapor phases 液相和汽相
limestone 石灰岩
lining the pores 包裹孔隙
liquid 液体
liquid droplet 液滴
literature 文献
lithology 岩性
location 部位
loosely 松散的
low energy material 低能量物质
low-shrinkage 低收缩
main 主要的
maintain 保持
manner 方式
market requirement 市场需求
Material Balance Equation（MBE）物质平衡方程
mathematically 从数学角度上讲
matrix 基质
measure 测定
media depth 中深度
meniscus 弯液面
mercury 水银
microscopic distribution of fluids 流体的微观分布
migrate 运移
millidarcy（md）毫达西
million 百万
miscellaneous investigation 综合研究
miscible applications 混相驱动设施
miscible displacement 混相驱
model 模型
modeling 建模
Modular Formation Dynamics Tester（MFDT）模块式地层动态测试器
moldic 溶膜的
more than 不止
morphology 形态学

movement 移动
multiple 多个
natural gas 天然气
naturally 自然地
near-critical gas-condensate 近临界天然气凝析油
near-critical 近临界
net 净
nitrogen 氮
nomenclature 命名法
non-porous 无孔的
nonuniform 非均质的
normal fault trap 正断层圈闭
normal and reverse faults 正冲断和逆冲断层
normal 正常的
numerical dispersion 数值弥散
observe 观察
obtain 获得
occupy 占据
occur 产生
of course 当然
oil bearing 含油
oil displacement 驱油
oil formation volume factor at the bubble point pressure 泡点压力原油地层体积系数
oil formation volume factor 原油地层体积系数
oil initially in place（OIIP）石油原始地质储量
oil layer open depth 油层裸深
oil wet 油湿
oil zoon 含油带
oil-bearing layer 含油层
on the basis of 以……为基础
on the other hand 此外
open channels 开放通道
opinion 意见，看法
opposite 对顶于
optimal completion 优化完井

order of magnitude 数量级
organization 构造
organize 搜集
origin 起源
originally dissolved gas 原始溶解气
overlain 上覆
overlying rock layer 上覆岩层
parameter 参数
particular system 特别体系
particular 特定的
pass through 穿过
pay zone 产油层
pelmicrites 球粒微晶灰岩
performance 特性
permeability stratification 渗透率成层分布
permeability to oil 油相渗透率
permeability 渗透率
petroleum 石油
petroleum-bearing rock 含油岩
phase diagram 相图
phases 相态
physical and chemical reorganization 物理及化学重组
physical rock properties 岩石的物理性质
physics 物理
pinch-out 尖灭圈闭
plant(s) 植物
plastic flow 塑性流动
play the role of 起……的作用
plot 标出（曲线）
plug 岩心样本
polyhedral 多面体的
polymer 聚合物
pore 孔隙
pore boundary 孔隙边界
pore interconnection 孔间通道
pore spaces 孔隙空间
pore volume compressibility coefficient 孔隙体积压缩系数
pore volume 孔隙容(体)积
pore volume 孔隙体积
pore-pressure depletion 孔隙压力递减
porosity 孔隙度
porous media 多孔介质
porous medium 多孔介质
porous rock 多孔岩石
porous 多孔的
pose 显现出
position 位置
positive value 正值
potential 潜力
predict 做预测
predicted abandonment pressure 预测枯竭压力
prediction 预测
preferential wettability 优先湿润性
preferentially 优选
present 出现
preserve 保存
pressure 压力
pressure coefficient 压力系数
pressure difference 压差
pressure drop 压力降
pressure gradient 压力梯度
pressure maintenance 压力保持
pressure-production performance 生产与压力动态
pressure-temperature diagram 压温图
pressurized fluids 加压流体
prevailing reservoir conditions 主导油气藏条件
prevent 防止
primary drive mechanisms 原(始)驱(动)采油机理
primary pores 一次孔隙
principle 原理
procedure 过程，方法
process 过程
processes 方法
producing rate 生产率
production 采油，生产
productivity 生产力
progress 行进
progressively 渐渐地
prolific 丰富的
property 性质
propose 提出
providing 倘若
publish 发表
pulse testing 脉冲试井
purpose 目的
push 推
PVT（pressure, volume, temperature）压力/体积/温度
quality 质量
quantitatively 定量地
quantity 定额
raise 升高
rare 罕见的
rarely 极少地
rate of flow 流量
ratio of...to... ……与……之间的比率
recommend 推荐
recoverable hydrocarbon fluids 可采油流
recoverable reserves 可采储量
recovery process 采收方法
recovery 采收
reduction 降低
refer to 指的是
region 区域
regionalized variables 区域化变量
relation curve 关系曲线
relationship 关系
relative diagram 相关图
relative permeability 相对渗透率
relatively 相对地
reliable 可信的
reliability 可信度

VOCABULARY

remain 保持
Repeat Formation Tester (RFT) 重复地层测试器
repel 排斥
represent 代表；描述
representing 代表
requirement 要求
reserve parameters 储备参数
reservoir behavior 油层动态
reservoir characteristics 油藏参数
reservoir depletion 油藏衰竭
reservoir depletion scheme 油藏衰竭示意图
reservoir engineering 油藏工程
reservoir heterogeneity 储层非均质性
reservoir performance 油层动态
reservoir properties 油藏性质
reservoir rock 储油岩
reservoir simulation model 油藏模拟模型
reservoir withdrawal 油层产量
reservoir 储层
reside 存在
respectively 分别地
respond to 对……作出反应
response 反应
restate 重申
retain 保持
retrograde gas condensate reservoir 反凝析气藏
robust 强势的
rock facies 岩相
rock layer 岩层
rough surface 粗糙表面
salinity 盐度
salt dome traps 盐丘圈闭
sandstone 砂岩
saturated oil reservoir 饱和油藏
saturated pressure 饱和压力
saturation 饱和度

scf 标准立方英尺
scientific principle 科学原理
seal 密封
secondary pores 二次孔隙
sedimentary rock 沉积岩
sediment 沉积物
seep 油苗
separate...from... 分隔
serious 序列
shale 页岩
shape 形状
sheet-like pore throat 片状孔喉
shringkage 收缩
shut in 关闭
simplify 简化
simulation software 模拟软件
simulator 模拟程序
simultaneously 同时地
skeletal grain 骨骼颗粒
slope 坡(梯)度
smearing 拖尾效应
Society of Petroleum Engineers 石油工程师协会
software 软件
solid surface 固体表面
solubility 溶(解)度
solution 溶解
solution 溶解作用
solution-induced porosity 溶解次生孔隙
solve 求解
solving for... 解出……
sorption isotherms 吸收等温线
source (资)源
span 跨越
spatial continuity 空间连续性
spatial distribution 空间分布
spatial location 空间位置
special features 特性
specialized software 特殊软件
specified 限定的

spherical shape 圆球状
spread on 分布在……
spread over 遍布
spreading tendency 扩散倾向性
stable production 稳定生产
stable 稳定的
stage 阶段
standard nomenclature 标准术语
static gradient diagram 静梯度图
static liquid density inside the bore hole 井眼内静(态)流体密度
static liquid pressure gradient inside the bore hole 井眼内静(态)流体压力梯度
static pressure after shut down 关井后的静压
static temperature 静温
static water column pressure 静水柱压力
STB 标准地面桶
steam flooding 蒸汽驱油
steam soaks 蒸汽浸泡
storage capacity 储量
storage capacity 存储能力
storage geometry 地层形态
storage potential 储藏潜力
straight line 直线
strata 地层
stratigraphic traps 地层圈闭
stress 应力
structural traps 构造圈闭
subdivision 分支
subsequent events 后期事件
subsequent 后期的
subsequently 随后
subsurface geology 地下地质
subtypes 亚类(型)
superhydrophobic surface 超疏水表面
supplement 补充
suppose 假设

surface 地表
surfactant 表面活性剂
surround 围绕
symbols 字符
syncline 向斜(层)
system 系统
tank model (理想)槽式模型
target 目标
task 工作
temperature 温度
tend to 往往,趋向于
tendency 倾向
tens of millidarcies 几十个毫达西
the concept of ……的概念
the contact angle 接触角
the degree of ……的等级
the law of conservation of mass 质量守恒定律
the ratio of... to... 与……(之间)的比率
the three-dimensional geological interpretation 三维地质分析
thickness 厚度
transmit 传送
throat passage 喉道
thrust faulted 冲断
thrust fault trap 冲断层圈闭
thrust and lateral faults 横向冲断
tilled layer 泥砾层
time and space 时间及空间
time-consuming and expensive 耗时耗力
tiny plant 地表植物
total pore space 总孔隙空间
total pore volume 总孔隙体积
total pressure drop 总压力降
total volume 总体积
transfer 转换
translate 解释
transmit 传送
trap 圈闭

treat... as... 把……看作是……
truncation 截顶圈闭
tubular 管状
twophase volume factor at initial reservoir 原始地层两相体积系数
two-phase reservoir 两相驱(动)油藏
type 类型
typically 典型的
ultimate hydrocarbon recovery 最终烃采收率
unconformities 不整合面
unconsolidated 未固结的
underlain 在……之下
undersaturated oil reservoir 欠饱和油藏
uniformity 均匀度
unit 单位
unrealistic 非真实的
utilization 应用
valid 有效
vapor 气体
vapor phase 蒸汽相
variation 变差
various types of 各种类型的
various 多种
vary 变化
varying degrees of 不同程度的
velocity 速率
verify 核实
vertical 竖直的
vertical heterogeneity 垂向非均质性
viscosity 粘度
visual map 视图
void space 空隙
volatile 挥发
vs. 与……相比
vuggy 晶洞的
water compressibility coefficient 水的压缩系数
water compressibility 水的压缩率

(系数)
water drive 水驱
water flooding 注水法
water influx 注水
water wet 水湿
well spacing density 井网密度
wet gas 湿气
wettability 湿润度
wetting characteristics 湿润特性
wetting phase 湿润相
with regard to 关于
with respect to 相对于
within short distances 在短距离之内
yearly rate 年产量
yield 产出
Young's relation 杨氏关系式
zero-dimensional (0-D) model 零维模型
zone of two-phase flow 两相流带(区)
zoning 分带

Chapter 2

a joint (of) 一根
a joint 接头;单根
a set of 一套
a volume of 一定体积的
ability 能力
AC electric power 交流电源
acceleration of gravity 重力加速度
accessible 可进入的
accomplish 完成
accumulator unit 蓄电池组
accurate speed 精确速率
achieve 完成
act as 充当
add 添加
additive 添加剂
adequate 适当的

VOCABULARY

adjust 调节
adsorption 吸附
aggravates 恶化
air source 气源
air 空气
amount 数量
amount of 一定数量的
annular flow path 环状流送通道
annular space 环(形)空(间)
annulus 环空
apply 实施;应用
applying pressure 施加压力
approximately 大约;近似
asphalt 沥青
assemble 组装
assembly 设施
attach 系上
attached to 安装到
auxiliary axle 辅轴
available 适用的
average 平均
backup tongs 卸扣大钳
balance 平衡
barge 驳船
barge rigs 船载钻机
barite (BaSO) 重晶石
based on 基于
be connected to 连接到
be determined by 由……决定
be made up of 由……组成
be rated as 分类为
be wound around 缠绕在……
bearing crown block (轴承)天车
bearing seal 轴承密封
beneath 在……正下方
bentonite clay 斑脱土
bentonite 膨润土
bit 钻头
blend 混合物
block diagram 方框图
block 堵塞

blowout preventer (BOP) stack 防喷器组
blowout 井喷
borehole 井眼
braid 编辫
brake 闸;刹车
break into 破碎成
break the gel 破凝
break 折断
breaking out 松扣
bridges 架桥
bridging agents 搭桥剂
brittle shales 脆页岩
button bit 镶齿钻头
cable-tool drilling 顿钻钻井
cake 泥饼
calcium carbonate 碳酸钙
calcium chloride 氯化钙
calcium 钙
cantilevered mast 悬臂式井架
carbon dioxide 二氧化碳
casing 套管
catastrophic failure 严重事故,突然失效
category 类别;目录
cathead 猫头
cat shaft 猫头轴
cause 引发
cave in 坍塌
centrifugal force 离心力
centrifuge 离心机
certain degree 某种程度
certain type of 某种类型
chemical composition 化学组分
chemical differences 化学药品的差异
chemical 化学物质
chemicals 化学药品
chip 钻屑
choke manifold 节流管汇
circular component 螺旋流送物

circular 圆形
circulation 循环
circumstances(周边)环境
clamp 卡住
clay 粘土
coefficient of friction 摩擦系数
combination 合成物
combine 复合
combined assembly 复合设备
common 普通
compare 比较
complete 完成
completion fluids 完井液
complicated 复杂的
component 组件
compressed 压缩的
concentration 浓度
concept 概念
condition(s) 条件
conduct a test 做试验
conductor pipe 导管
cone 牙轮
confirm 确认
conservative 守恒的
consists of 包含
constitute 构成
contact 接触
content 含量
continuous spool 卷(动)轴
continuous 连续的
cooling and lubricating of equipment 设备冷却及润滑
corresponding opening 对应开口
corrosion 腐蚀
corrosion coupons 腐蚀取样器
cost 费用
create 创造,生成
crown block 天车
crush 粉碎
curved pipe 弯管
cutting edge 切削刃

215

damage 破坏
dead line 死绳
dead-line anchor 死绳固定器
debris 碎屑
decrease 下降
degasser 除气器
density of drilling fluid 钻井液密度
density 密度
depend 依靠
depending on 依据
deposite 沉积
derrick 井架
desander 除砂器
design 设计
desilter 除泥器
detect 检测
determine 确定
detonater 雷管
detrimental 有害物
device 设备
diameter 直径
diamond bit 金刚石钻头
diesel engine 柴油机
diesel fuel 柴油
dilution 稀释
disconnect 卸扣
dispersed 扩散的
dissolved gases 溶解气
doghouse 值班室
double pumps 双泵
drag 拖拽
drawworks drum 绞车转鼓
drawworks 绞车
drill collars 钻铤
drill line 钢丝绳
drillship 钻井船
drill solids 钻屑
driller console 司控台
driller 司钻
drilling assembly 钻具组合
drilling floor 钻台

drilling fluid 钻井液
drilling line 钢丝绳
drilling mud weight 钻井液比重
drilling parameters 钻井参数
drilling program 钻井程序
drilling rate of penetration 钻井穿透速率
drilling stem 钻柱
drillpipe section 钻具总成
drillpipe 钻杆
drillship 钻井船
drill-string 钻杆
drum brake (绞车) 主刹车
drum 转鼓
dry mud components storage 干浆储备装置
dump 倾卸
dust 尘埃
effectiveness 有效性
efficiency 效益
electric driven rotary 电动转盘
electrical power 电力
electricity 电气
elevator 吊卡
embed 嵌入
emulsified brine phase 乳化盐水
emulsion 乳浊液
enclosed space 封闭空间
end cutting tool 端面切削工具
engine 引擎
enhance 增强
enlarge 扩大
environment (地理) 环境
environmental considerations 环保理由
equal to 等于
equipment 设备
evaluate 评价
exceed 超出
exert 施加
exploration 勘探

extremely 及其
fast line 快绳
feature 特有功能；优点
fill 填充
filter cake 浆饼
filter 过滤器
fine particles 细小颗粒
fire drill 消防演习
fit 适合
fit into 嵌入
flake away 剥落
flat-sided kelly 四面方钻杆
flow line 流送管线
flow rate gauge 流量计
flow rate torque 转矩
fluid fume 流体蒸发气
flush 冲刷
foaming 起泡
foaming agent 发泡剂
for this reason 由于此原因
force 强迫，施力于
form 形成，形状
formation evaluation 地层评价
formation matrix 地层基质
formation pressure 地层压力
formulated 列出
fracture 裂缝
free-flowing state 自由流送状态
frequently 频繁地
function 功能
gaseous drilling fluid 气化钻井液
gel 凝胶
generate 发电；产生
generator 发电机
geotechnical engineering 岩土工程
gilsonite 黑沥青
glycols 乙二醇
gooseneck 鹅颈管
grip 夹住
ground cellulose
hang suspended 吊装

VOCABULARY

hardness formation 硬地层
height 高度
helical flow 涡流,螺旋流
helicopter 直升机
high-pressure hose 高压软管
hoisting system 举升系统
homogenous 均质的
hook load 大钩负荷
hook 大钩
hydraulic break system 液压制动系统
hydraulic energy 液压能
hydraulic forces 湍流力
hydraulics system 水力系统
hydrogen sulfide 硫化氢
hydrostatic pressure 流体静压
improve 改善
in combination with 联合
incorporate 合并
in position 就位
in practice 实践上讲
in rate of 以……的速率
in turn 依次
inch 英寸
incorporated 加入
increase 增加
induction motors 感应电机
influx 注入
information 信息
inhibitor 抑制剂
insoluble salts 非脂肪盐
instability 不稳定性
instruments 仪表
interactions 相互作用
intermediate casing 技术套管
invade 侵入
involve 包含
jackknife 折叠式井架
jack-up or self-elevating rigs 自升式钻机
journal bearing 径向轴承

kelley 方钻杆
kelly bushing 方钻杆补心
kelly cock 方钻杆旋塞
key seating 钻具卡槽
kick 井涌
kill material 压井材料
kink 扭折
land 陆地
large opening 大开口
larger-diameter 大直径
leading to 导致
level sensor 液面传感器
lime polymer mud system 钙质聚合物泥浆
limit 限制
log 测井
loosen 松扣
lost circulation 井漏
low annular velocities 低环空粘度
low density mud 低密度泥浆
low pH (acidic) 低pH(酸度)值
low-maintenance 低维修率
lubricant reservoir 润滑油箱
lubricate 润滑
lubricity 润滑能力
LWD (logging while drilling) 随钻录井
main categories 主要分类
main functions of ……的主要功能
maintain wellbore stability 保持井眼稳固
maintaining 维修
maintenance costs 维修费用
major 主要的
majority 大多数
make reference to 涉及
makeup tongs 上扣大钳
making a joint (connection) 接单根
making a trip 起下钻
malt 麦芽
master bushing 主补心

material 物料
maximum density 最高密度
mechanical action 机械作用
mechanical brake 机械制动
mechanical force 机械力
mechanism 机理
method 方法
minimizing 极小化
minimum 最小值
mist 气雾
mixture 混合物
modern 现代的
monitor 监控
monkey board 二层平台
mousehole 大鼠洞
mud aeration 泥浆充气
mud cleaning equipment 泥浆净化设备
mud column 泥浆柱
mud filtrate 泥浆滤液
mud hog 浆泵
mud parameters 泥浆参数
mud pit 泥浆池
mud program 泥浆设计
mud properties 泥浆特性
mud property 泥浆性能
mud pump 泥浆泵
mud recorder 泥浆记录仪
mud return line 泥浆返还管线
mud solids size 泥浆固化物多少
mud system 泥浆系统
mud tanks (pits) 泥浆池
mud weight 钻井液密度(比重)
mud-gas separator 泥浆-气体分离器
multipoint 多(端)点
must 桅杆式井架
MWD (measure while drilling) 随钻测井
native clays 天然粘土
native rock 原生岩
natural gas wells 天然气井

necessary 必要
non-aqueous muds 非水基泥浆
non-dispersed 非扩散的
nozzles velocities 水眼流速
O_2 trapped condition 氧气滞留（条件）
occur 产生
offshore rigs 海上钻机
off-shore 海上
oil-based mud 油基泥浆
on trips 起下钻
onshore rigs 陆地钻机
osmotic forces 渗透力
overbalance 过平衡
oxygen 氧气
parameter 参数
particles 颗粒
pay zone 产层
penetration 钻穿
performance 操作特性
permanently 永久地
permeability 渗透率
pH fluids 钻井液pH值
pick up 拉起
pin 锁销
pinned together 拼装到一起
pipe joints 管柱接头
pipe rack 管架桥
pipe ramp（运管）坡道
place 地点
plan 计划
plastic viscosity 塑性粘度
polymer fluids 聚合物钻井液
polymer 聚合物
pop off valve 地压阀销
pore spaces 空隙空间
pore throats 毛管孔
portability 可携带
portion of 一部分
position 方位
potassium formate 甲酸钾

potassium 钾
power system 动力系统
power 动力
precipitation 沉淀
precision 精确度
prefabricated sections 预制部件
pressure 压力
pressure gradient 压力梯度
pressure pulse 压力脉冲
pressure-tight system 密闭系统
pressure-tight 压力密闭
prevent 防止
previously 先前地
procedures 方法；过程
processed and sold 加工销售
production casing 生产套管
property 特性
provide 提供，假设
pull up 提升
pump pressure gauge 泵压计
pump pressure 泵压
pumping force 泵送压力
quality 质量
quantity 数量
quiet 静默
rathole 小鼠洞
re-circulated 反复循环
reduce 降低
reel 卷轴
refer to 指的是
relatively 相对地
rely on 依赖
removal 除掉
replace 替换
require 要求
resembling 就好像
reserve pit 泥浆储备池
resist 抵制
respectively 分别地
responsibility 责任
responsive 灵敏的

resume 恢复
rig floor 钻台
roller bearing 滚动轴承
rotary gauge 转速表
rotary hose 水龙带
rotary rig 旋转钻机
rotary speed 转速
rotary table 转盘
rotary tongs 大钳
rotation 转动
rotating spool 转鼓
rotating system 旋转系统
rotational viscosimeter 旋转粘度计
routinely 常规地
rub 摩擦
running casing 下套管
sag 滞留物
salt 盐
sample trap 岩粉收集器
sand content 含沙量
screens out 筛选出
screw into 旋入
seal of permeable formations 透水地层的密封
seal 密封
semisubmersible rigs 半潜式钻机
set 装置
shale inhibition 页岩抑制性
shale shaker 振动筛
shale 页岩
shale stability 页岩稳定性
shallow 浅
shear thinning drilling fluids 剪切稀释钻井液
similar 相似的
situations 位置条件
six-sided 六面体
skin damage 表皮破坏
skin effect 表皮效应
slipped 滑动
slow pump stroke test 低泵速泵冲试验

smaller pieces 细小物
softening 软化
solid 固化物
solid content 固体成分
solid mud particles 固体泥浆颗粒
solids control equipment 固相控制设备
solids loading 固化物载荷
special considerations 特殊理由
special valve 特种阀
specific 特定的
speed 速度
spool 转轴
stabilize 使稳定
stable 稳定的
stack 堆栈
stand pipe 立管
static fluid 静液
steel cable 钢缆
steel pin 钢销
stiff foam 静止泡沫
storage spool (reel) 储线卷轴
store 贮存
stress 应力; 紧张
structure rigs 组装式钻机
structure 构造
stuck pipe 卡钻
stuck-pipe 管道堵塞
submersible rigs 潜式钻机
subnormal 亚正常
subset 分支
substructure 底座
suction pit 吸浆池
suction tank 吸入罐
sufficient 充足的
suit 适合
sulfide scavenging chemical 清硫化学药品
support 支撑
supporting 支持
surface casing 表层套管

surrounding rock 围岩
surrounding 周围的
suspend 悬挂
suspended drillpipe 钻杆悬挂
suspension 悬挂
swelling of formation clays 地层粘土膨胀
swivel 水龙头
symptom 征兆
synthetic oil 合成油
synthetic polymer 合成聚合物
synthetic-based fluid 合成基泥浆
system 系统
tectonic force 构造作用力
term 术语
thief zoon 漏失层
thin 稀薄
thread 缠绕; 螺纹
tight hole 井径缩小
tighten 系(扣)紧
tool 工具
torque control 扭矩控制
torque gauge 扭矩仪
torque 扭矩
total depth 完钻井深
toxicity 毒性
transfer 传送
transmit 输送
transport regions 传送区
trap 捕集
traveling block 游动滑车
tricone bit 三牙轮钻头
trip 起下钻
trouble shooting 故障排除
trouble 故障
true vertical depth 真垂向井深
tungsten carbide buttons 钨合金钻头
turn 转动
type 类型
types of drilling fluid 钻井液类型;
typical 典型的

unexpect 没预料到
unit 单位
valve 阀门
variety 广泛
various 各种
vast 广阔的
vast majority 绝大多数
vertical movement 竖直方向运动
vertical position 竖直位置
vertical 垂直的
via 通过
vibrating screen 振动筛
viscosity control 粘度控制
viscosity 粘度
washout 冲蚀
water loss 失水
water sensitive formations 水敏感地层
water storage 储水罐
Water-based Mud (WBM) 水基泥浆
wear 磨损
wearing out time 磨损期
weight indicator 指重表
weight material 重物
weight materials 加重材料
weight on bit 钻压
well control 井控
wellbore 井眼
well spacing density 井网密度
withdraw 抽(拉)出
withstand 耐受
workover 修井
workpiece 工作面
workspace 作业空间
worn bit 已磨损钻头
wrap 缠绕
zinc 锌

Chapter 3

abandon 废弃

according to 根据
actual steel strength 实际钢质强度
adaptor 转换接头
additional amount 附加量
adds to 增加
affect 影响
amount 数量
anchor...in place 固定到位
annular clearance 环空间隙
annular steel tube 环空钢管
annulus 环空
assemble 安装
at a rate of 以……的速率
at the top end of 在……上顶端
attachment 附件
average 平均
barrel 桶
basic requirement 基本要求
be identified by 通过……识别
bit sizes 钻头尺寸
blowout preventer（BOP）防喷器组
body 管体
bond...to... 将……固定到……
borehole face 井壁
borehole 井眼
bottom 底部
box(coupling) 管箍
break 破裂
case 案例
casing length 套管长度
casing shoe 套管鞋
casing size 套管尺寸
casing string 套管柱
casing 套管
cave in 坍塌
cavy 易坍塌的
cellar 圆井
cement 水泥
cement displacement 水泥驱替
cement head 水泥头
cement plug 水泥塞

cement slurry 水泥浆
cement top 水泥面
cementing 注水泥
cementing chemical 固井药品
cementing engineering flow diagram 固井流程图
cementing engineering 固井工程
cementing head 固井水泥头
cementing job 固井作业
cementing line 固井管线
cementing operation 固井操作
centralized string of casing 同心管柱
certain depth 一定深度
certain value 定值
check valve 止回阀
chemical 化学药品
check 检查
choke ring 阻流环
circulating 循环
classify 分类
collapse 折断
collapsing 破裂
common lengths 通用长度
compare 比较
completely 完全地
complicated formation 复杂地层
conduit 导管
connection 接头
consist of 包含
constant 常数
control 控制
conventional 常规
corrosion 腐蚀
cost 费用
coupling 接箍
critical operation 临界操作
cross flow 窜流
density 密度
designed depth 设计深度
device 设备
difference 差异

dimensions and strengths of casing 套管尺寸及强度
directional drilling 钻定向井
displace 替浆
displacement of the slurry with drilling fluids 用钻井液替浆
displacement 替浆
double pump 双泵
drilling fluids 钻井液
economical 经济的
encounter 遭遇
exert 施加
external force 外力
extra 额外的
fabricate 制做
factory 工厂
female connector 母扣
fill up 填满
fill 填充
fix 安装，固定
flatten 压扁
float collar 浮箍
formation pressure 地层压力
formation test 地层测试
formation testing 地层测试
fresh water formation 净水层
fresh water 清水
function 功能
further 进一步
gel 凝胶
generally 一般地
go up 上升
grade 等级
guide shoe 引鞋
hardware 固体填充物
high viscosity gel 高粘度胶液
high-pressure line 高压管线
hold on 保持
hollow 中空的
hydrocarbon zone 油气层
identify 识别

VOCABULARY

immediately 马上
in case that 以防
in case 以防
in position 到位
indicate 表明
inject 注入
inner side 套管内部
inside capacity of the casing 套管内容积
inside diameter(ID) 内径
install 安装
integral sheath 水泥环
interpolation cementing head 插入头
interpolation cementing 插入式固井
isolate 隔离
joint 接头
keep away from 远离
key procedure 关键过程
leaking formations 渗漏地层
leaky 渗漏的
load 负荷
loose 松软的
lost circulation 井漏
lost circulation control 井漏控制
lower rubber plug 下胶塞
main type 主要类型
make up 接上
making the connection 接单根
male connector 公扣
measure 测定
mechanically 机械地
migration 运移
mix the chemicals 混合药品
mixture 混合物
mud pump 浆泵
obtain 常常选用
occur 发生
on each end 在两端
on site 在现场
operation 操作
outside diameter(OD) 外径

part 部件
per foot 每英尺
per-foot basis 以每英尺计(算)
perforate 射孔
perform 实施
pin（阳螺纹端）管销
pipeline 管线
plug-cementing 柱塞式固井
plug 柱塞
point 接点
possible failure 可能破裂
pounds per foot（lb/ft）磅/平方英尺
ppg（pound per gallen）磅/加仑
prefer 挑选
prepare 制备
pressure gage 压力表
prevent 防止
primary cementing procedure 一次固井过程
primary cementing process 一次固井方法
principal objective 主要目标
process 过程
programmed slurry weight 配制好的水泥浆比重
property 性能
protect 保护
provide 实施
psi（pound per square inch）磅/平方英寸
pump the slurry 泵送水泥浆
pump 泵
purpose 目的
pushing...out 将……挤出
put the rubber plug into the cementing head 将胶塞放入水泥头内
range 范围
rapidly 快速地

reach 到达
reinforce 增强
release sign 释放标志
release the pressure 泄压
remedy job 补救工作
require 需要
restrict 限制
rig foundation 钻机底座
rock salt 石岩
rotary hose 水龙带
rubber membrane 橡皮膜
running casing 下套管
screw together 扣接在一起
screw-type connectors 丝扣
seal off 封隔
seat 坐在……上
seating the rubber plug 使胶塞坐在上面
secondary cementing process 二次固井过程(方法)
select 选择
separate 分隔
separately 分别地
set cement plug 下水泥塞
set 下(套管)
setting the casing 下套管
shale shaker 振动筛
shock load 冲击载荷
shrinking layer 缩孔层
signal 标志
slurry 水泥浆
solid 实心的
solidify 固化
solve 解决
spacer fluid 隔离液
specific intervals 特定区段
squeeze cementing 挤压式固井
squeezing pressure 碰压
stand(s) 钻杆
steel casing 钢管
stream 油流

strokes per minute 冲程/每分钟
supply 供应
support 支撑
surface pressure 井口压力
take place 进行
tank 泥浆罐(槽)
tensile strength 抗张强度
the casing weight 套管重量
the joint of casing 套管接头
the top of cement 水泥面
thief zones 漏失层
tool 工具
top cementing 顶部固井
trouble 问题
tube 管体
tubing 油管
typical 典型的
union 由壬接头
unpack the backing pin of the lower rubber plug 打开下胶塞的底销
unpack the backing pin of upper rubber plug 打开上胶塞的底销
unpredicted 没预料到的
unscrew the circulating head 卸下套管循环头
upper rubber plug 上胶塞
vary 变化
vertical movement 竖直移动
vertical 竖直的
viscosity 粘度
vital 必要的
wait on cement 候凝
water slurry samples 水泥浆样
weight 重量
well head 井头
zone 层,带

Chapter 4

a broad view of 展望

a jet of 喷射流
a variation 变量
accurately 精确地
afford 给予,提供
aim 目标
assembly 装置
associated 相关的
at the same time 同时
attach...to 连接到……
be accomplished by 用……完成
be considered as 被认为是
be different from 不同于
be equipped with 装配有
be linked to 与……有联系
be restricted to 受限于
be suitable for 适合于
blast 爆炸
blasting cap detonator 点火雷管
borehole face 井壁
build up 恢复,建立
bullet 子弹
cap detonator 帽式引爆装置
case 火药箱
cased hole completion 下套管完井
cause no problems 无引发问题
cement sheath 水泥环
cemented casing 封隔套管
cemented liner 封隔尾管
cementing job 固井作业
ceramic case 陶瓷引爆室
charge 装料
circulating device 循环装置
classify 分类
closed ports 封闭式弹仓
commonly 普通地
completion 完井
complex 复杂
complicate 使复杂
complicated 复杂的
connection 连接
consist of 包含

consolidate 加固,压实
conventional completion 常规完井
conventional single-zone completion 常规单区完井
cross section 剖面图
cut away of a hollow cylindrical steel carrier 射孔枪架剖面图
depending on 依据
design 设计
designed depth 设计深度
detonating cord 导火索
detonator 雷管
develop 开发
diameter 直径
differ 不同于
directional explosions 定向爆破
disintegrate on firing 爆炸分解
double-zone completions 二层完井
downhole tools 井下工具
downhole equipment 井下设备
drilling phase 钻井阶段
dual packer 双封隔器
due to 由于
effectively 有效地
effluent seepage area 渗出区(域)
electric current 电流
electric detonator 电雷管
enclose 包含
ending in 末端至
energy consumption 能量消耗
equipment 设备
exist 存在
expendable gun 销毁式射孔枪
expendable gun with frangible aluminum charge case 配有生铝弹仓的销毁式射孔枪
experience 经历
explosive charge 火药
fire 爆破
flow rate 流量
form 形状,形式

VOCABULARY

frangible aluminum 生铝
fundamental characteristic 基本特性
gas breakthrough (GBT) 气窜入井
geological characters 地质特性
gravel pack 砾石充填
hanging tubing 尾管悬挂
high-energy gases and particles 高能气体颗粒
hollow-carrier 射孔器枪身
hydrocarbon reservoir 油藏
hydrocarbon zones 油层
ignite 点火
in case of 以防止
in comparison with 与……相比较
in conjunction with 与……协力
in order to 为了
in relation to 关于
in terms of 根据
in this way 用这种方法
individual well 单井
initial investment 最初投资
installation 安装
intense 强烈的
interface 界面
interface problems 界面问题
intermediate casing 技术套管
involve 包含
isolate 隔绝
isolate zones 绝缘区
jet perforating 聚能射孔
kill string 压井管柱
known as 称为
landing nipple for plug 用于填塞的定位短节
leading to 导致
lift 举升
limestone reservoirs 石灰岩油藏
limit 限度
liner 衬垫；尾管
liner hanger 尾管挂
long string 长管柱

lower end 下端
lower perforated reservoir 下射孔油层
low-pressure formations 低压地层
main explosive charges 主爆炸药
maintenance 维修
make the correct decision 作出正确决定
master 掌控
mediocre production 中等产量
metal case 金属箱体
metal strip carriers 金属条托架
methods 方法
minimize 减少
multiple 多……；复杂
multiple-zone completion 多区完井
multiple-zone tubing-less completion 多区无油管完井
neutralize 中和
obtain 获得
oil layer 油层
on the other hand 另一方面
open-hole completion 裸眼完井
open-hole gravel packing 裸眼砾石充填
opposite 在……之上
optimum condition 最佳条件
packer 封隔器
packing device 充填设备
parallel dual string completion 并行双油管完井
parallel string completions with two tubings 双油管并行完井
pay zone 产油层
penetrate 穿透
perforated casing 有孔套管
perforated completion 射孔完井
perforating charge carriers 射孔弹仓
perforating gun 射孔枪
perforation intervals 射孔间隔
pierce 钻穿

port plug 射孔塞
position 位置
positioned 定位
preceding 先前的
precisely 精密地
pressure drops 压力降
prevent...from ……防止
primer 引信
procedure 过程，方法
proceed 着手进行
process 方法，过程
production casing 生产套管
production liner 生产尾管
production packer 采油封隔器
production strings 生产管线
production tubing 生产尾管
proper perforating 正确射孔
protect 防护
quality 品质
rarely 很少地
rather than 胜于
relative 相关的
relatively 相对应地
rely on 依靠
replace 更换
require 要求
required specifications 所要求的技术指标
reservoir conditions 油藏条件
reservoir fluids 储层流体
reservoir perforation 油层射孔
restore 再生
retrieve 补偿，回收
retrievable hollow carrier guns 回收式射孔枪
sand control 防沙
schematic 示意图
scientifically 科学地
screen 筛网
secondarily 其次
selectivity 选择性

semiexpendable gun with wire strip carrier 配有引爆线托架的半销毁式射孔枪
semiexpendable guns 半销毁式射孔枪
separate 不同的
set 下（套管）
set off 发射
shape 形状
shaped charges 固体炸药
shaped-charge gun 固体炸药发射装置
sheath 水泥环
shoot 射孔
short string 短管柱
similarly 同样地
simplicity 简单
single packer 单封隔器
single tubing 单尾管
single-zone 单区
single-zone tubing-less completion 单区无油管完井
special explosive charges 特种炸药
specific 特定的，单位的
steel 钢制
steel carrier 钢架
stimulating 增产
subsequent 随后的
surface casing 表层套管
technical requirement 技术要求
technique 技术
the producing formation 产油层
theoretically 理论上的
triple completion 三层完井
trouble free 无故障
tubing-annulus completion 油管-环空完井
tubing-less completion 无油管完井
tubing strings 油管柱
type 类型
unrestricted 自由的，不受限制的

upper perforated reservoir 上射孔油层
utilize 使用
valid 有效
various 各种各样的
velocity 流速
water break through（WBT）水窜入井
wellbore 井眼
whereas 而，鉴于
wire screen 筛网
wire-wrapped Screen completion 绕丝筛管完井
with respect to 相对于
workover jobs 修井作业
workover operations 修井操作
wrap 包，缠绕

Chapter 5

a certain extent 某种程度
a finite volume of 有限的容积（体积）
a limited number of 有限的数量
a maximum oil recovery 最高油采收率
a minimum of produced water 最低产水率
a number of 一定数量的
a quantity of 一些
a rapid pressure decline 快速压力衰减
a slug of 一段，一股
a special case of 一个……的特例
a unit volume of 一个单位的体积（容积）
a wide variety of 广袤的
accumulation-and-migration process 累积、迁移过程
achieve 完成

acid 酸
act on 作用于
adding costs 增加费用
additional 附加的
address 处理
adequate production 足量生产
adjoin 毗邻
advanced form of steam stimulation 蒸汽吞吐的高级形式
aeration 充气
affect 影响
aforementioned 上述的
agitate 搅拌
ahead of 在……前
aid 援助
alcohol 乙醇
allow 允许
alter 升高，改造
alternative enhanced oil recovery mechanisms 提高采收率的变通机理
alternative method 变通方法
anticipate 预先处理预期
any four injection wells 任意四口注入井
application 设备
approach 方法
appropriate 适当的，合理的
approximately reservoir pressure 油藏压力近似值
aquifer geometries 含水层几何尺寸
aquifer 含水层
arrangement 布局，安排
artesian water drive 自流水驱
artificial drive 人工驱油
artificial recovery method 人工采收方法
as a result of 作为结果
associated with 与……有关
assume 假定
at some point 在某一区段

VOCABULARY

at the corner of 在……的拐角处
at the desired rate 以所需速率
at the edge of 在……的边缘
at the middle of each side of the square 在正四边形的四个边线中间
attractive 有吸引力的
availability 利用率有效性
back pressure 背压
bacteria 细菌
bacterial cultures 细菌培养物
be bounded by 束缚于
be bounded on 束缚在
be characterized by 通过……表示出……的特性
be converted into 转换成
be directly opposed to 直接对立于,与……相抵
be displaced by 被……替换
be divided into 划分成
be equal to 等于
be identified by 通过……加以识别
be in equilibrium 处于均衡状态
be insensitive to 对……反应迟钝
be large enough 足够大
be opposed to 反对对立于
be projected to 达到了……的预期效果
be referred to by 表述为
be similar to 与……相似
be subjected to 受……的支配（影响）
be trapped in 滞留于……
beam pumps 游梁泵
beneath 在……之下
beneficial effect 有效作用
best available data 现有最佳数据
biosurfactants 生物表面活性剂
bitumen 沥青
blends of 混有
bottom water 底水

bottom-hole pressure 地层压力
break down 打破出故障
breakthrough 突破, 穿过
bubble-point pressure 泡点压力
buildup of a liquid column 液柱压力恢复
bypass 旁路, 侧通
by various means 由于各种原因
capillary pressure 毛细管压力
carbon dioxide 二氧化碳
category 类别目录索引
cause 原因引发
caustic flooding 碱水驱油
chemical flooding process 化学驱油法
chemical injection 化学剂注入
chemical 化学药品
christmas tree 采油树
close to 接近于
closed（volumetric）unit 封闭（立体）单元
cogeneration plant 热电厂
combination drive 混合驱
combination 联合
combustion front 燃烧前缘(峰)
common 共同的, 普通的
commonly 通用地
compare to 比作
compare with 与……相比
completing ignition 实施点火
complex arrangement of valves（采油树）组阀
component 组分
compressibility 可压缩性
concentration 浓度
concentric tubing string 同心管柱
conceptually 理论上
concurrently 并发的, 并行的
condensed water 冷凝水
conduct 传导, 导出
congealment 凝结, 冷却

connate water 原生水
connect...to... 将……连接到……上
consists of 包含
constant 常数
consume 消耗
contact 接触
contain 包含
content 内含物
countercurrent 逆流
continuous air injection 连续注空气
continuous flow gas lift 连续流动气举
contribute to 有助于
control 控制
conventional methods 惯例, 常规方法
convert 转换
countercurrent 逆流
create 创造产生
cross section view 剖面图
crude oil 原油
crystal and basal injection patterns 顶部注气、底部注水模式
curtailed 消减
cyclic steam stimulation (CSS) process 周期注蒸汽增产法
decline 降低, 下降
decrease 减少
density 密度
depleted 衰竭的
depletion drive 溶解气驱
deposits 沉积(物)
describe 描述
design 设计
desire 要求
detergents 洗涤剂, 去污剂
determine 决定
difference 差异
differential thermal expansion 热膨胀差异

· 225 ·

digest 消化，蒸煮
diminish 缩减
direct line drive 直线驱
directional permeability 定向渗透率
displace 驱替
displacing fluids 置换液
dissolve 溶解
distance between lines of injectors and producers 注入井及生产井之间的直线距离
distance between wells of the same type 同类井之间的距离
downhole valve 井下阀
drainage 排驱，排水设备
drilhead 井底
driving force 驱动力
driving mechanism 驱动机型
due to 由于
due to the fact that 基于……的事实
duty 职责
economic 经济的
edge water 边缘水
effects 效果
efficient 有效的
electric heater 电热器
electric submersible centrifugal pumps 电动潜水泵
Electro-Thermal Dynamic Stripping Process（ET-DSP）电热式动力洗提方法
eliminate 消除
emit 逸出，排放
encounter 碰撞遭，遇
enhanced oil recovery（EOR）提高采收率
enriched gas process 富气驱油法
ensure 保证
entirely 全部地
equal to 等于
equilibrium 均衡
essentially 本质上

evaporation front 汽化前缘
even production 平稳生产
evidence （通过）……证实
excellent review of the peripheral flood 边缘注水最佳效果
exist 存在
expand 膨胀
expansion 膨胀
expansion of the individual rock grains 个体岩石颗粒膨胀
experience 经历，经验
exploitation 开发
extensively 广泛地
exteriors 外部的
external boundary 外边界
external energy 外部能量
extra injection well 附加注入井
extra 额外的
extract 提取，抽提
extraction method 抽提法，萃取法
extraction rate 萃取率
factor 因素，系数
fall 下降
fatty acid 脂肪酸
faulting and localized variations 断层及局部变化
fill up 充满
five-spot 五点（井网）
flank 侧翼
flood life 注水开发阶段
flood pattern 注采井网
fluid column 液体柱
fluid density 流体密度
fluid injection 流体注入
force 强制力
form a square 形成一个正方形
form 形状，形成
formation compaction 地层压实
formation of a miscible phase 混相地层
formation permeability 地层渗透率

fracture 裂缝
free gas 游离气，自由气
fuel 燃料
gain 获得，增益
gas bubbles 气泡
gas burner 天然气燃烧器
gas cap drive reservoir 气顶驱油藏
gas cap drive 气顶驱动
gas injection 注气
gas lift 气举
gas turbine 燃气轮机
gas-oil ratio 油气比
gene mutation 基因突变
generate 发生，产生
generic term 专业术语
gravitational forces 重力作用
gravity 重力
gravity drainage drive 重力驱油
gravity driven drainage 重力排放
gravity segregation 重力分层，重力分选
heat utilization 热利用率
heterogeneity 非均质性
hexagon 正六边形
high-power ultrasonic vibrations 大功率超声波震动
high-pressure lean gas process 高压干气法
high-pressure steam processes 高压闪蒸法
high-viscosity fluids 高粘度流体
high-viscosity oil 高粘度油
horizontal 水平的
huffand puff 蒸汽吞吐
hydraulic pumps 液压泵
hydrocarbon chain 烃链
hydrogen sulfide 硫化氢
hydrophilic 亲水的
hydrostatic column 静液柱
identical 同形异构
identify 鉴定，标识

VOCABULARY

ignite 点火
illustrate 图解
immiscible fluids 不互溶流体
immiscible 不互溶的
impede 阻碍
impermeable rock 不渗透岩层
imply 隐含表达
in addition to 除……之外还……
in general 一般地
in some cases 在一些情况下
in some degree 在某种程度上
in the form of 以……的形式
in turn 反过来
include 包含
increase 增加
indicate 表明
individual compressibility 个体可压缩性
inefficient 无效的
inefficient process 无效的方法
infinite 无限的
influx 注入
initial fluids distribution 原始流体分布
initially 最初的
inject 注入
injection patterns 注入网
injection point 注入点
injection rates 注入率
injection well 注入井
injection-production well arrangements 注入-生产井布局
injectivity 注入能力
injector 注入井
insensitive 不灵敏的
in-situ combustion 火烧油层
instability 不稳定性
installation 安装
insufficient 不够的
insulating heat blanket 隔热带
interior 内部

intermittent gas lift 间歇气举
invading water 驱替水
inverted nine-spot 反九点（井网）
investigator 调查人员
involved in 包含在内
irregular 不规则的
irregular injection patterns 不规则注入井网
ISC approach 火烧油层法
jar 罐
lack of 缺乏
lead to 导致
lean gas and water 干气与水
least efficient 最低效的
liberation 释放
liquid hydrocarbon slug 液态氢流体
liquid hydrocarbons 液态氢
located 位于
long periods of time 很长一段时间
low pressure steam 低压蒸汽
low-gravity oil 低比重油
"macaroni" string 小直径管
maintain 维持，保持
manage 管理
map view 俯视图
marginal 边缘的
maximum 最大的
mechanical device 机械装置
mechanism 机理
melting point 熔点
metabolize 使……新陈代谢
methane 甲烷
microbes 微生物
microbial enhanced oil recovery 微生物强化采油
microbial injection 注入微生物
microbial treatments 微生物处理
microscopic pore spaces 微观孔隙空间
migrate 运移
miscibility 混相能力，混溶性

miscible front 混相前缘
miscible phase 混相
miscible slug process 混相段塞驱油法
mixture 混合
mobility 流动性
mobilizing 使……流动
molasses 糖浆
movement 运动
moving the location of injection wells frequently 频繁地改变注入井的方位
multilateral wells 多边井
mutual solvent process 互溶剂法
natural drive mechanisms 自然驱动机理
near-shutdown mode 近关井状态
negligible 可忽略的
nitrogen 氮
non-uniform pattern 不均匀井网
normal nine-spot 正九点（井网）
nurture 培育
nutrient 养分
objective 目标
occasionally 偶然地
occupied by 被……占据
occur 发生
oil bank 集油带
oil leases 油租赁（合同）
oil mass 油量
oil producing wells 产油井
oil swelling 油膨胀
oil zone 油区
original condition 原始状态
otherwise 否则
out crop of sand 砂岩露出
over the distance of several well spacings 越过若干井距
over the lifetime of 在……的使用期间
overall 所有的

oxygen 氧气
paraffin chains 链烷烃链
paraffin components 链烷烃组分
parameters 参数
partially 部分地
past 越过
patented process 已获专利的方法
patterns 井网
patterns termed inverted （定义为）反井网
percentage 百分率
performance 特性
peripheral flooding 边缘水驱，环状注水
peripheral flooding 边缘水驱
peripheral injection patterns 边缘注水井网
periphery 边缘，外围
permit 允许
petroleum derivatives 石油衍化物
phase behavior 相态特性
piezoelectric vibration unit 压电振动器
pipeline network 管道系统
piston-like displacement of liquid slugs 活塞式流体驱替
place a rest 静置
plague 严重影响
play an important role in 扮演重要角色
plunger lift 活塞气举
polymer flooding process 聚合物驱油法
polymer slug 聚合物段塞瓶
polymer solution 聚合物溶液
pool 油区
pore space 孔洞，孔腔
pore volume 有效孔隙体积
portion 部分
possible 可能
potential problems 潜在的问题

practical purposes 实际目的
practice 实施
precisely 精确地
presence 存在
present 出现
pressure-driven steam process 加压蒸汽驱油法
pressure dedine 压力下降
previously 先前的
primary recovery 一次采油
processing 处理，加工
produce fluids 产出流体
production stream 采出液流
production tubing 生产油管
productivity 生产力，生产率
profitably 有利地
progressive cavity pump 螺杆泵
project 方案，设计
propel 推动
propagation 蔓延;传播
propose 提出
provide 提供
push...out of... 将……推出……
quarter square miles 四分之一平方英里
quaternary recovery 四次采油
raise 举升，提高
range 范围
range from...to... 由……到……的范围内（变化）
rapid 快速的
rarely 极少地
react 反应
receive attention 引起注意
recovery engineering 采收工程
recovery factor 采收率
reduce 减少
reduction 降低
refer to 指的是
regardless of 不管
region 区域范围

regular four-spot 正四点（井网）
Regular Injection Patterns 规则注入井网
relative position 相对位置
relatively 相对地
release 释放
rely on 依靠
remain 保持
remainder 残留物
replace 替换，置换
replenish 补充
reservoir having artesian water drive 自流水驱油藏
reservoir pressure 油藏压力
reservoir rock compressibility 储油岩层可压缩性
residual oil 残油
respective economic limits 各自的开采极限
response to 回应
result in 引起
retrograde evaporation 逆蒸发
rhamnolipids 鼠李糖脂
rise 上升，隆起
rock and liquid expansion drive 岩石及流体膨胀驱
rock matrices 岩石基质
rock stratum 岩层
schematic illustration 规划图
selection 选定
separate 分离，析出
separation & storage facilities 分离及贮存设施
settle 沉淀
shake 震动
shale streaks 页岩拖延作用
similar condition 类似条件
situ sodium salts of fatty acids 脂肪酸钠盐
skewed four-spot 斜四点（井网）
slant-hole drilling techniques 斜孔钻

井工艺
slightly 轻微地
slug 段塞,一段流体
so...as to 如此……以至于
solidify 固化
solubility 溶解度
solution gas 溶解气
solution gas drive reservoir 溶气驱油藏
solvent 溶剂
source 资源
spacing 间距
speculative 前景辉煌的
square miles 平方英里
stage 阶段
staggered line drive 交错的行列注水
Steam Assisted Gravity Drainage (SAGD) 蒸汽辅助重力驱油
steam chamber 蒸汽带
steam flooding 蒸汽驱油
steam injection 蒸汽注入
steam soak 蒸汽浸渍
stimulate 强化,刺激
steam stimulation 蒸汽增产法
storage 储存
strains 应变;变形
stratum 地层,岩层
structure 结构
subsequent 随后的
substantially 实质上
subsurface pumping 潜油泵抽油
sufficient 充足的
superheated steam 过热蒸汽
supplement 补充
surface tension 表面张力
surface water lines 表层水管线
surfactant flooding 活性溶剂驱油
surfactants 表面活性剂
surrounding 周围的
suspended solids 悬浮固体颗粒

swap formation 交换地层
sweep...from... 将……从……中驱除
technique 方法,工艺
technological measure 技术手段
tend to 往往,倾向于
term 术语
tertiary recovery 三次采油
THAI(Toe to Heel Air Injection)水平井注气(技术)
the movement of the injected water 注入水的运移
the reservoir gas space 油层气空隙
the waterflood front 水驱前缘
thermal recovery 热力采油
thermally enhanced oil recovery methods (TEOR) 热力提高采油率方法
thin shale barrier 薄页岩隔层
through 通过
to some degree 至某种程度
transport 运送
trap 圈闭
treat 处理,加工
typical peripheral waterflood 典型的边缘注水
ultra-low interfacial tension 超低界面张力
ultrasonic stimulation 超声波增产措施
underground pressure 井下压力
underlying 下覆
undersaturated oil reservoir 欠饱和油藏
uniformly 均匀地
unit 单元
unprofitable wells 无开采价值井
utilization 利用
VAPEX (Vapor Extraction) 蒸汽抽提
variable permeability 可变渗透率

variations 变形
versus 与……相比较
vertical barrier 垂向隔层
vertically 垂向地竖直地
viable 能持久,能存活
vicinity 毗邻
viscosity 粘度
void space 空隙
water basin 水域
water bearing rocks 含水岩层
water drive 水驱
water flooding 注水
watered-out producers 水侵生产井
waterflood front 水驱前缘
well arrangements 布井
well arrangements for dipping reservoirs 倾斜油藏布井
well head 井口
well spacing 井距,布井
wet combustion 湿式燃烧
with a production well at the center 将生产井围在中央

Chapter 6

a series of 一系列的
accordingly 相关的
accumulate 累积
affect 影响
analogous 模拟的,类似的
analysis 分析;处理
analyze 分析
approach 方法
approximate 大约的
approximate end of wellbore storage effects 井眼储液影响末端
aquifer 含水层
assess 估价
assuming that 假设
axis 轴

barrier 阻挡层
behavior 状态
bottom-hole flowing pressure 井眼流送压力
boundary 边界;边缘
brine 盐水
brine injection 盐水注入
buildup 恢复;建立
by way of 通过……方法
calculate 计算
categorization 分类
chart 图表
circular and square drainage areas 圆形及方形泄油面积
classify 分类;分选
coefficient 系数
column 柱;栏
combine 复合
communication 交流;通信
compare 比较
completion practices 完井作业
complicate 复杂的
composite effect 复合作用
composite reservoir 复合地层
compressible 可压缩的
conductivity 传导率
constant pressure 恒定压力
constant producing rate 稳定产量
construct 建造
coordinates 经纬度
corresponding 相对应的
cycle 周期;
decline 下降
definite trend 明确的趋向
definition 定义
denote 表示
depend on 依据
deviation 偏差
deviation from straight line 偏离直线
diffusivity equation 传导方程;扩散方程

dimensionless 无维的;无量纲的
dimensionless pressure 无维压力
dimensionless shut-in time 无维关井时间
distance 距离
distinct 个别的;明晰的
distribution 分布;分配
disturbance 干扰;障碍
dominated data 有效数据
drainage area 排油面积
Drill-Stem Test (DST) (钻杆)中途试井
duration 持续期
Earlougher's pressure buildup data Earlougher 的压力恢复数据表
Earlougher's semilog data plot for the drawdown test Earlougher 的压降试验半对数曲线
effectively 有效地
efficiency 效益
end of transient flow 瞬变流末尾
equalize 均衡
equilateral drainage areas 等边形泄油面积
equivalent 等效的
erroneous 错误的
essentially 基本的
estimate 估算
evaluate 评价
exceed 超出
exhibit 展示
expand 扩张;膨胀
expansion 扩张;膨胀
Exploration Well Test 探井试井
expression 表达(式)
extension 伸展
extrapolate 推断
falloff 下降;衰减
falloff testing 注水井压降试井
false pressure 视觉压力;假压
fault 断层

flat 平缓的
flow properties 流动性
flow rate 流量
flowing period 开井时间
fluid distribution 流体分布
formation transmissibility 地层传导率
fracture length 裂缝长度
front tracking 前缘跟踪(法)
fundamental 基本的;主要的
fundamental objectives 主要目标
geometry 几何形态
graphically 图形地
gravity effect 重力效应
horizontal 水平的
idealized drawdown test 理想压降试井
idealized rate schedule 理想产量表
illustration 插图
in prior to 早于
in terms of 根据
individual phase 单相
induce 诱导;感应
infinite 无限的
inhomogeneity 非均质性
initiation 激发;起始
injected fluid bank 已注入流体区域
injection time 注入时间
Injection Well Test 注入井试井
injectivity test 注入能力测试
intercept 截距
interference 干扰;妨害
interpret 解释;说明
intersect 横贯
interwell permeability 井间渗透率
involve 包含
isotropic 各向同性的
judge 判断
laminar flow 层流
layer pressure 层压
lg-lg data plot 双对数数据曲线

VOCABULARY

linear form 线性型
location of front 前锋定位
log cycle 对数周期
logarithm 常用对数
log-log scale 双对数图尺
mathematical expression 数学表达式
maximum pressure 最高压力
methodology 方法论
mobility ratio 流度比
Multiple Well Test 多井试井；干扰试井
multirate 多率
negative skin factor 负表皮因子
net change 纯变化
no flow across drainage boundary 泄油边界对面无油流
non-unit-mobility ratio systems 流度不为一的油藏
obtain 获得
outline 轮廓；概要
override 替换值；重叠
packer 封隔器
parameter 参数
portion 部分
positive value 正值
pressure behavior 压力动态
pressure buildup 压力恢复
pressure difference 压差
pressure drawdown 压降
pressure drawdown test 压降试井
pressure falloff test 压降试井
pressure profile 压力分布图
pressure response 压力响应
procedure 过程；步骤
proceed 着手；进行
Production Well Test 生产井试井
propose 提出
provide 提供；装备
pseudosteady state 拟稳定态
pseudosteady-state region 拟稳定态区域

pulse 脉冲
radius 半径
recognize 识别；认可
reflect 反射；反映
region 地区
relationship 关系；比例
represent 描述；代表
representative samples 典型示例
reservoir behavior 油层动态
reservoir heterogeneity 储层非均质性
reservoir limit 油层边界
reservoir limit and shape 油层边界模型
respectively 分别地
rule of thumb 经验法则；近似值
saturation 饱和度
scale 规模
schematic 图解的
schematic diagram 原理图
select 选择
semilog graph paper 半对数坐标纸
semilog plot of pressure drawdown data 压降数据半对数曲线
sequence 顺序；关连
shut-in period 闭井期间
simultaneous measurements 并行测量
Single Well Test 单井试井
skin 表皮；井壁
skin and wellbore storage effects 井壁及井眼储液影响
skin effect 表皮效应
skin factor 表皮因子；井壁污染系数
slope 坡度
slope ratio 斜度比
slope ration 倾斜度分配率
static condition 静态条件
static pressure 静压
step rate 梯度递降产量

storage ratio 储量与产量比
subscript 下标；记号
sufficient 充足的
sum 总数；和
superposition 叠加
symbol 符号
symmetric 对称的；平衡的
systematic analysis 系统分析
technique 方法；技术
tend to 往往；倾向于
throughout 贯穿；遍布
time ratio 时间比
transient flow region 瞬变流区域
transient flow 不稳态流
Transient Well Test 不稳定试井
transition 转折点
transmissibility 传导能力
treatment 处理；论述
two-bank system 双油带系统
unaffected region 未受影响区域
underride 落后
uniform thickness 等厚
unit slope 斜率为1
unsteady-state 不稳定状态
vacuum 真空的
valid 有效的
various banks 各种层面（油带）
versus 与……比较
vicinity 附近
viscosity 粘度
well testing 试井
wellbore storage region 井眼储存区域
wellbore-storage-influenced pressure 井眼影响压力
yield 产额；屈服点

Chapter 7

abrasive 摩蚀

absorber 吸收塔
accumulator compartment 蓄热室
adherence 吸附
adjustable water siphon 可调虹吸水
advance 升高；前进
agent 剂；代理
agitation 搅拌
anchor（套管）固定器
anticipate 预期
API pump classification schematic API（美国石油学会）油泵分类示意图
auxiliary gas outlet 辅助气出口
auxiliary 辅助的
baffle 挡板；隔层
baffle plates 挡板
barrel 筒；桶
beam pumping classification 游梁式抽油机分类
bearing 轴承
belt cover 皮带护罩
blade 刀片；刀闸
blast joint 防磨接头
bonnet 盖；帽
bottom anchor 底部固定
brake 刹车
bubble cap 泡帽
bubble cap during operation 运行过程中的泡帽
bubble tray 集泡盘
carbonate 碳酸盐
carrier bar 承载环（杆）
casing hanger 套管悬挂器
casing head 套管头
casing spool 井口套管短节
casing-tubing annulus 套管-油管环空
cement 水泥
centrifugal compressor 离心式压缩机
ceramic 陶瓷

chamber 泵室
christmas tree 采油树
clamp-type connection 钳形连接
clog 堵塞
close power fluid (CPF) system 闭式动力液系统
close-fitting plunger 紧密结合式柱塞
coalescence 凝聚；并和
collision 撞击
combustible 可燃的
combustion 燃烧
commingle 混合
concentration 浓度
conductor pipe 导管
contaminant 污染
control manifold 控制管汇
convert 转换；倒置
counter balance 平衡锤
counterweight 平衡块
crank pin bearing 曲柄销轴承
crude stabilizer 原油稳定器
cylindrical 圆筒的
dehydrator 脱水器
dipole 偶极子
discharge 排泄
disperse 扩散
divert 转换；转化
double barrel horizontal 双筒卧式
downhole components 井下组件
drain 排放口
dry gas outlet 干气出口
dual tubing comletion 双油管完井
dump 倾卸
dump valve 排油阀
eductor 气举管；喷射器
eductor jet nozzle 喷嘴
elastomer-lined stator 弹性材料衬里定子
electric coalescing section 静电聚合部位

electrostatic coalescence 静电并和
electrostatic treater 静电处理器
emulsify 乳化
emulsion and free-water inlet 乳液-游离水入口
emulsion conductor pipe 乳化液导管
emulsion inlet 乳化液入口
emulsion spreader 乳化液喷洒器
equalizer 均衡器
evacuate 抽空
exchanger coil 换热蛇形管
exhaust hose 排气管
facility 方便；设施
feasible 可行的
firebox 燃烧室
first stage free-water knockout 一级游离水分离
flame 火焰
flow coupling 流送接箍
fluid intake 液力摄取
flume 渡槽
force 动力
friction 摩擦
fulcrum 支点
gas boot （压力）缓冲立管
gas outlet 气体出口
gas separator 抽气器；油气分离器
gas valve 气阀
gas-lift mandrels 气举工作筒
gate valve 闸阀
gauge glasses 玻璃液面计
gear box 变速箱
gear reducer 齿轮减速器
glycol downcommer pipe 乙二醇下行管
glycol liquid 乙二醇液
glycol pump 乙二醇泵
glycol-gas seperator 乙二醇-天然气分离器
grid 隔栅
grid transformer 栅极变压器

VOCABULARY

groove 沟;槽
gunbarrel treater 油水分离器
heat or fire 加热或燃烧
heating coil 加热盘管
heavy wall barrel 厚壁钢桶
heavy-duty 重型的
helical-shaped 螺线型的
horizontal 卧式;水平的
horsehead 抽油机驴头
hydraulic 湍流
hydraulic pumping system 液压抽油系统
hydrogen sulfide 硫化氢
ignite 点火
impingement 撞击;震击
inert 惰性的
inertia 惯性
initial 初始的
instrumentation 检测设备
insulating oil blanket 绝缘油缓冲层
interaction 相互作用
interior 内部的
internal combustion engine 内燃机
intimate 亲密的;直接的
junction box 接线盒
kinetic 动力的
knit 编织
knockout 分离
landing nipple 定位短节
lever system air-balanced system 气动平衡式抽油机
lever system conventional unit 常规游梁式抽油机
lever system iunfkin mark lunfkin mark 式抽油机
linear 线性的
liner barrel 衬套
linkage 联动
log 记录
LPG 液化石油气
maintenance 维修

manifold 管汇
manway 检修孔
mechanical linkage 机械联动装置
mechanism 机理
metal fin 金属翼片
mist extractor 除雾器
motor 电动机
mount 安装
multiple casing string 多套管柱
multistage 多级
multistring packer 多管封隔器
needle valve 针阀
oil and gas outlet 油气出口
oil inlet 油入口
oil outlet weir 油出口堰板
oil outlet 油出口
oil valve 油阀
open power fluid system（OPF）开式动力液系统
oscillation 震动;颤动
packing assembly 密封部件
pack-type 密封类型
passage 通道
PC pump 螺杆泵
phase 相
pitman 游梁拉杆
pitman crank 拉杆曲轴
pitman 游梁拉杆
plunger pump 柱塞泵
pneumatic 风力的
polished rod 光杆
polished rod clamp 光杆夹具
portion 部分
power cable 动力电缆
power fluid system 动力液系统
power fluid tank 动力液罐
pressure gauge 压力表
prime mover 原动机
producing sand 沙层
production casing 生产套管
production manifold 生产管汇

profiles 纵断面图;扼要说明
progression 前进
protector 保护装置;护罩
pump cavity 泵腔
radial 径向的
reboiler 再沸器
reciprocating compressor 往复式压缩机
refinery 炼油厂
reflux coil 回流旋管
responsibility 响应性
restrictions 限制;节流
retention time 滞留时间
retrieval 恢复;取回
reverse 反转
revise 矫正
rod 光杆
rod pumping component 有杆泵抽油部件
rodless pumping 井下无杆泵
roller 辊
rotation-proof 防转
rotor 转子
rupture 使破裂
saddle 鞍状
safety head 安全头
safety valve 泄压（安全）阀
salinity 盐度
sampson post 游梁支架
sand-laden 含沙
schematic 示意图
schematic of a basic casing installation 套管安装示意图
schematic of a basic tubing installation 油管安装示意图
schematic of a heater-treater 加热破乳脱水器示意图
schematic of a low pressure free-water knockout 低压游离水分离器示意图
seating nipple 座节

second stage free-water knockout 二级游离水分离
segregation 分离
self-aligning 自动校准
separation 分离
separator 分离器,隔板
side-pocket mandrels 偏心气举阀工作筒
single tubing string 单油管柱
siphon 虹吸
siphon equalizing pipe 虹吸平压管
siphon valve 虹吸阀
(sliding)sleeve 滑套
soft packed plunger pump 软盘根柱塞泵
sophisticated 复杂的;高级的
spherical 球形
stack 烟囱
standing valve 固定阀
stationary 固定的
stator 定子
steam turbine 蒸汽轮机
stock tank 库存罐
strip 条,带
stripper column 洗提塔
stroke 冲程
stubborn 顽固
stuffing box 盘根盒
subsurface pump 深井泵
subsurface pump portion of a rod pump 有杆泵井下部分部件
subsurface safety valve 井下安全阀
sucker rod 抽油杆
sucker rod coupling 抽油杆接箍
suction chamber /vessel 吸入室
sulfate 硫酸
surface flow control installation 地表流送控制安装
switchboard 配电盘
"Tee" fitting 三通管
tank-shaped 罐状的

tapered nozzle 锥形喷口
thermometer 温度计
thermostat 热动开关
thrust 刺,插
tolerance 耐受力;公差
top anchor 顶部固定
torque 扭矩
transformer 变压器;转换器
transition 转折点
travelling valve 游动阀
trial-and-error process 反复试验法
trigger 触发器
tubbing bonnet 油管帽
tubing anchor 油管锚
tubing hanger 油管挂
tubing hanger adapter 油管挂接头
tubing head 油管头
tubing head adapter 油管头接头
turbulence 湍流
vane 叶轮
velocity 速度
vent 通气孔
vertical 立式的;垂直的
vessel 器皿;容器
voltage 电压
walking beam 游梁
water siphone 虹吸水
water valve 水阀
weight 承重
weighted float 加重浮标
weir 堰板
wet gas inlet 湿气入口
wire mesh 钢丝网
wireline hanger 悬绳器
wireline-operated 铠装电缆操作的
working barrel 深井泵工作筒

Chapter 8

accelerometer 加速器

access 存取,访问
accommodate 容纳,调节
accomplish 实行
accurate 精确
activator 催化剂,触媒剂
adjustable 可调节的
adopt 采用
advanced 高级的
aeronautics 航空学
air bath 空气浴
air hole 气孔
alarm 报警
ambient 周围的
amplitude 振幅
analyze 分析
anti-shock 防震
anti-vibration 抗震
appendix 附录
application 应用
arrested water film technology 滞留水膜技术
artificial intelligence technology 人工智能技术
assembly 安装
auto-gain mode 自动增益模式
automatic 自动的
automatic equipment 自动设备
back up facility 备用设备
background colour 背景色
balsa wood carrier 轻木载物器
battery module 蓄电池模块
battery 电池
behavior 动态
biaxial inclinometer system 双轴测斜系统
Bluetooth transmission 蓝牙传送
bob 测锤
boiler pressure vessel 锅炉压力容器
Brookfield viscometer 布氏粘度计
buffer system 缓冲系统
built in 内置

VOCABULARY

burnish 磨光
cable electrical resistance 电缆电阻
cable reel 电缆盘
calculation 计算
calibrated scale 标定刻度
capacity 容量
capture 俘获
cell 电池
characteristics 规格参数表
charge 充电
chemical-resistant 防化
circuit 电路
collaboration 协作,合作
composite top surface 合成顶面
comprise 包含
computer integrated access 计算机集成存取
computerization 计算机化
conductivity 传导性
configuration channel 配置频道
consecutive 连续的
consumption 消耗
conversion joint 转换接头
crack 裂缝
cross-section 横断面
curve 曲线
customize 定制
DAC (Distance Amplitude Correction) 远程振幅矫正
DAC/AVG curve DAC/AVG 曲线
dam 堤,堰
damping 阻尼
database 数据库
dataset 资料组
defect 故障,缺陷
depth 深度
destruction 破坏
detection circuit 传感电路
detector 检波器
determination 测定,计算
diagnose 诊断

diameter 直径
digital 数码
digital-indicating 数码显示
directional tracks 定向跟踪
disassembly 拆卸
display 显示
Distance Gain Size curve function (AVG) 远程增益曲线
distance 距离
distortion 变形
dual element 双码元
duplicate 使成双倍
echo envelope 回波包
electrical resistance 电阻
eliminating 消除
embankment 堤
environment 环境
equivalent 相等的
equivalent diameter 当量直径
evaluate 评价
exceed 超出
excellence 优秀
excitation 集电
external pressure 外部压力
facility 设备
feature 优点
finished steel 精制钢
flaw 裂痕
fluid density 流体密度
fluorescent lighting 荧光照明
foundation 基础
full wave 全波
function 功能
gear oil 齿轮油
gel strength 凝胶强度;
glare-free 防耀眼的
graduated arm 刻度指针
graduated cable 分度缆,测绳
graduated scale 分度(比例)尺
guide wheel 导向轮
half wave 半波

hermetic 密封的
IC technique 集成电路技术
immerse 浸没
inclinometer 测斜仪
index 索引,转位
ingress 进入
inherent risk 内在危险
inherent 原有的
inspection 检查
instrument operating parameters 仪表操作参数
instrumentation 检测仪表
intact 原封不动的
integrated 集成的
Intelligent judging system 智能判断系统
intelligent 智能的
intensity 强度
interactive 交互的
interface 界面
interior 内部
judging 判定
kit 成套设备:
knife-edge 刀口
knob 按钮
lab 实验室
language version 语言版本
lard 油污
latching controller 闭锁控制器
LCD 液晶显示
lead industry trend 工业领先地位
liquid bath 液池,液浴
Lithium-ion battery 锂离子电池
localization 定位
manage 管理
master-slave menu 主-从菜单
measurement 测量
MEMS 微型机电系统
memory 内存
mode 状态
module 模块

· 235 ·

Mud Balance 泥浆比重秤
negative 负值
offline 脱机
offset 偏移
orient 定位,定向
orientation control 定向控制
PC 个人电脑
PDA 掌上电脑
peak echo 回波
Peak Hold 峰值存储
peak 峰值
performance index 性能指标
PID temperature control 比例积分微分温度控制
pipe fittings 管件
pivot tables and charts 核心图表
plane projection 平面投影
plastic viscosity 塑性粘度
polyester-epoxy 聚酯-环氧树脂
portable 便携式
positioning 定位
positive 正的,阳的
power-off protection 断电保护
precisely 精确地
presentation 呈现,陈述
preview 预览
probe 探头
profile 剖面图
programmable 可编程的
pulse 脉冲
pulse energy 脉冲能量
Pulse Repetition Rate 脉冲重复频率
pulse width 脉冲宽度
pulser 脉冲发生器
rail transportation 铁路运输
rated power 额定功率
real-time sampling 实时取样
receiver 接收器
record 记录
rectification 矫正,整流

redundant 冗余
refrigerant 制冷剂
reliable 可靠
repetition 重复
resolution 分辨率
RF 射频,高频
rheological 流变学的
rheometer 电流计
Rotational Viscometer 转动粘度计
sample cell 样品管
sample soaking 样品浸泡,样品吸收
sample 采样
save 保存
scanning 扫描
schematics 图表
scheme 示意图
security-guarantee 安全保障
selectable 可选
self-checking function test data 自检功能测试数据
self-checking 自检
sensitivity 敏感性
sequence 顺序
settlement
setup 设置
shear rate 剪切速率
shortcut key 快捷键
single element 单码元
Single Phase 单相
site 现场
soaking 吸收试验
solid state electronics 固体电子学
specification 说明书
specifications 规格
spike 尖峰
spirit level 水平仪
stability 稳定性
Stainless Steel 不锈钢
state stability 定态
steady 稳定的

steel 钢
store 储存
survey process 检验过程
survey 测量,测绘
swiftly 很快地
technique 技术
template 模板
test block 试块
thermo cup 量热杯
thermometer 温度计
Time Tracks 定时跟踪
tool face 刀面
track 轨迹
transmission 传送
transportation 输送
trench 地沟
trend 趋向
Ultrasonic Flaw Detector 超声探伤仪
ultrasonic inspection equipment 超声波检测设备
uniformity 均匀性
unique 单值,唯一
USB port USB 接口
utilization 使用
vapor 蒸汽
velocity 速度
vertical heave 举高
vessel 容器,槽
via 通过
vibration 震动
viscometer 粘度计
wave 波
weld 接缝,焊接
winch 摇柄,绞车
workflow 工作流程
workpiece 工件
zoom in 放大
zoom out 缩小

参 考 文 献

[1] AHMED T H. Reservoir Engineering Handbook [M]. 2nd ed. Houston Texas: Gulf Professional Publishing, 2001.

[2] 陈涛平,胡靖邦.石油工程[M].北京:石油工业出版社,2000.

[3] 陈铁龙,孙艾茵.石油工程专业英语[M]. 北京:石油工业出版社,2006.

[4] 康勇.石油科技英语基础教程[M]. 北京:石油工业出版社,2005.

[5] 江淑娟.石油科技英语[M]. 北京:石油工业出版社,2007.

[6] 张继芬,赵明国,刘中春.提高采收率基础[M]. 北京:石油工业出版社,1997.

[7] 刘怀忠.涉外钻井英语培训教程[M]. 东营:中国石油大学出版社,2003.

[8] 刘德华,刘志森.油藏工程基础[M]. 北京:石油工业出版社,2004.

[9] 张明昌.固井工艺技术[M]. 北京:中国石化出版社,2009.